The Story of Romans

The Story of Romans

*A Narrative Defense
of God's Righteousness*

A. KATHERINE GRIEB

Westminster John Knox Press
LOUISVILLE • LONDON

Scripture quotations marked NRSV are from the New Revised Standard Version of the Bible, copyright © 1989 by the Division of Christian Education of the National Council of the Churches of Christ in the U.S.A., and are used by permission.

Book design by Sharon Adams
Cover design by Lisa Buckley
Cover art: PhotoLink © PhotoDisc

First edition
Published by Westminster John Knox Press
Louisville, Kentucky

This book is printed on acid-free paper that meets the American National Standards Institute Z39.48 standard. ♾

PRINTED IN THE UNITED STATES OF AMERICA

05 06 07 08 09 10 11 — 10 9 8 7 6 5 4 3

Library of Congress Cataloging-in-Publication Data
Grieb, A. Katherine.
    The story of Romans : a narrative defense of God's righteousness /
A. Katherine Grieb.
        p. cm.
    Includes bibliographical references and index.
    ISBN 0-664-22525-X (alk. paper)
    1. God—Righteousness—Biblical teaching. 2. Bible. N.T. Romans—
Criticism, interpretation, etc. I. Title.

BS2398.G75 2002
227′.107—dc21
                                                                2002016859

For all God's beloved in Washington, D.C.,
who are called to be saints,
and especially for Gordon and Mary
and the church in their house

Contents

Preface

Romans is a sustained argument for the righteousness of God that is identified with and demonstrated by the faithfulness of Jesus Christ, understood primarily as his willing obedience to suffer death on the cross. The title of this book, *The Story of Romans: A Narrative Defense of God's Righteousness*, reflects its claim that Paul's argument in defense of God's righteousness is constructed on a series of stories nested within the one great story of what God has done for Israel and for the Gentiles in Jesus Christ. Paul's theology of the cross results in a redefinition of the imitation of Christ that has dramatic implications for the church's life together and its apostolic vocation as the body of Christ in the world. In this book, I identify the narrative substructure of Romans by retelling the stories Paul references in order to make his argument. I am convinced that many readers are intimidated by the argument of Romans because they have not been alerted to Paul's narrative strategy. This book is designed to underline the key moves in that argument, to explain why Paul alludes to the stories he does and how they are related to his defense of God's righteousness, and to show what difference Paul's argument in Romans makes to church members today.

As a seminary professor of New Testament theology, I am often asked to address church groups on the subject of Paul's theology as seen in his letters. This book grows out of my experience that Romans—arguably Paul's most important letter—is largely unavailable to the people of God today. One of my working assumptions in writing this book is that if pastors and Christian educators become excited about Paul's argument in Romans, they are more likely to preach from Romans and to teach it in adult education classes. The importance of Romans in the history of the church is well known: a passage from Romans was instrumental in the conversion of Augustine[1]; the commentaries

---

1. Augustine, Saint, Bishop of Hippo, *Confessiones, The Confessions of Saint Augustine: A New Translation with Introduction*, ed. E. M. Blaiklock (Nashville: Thomas Nelson, 1983). Augustine's powerful description of his conversion is found in Book VIII, 29 of the *Confessions*. A short version is found in question 4 in "For Further Reflections" of chapter 6, in connection with Romans 13:13–14.

of Luther[2] and Calvin[3] on Romans helped to shape the Protestant Reformation; John Wesley's heart was "strangely warmed" while hearing someone read Luther's *Preface* to Romans[4]; and Karl Adam once described the impact of Karl Barth's commentary on Romans by saying that it fell like "a bombshell on the playground of the theologians."[5] Hardly any other book of the Bible has had such an influence on the church.

In today's church, too, there is considerable interest in Paul and in his letter to the Romans. However, since the Epistles are rarely the subject of sermons or classes, church members have few opportunities to develop the reading and listening skills needed for Paul's complex argument in Romans. Readers who don't know what to look for in the argument can easily get lost in Paul's long sentences and seemingly obscure references to the Old Testament. But Romans is well worth the time and energy spent to understand it. This book is written to facilitate your understanding of Romans by explaining Paul's argument through the story that he and his first hearers and readers shared.

---

2. Martin Luther, *Lectures on Romans*. Library of Christian Classics XV, trans. and ed. Wilhelm Pauck (Philadelphia: Westminster, 1961). Luther's "Preface to the Letter of Saint Paul to the Romans" contains these words: "This epistle is really the chief part of the New Testament, and is truly the purest gospel. It is worthy not only that every Christian should know it word for word, by heart, but also that he should occupy himself with it every day, as the daily bread of the soul." *Luther's Works*, vol. 35 (Saint Louis: Concordia, 1960) 365. Quoted in Peter Stuhlmacher, *Paul's Letter to the Romans: A Commentary*, trans. Scott J. Hafemann (Louisville, Ky.: Westminster John Knox, 1994) 1.

3. John Calvin, *Calvin's New Testament Commentaries: The Epistles of Paul the Apostle to the Romans and Thessalonians*, trans. R. MacKenzie, ed. D. W. Torrance and T. F. Torrance (Grand Rapids: Eerdmans, 1960). Calvin's own high regard for Romans is evident from his first words about it, page 5: "I am in doubt whether it would be worth while to spend much time in speaking of the value of this Epistle. My uncertainty is due only to my fear that since my commendation of it falls far short of its grandeur my remarks may merely obscure the Epistle. It is due also to the fact that at the very beginning the Epistle introduces itself better and explains itself better than any words can describe. It will, therefore, be better for me to come now to the theme itself. This will prove to us beyond any doubt that among many other notable virtues the Epistle has one in particular which is never sufficiently appreciated. It is this—if we have gained a true understanding of this Epistle, we have an open door to all the most profound treasures of Scripture."

4. John Wesley, "In the evening I went very unwillingly to a society in Aldersgate Street, where one was reading Luther's Preface to the Epistle to the Romans. About a quarter before nine, while he was describing the change which God works in the heart through faith in Christ, I felt my heart strangely warmed. I felt I did trust in Christ, Christ alone for salvation, and an assurance was given me that he had taken away *my* sins, even *mine*, and saved *me* from the law of sin and death" (Journal, May 24, 1738, emphasis original; *The Works of John Wesley, Vol. 18, Journal and Diaries I (1735–1738)*, ed. W. R. Ward and R. P. Heitzenrater [Nashville: Abingdon, 1988] 249–250).

5. Karl Barth, *The Epistle to the Romans*, 6th ed. trans. Edwyn C. Hoskyns (London: Oxford University Press, 1933, 1950).

My own reading of Romans was formed most concretely through exegetical studies done towards a doctoral dissertation submitted to Yale University in 1997.[6] I argued there, in the more technical manner characteristic of most biblical scholarship, that paying attention to the narrative substructure of Paul's argument results in a new and distinctive reading of Romans that could be significant for the contemporary church. This book is my opportunity to show how that is true. Reading Romans as a defense of God's righteousness, based on the story that demonstrates it, has proved to be a powerful way into the text in my own subsequent teaching of Romans, both in suburban parishes and in inner-city communities.

Moreover, this approach to Romans has proved particularly useful to seminary students when used in conjunction with more technical commentaries. Not all seminaries teach Greek, and even where students can read Romans in the original language, much interpretive work is required to move from Paul's argument to contemporary applications for teaching and preaching. We need books that can model these hermeneutical moves at the same time that they explicate the structure of Paul's argument. Narrative approaches to the Bible have proved extraordinarily effective in connecting believers to the text. To my knowledge, no one has yet made use of this insight at the level of either a seminary textbook or a parish study guide on Romans. It is my hope that this book will assist preachers and teachers to place Romans into the hands of the people of God, for whom Paul says it was written.

A few words about the working assumptions of the book are in order. First, I assume that chapters 9–11, Paul's anguished lament for unbelieving Israel, are central to the argument of the letter. This is not because of the recent emphasis on postholocaust theology, however important that work is for Jewish and Christian conversation, but because it has been true from the beginning that God's gracious election of Israel is the nonnegotiable foundation of Christian theology. As Karl Barth said long ago, any Christians who try to do theology without Israel are sawing off the very branch on which they are sitting.[7] "The righteousness of God" is much discussed in this book, especially

---

6. A. Katherine Grieb, "Affiliation with Jesus Christ in His Sacrifice: Some Uses of Scripture to Define the Identity of Jesus Christ in Romans" (Ph.D. diss., Yale University, 1997).

7. Karl Barth, *Church Dogmatics II/2*, trans. G. W. Bromiley et al. (Edinburgh: T&T Clark, 1957) 285–290. Also on point is the following quotation: "Without any doubt the Jews are to this very day the chosen people of God in the same sense as they have been so from the beginning, according to the Old and New Testaments. They have the promise of God; and if we Christians from among the Gentiles have it too, then it is only as those chosen with them, as guests in their house, as new wood grafted on to their old tree" (K. Barth, *Against the Stream: Shorter Post-War Writings 1946–52* [New York: Philosophical Library, 1954] 200).

in chapter 2, but its primary and most important meaning in Romans is God's covenant fidelity to Israel. God's righteousness means that the gifts and calling of God to Israel are irrevocable.

Second, I make a point of using the work of women scholars, who are still consistently underrepresented in biblical commentaries. After all, Romans is distinguished among the Pauline letters by the fact that the theological leadership of women is such a nonissue. Paul's colleague, Phoebe, probably carried the letter to Rome and expounded its theology on behalf of Paul, then provided oversight in the preparation of the community for the next phase of Paul's missionary program. I have learned a great deal from my colleagues here, especially Jouette Bassler, Beverly Gaventa, and Elizabeth Johnson, who have worked extensively in Romans. The scholarship of Jewish women, such as Paula Fredriksen, Tessa Rajak, and Claudia Setser, has been especially useful for describing first-century Jewish and Jewish-Christian communities at Rome.

Third, Paul spent most of his career laboring for church unity. In the same spirit, this guide to Romans is intended to prepare seminarians and pastors to teach it both in adult education programs of suburban parishes and in Bible study groups in the inner city or rural areas. The examples chosen to clarify Paul's meaning are designed to bring Christians of different social and economic locations into conversation with one another. For example, Paul personifies Sin and Death as powers that take control of people and enslave them. (Paul's theology is reflected in my consistent capitalization of these terms.) Contemporary analogies such as addiction, imprisonment, and abuse are real experiences for many readers, and not just those in the ghetto. Academic commentaries often avoid such examples, as if the text were too holy to deal with *real* Sin and Death. But Paul spent much of his time raising funds for the poor of Jerusalem, and Paul's own language is distinctly concrete. While the book is written primarily for preachers and teachers and is not addressed directly to the poor (who are often more effectively reached with an oral tradition of Bible study), it should require less "translation" than most others for use with low-income groups.

Finally, in this reading of Romans I take seriously Paul the pastor and evangelist. Romans was written to be heard by an actual congregation of Roman house churches, made up of particular people with specific problems. Paul writes to tell them that nothing can separate them from the love of God that is in Christ Jesus their Lord. He also writes to urge them to confess with their lips that "Jesus is Lord" and to believe in their hearts that God raised him from the dead, then to imitate the faithfulness of Jesus Christ by showing hospitality and grace to their brothers and sisters for whom Christ died. Romans can be, and has been, read effectively in a variety of ways. But when Romans is

read *only* as a theological treatise, or as a rule book, or as the data for a socio-
logical study of the early Christian church, Paul the pastor and missionary is
not heard.

A word about the organization of the book is in order. The introduction
summarizes my argument by introducing Paul and the importance of stories,
both in his world and in ours, before closing with an overview of Paul's narrative defense of God's righteousness in Romans. Subsequent chapters are concerned primarily with my exposition of the text of Romans and discussion of
theological issues within it. Each chapter opens with an epigram or two, chosen to complement that particular section of Paul's argument. Usually a brief
introduction to the chapter orients the reader to the often complex discussion
that follows. Particularly long chapters are punctuated by partial summaries of
the argument thus far, and every chapter concludes with a summary of Paul's
argument in that section of Romans. Comments relating Paul's argument to
the church today are scattered throughout the chapters, but at the end of every
chapter, under the heading "For Further Reflection," appears a set of questions specifically designed to bridge the gap between the classroom and the
church. Some of them anticipate apologetic or pastoral concerns that may help
in sermon preparation. Others are discussion starters for adult education
classes. Still others are designed to encourage the personal reflection by which
a reader engages Paul and Romans at a deeper level.

A word to those who have studied Greek at whatever level: Wherever possible, Romans should be read in Greek, for much of the subtlety of Paul's
thought is lost in any translation, no matter how excellent. Readers who have
even a little Greek will benefit from using an interlinear New Testament that
shows the Greek and a literal English translation in word-by-word correspondence. The following exercise will clarify many things in Romans for
readers with enough Greek to recognize the alphabet. Go through Romans,
or a photocopy of Romans, and underline every occurrence of words with the
roots transliterated *dikaio-* and *pist-*, which relate to righteousness and faithfulness. Notice where they occur and where they are most concentrated. I have
sometimes called attention to these words but not always, since that would be
tedious for my English readers.

Most of the church in the United States reads Romans in English or in
Spanish. The best strategy is to read two or more different translations of
Romans at the same time, avoiding the standard paraphrased and amplified
versions. Most of the biblical translations in this book are my own. Where they
are not, I have indicated the translation used. I use square brackets to show
that (1) I have added a word or phrase, usually for reference, that does not
appear in the Greek, as in Romans 4:8: "Was this blessing [from David] pronounced only on the circumcised or also on the uncircumcised?"; (2) I have

noted a text-critical issue (a point at which the ancient Greek manuscripts differ), as in Romans 5:1: "We have peace [or "let us have peace," as in some ancient texts] with God"; or (3) I have substituted a word for the original word in Greek, sometimes for clarity and other times to avoid the exclusive use of the masculine pronoun for God, as in Romans 11:1: "Has God rejected [God's] people?" I use parentheses or a backslash to show alternative translations, as in Romans 5:11: "We even rejoice (or boast) in God" or the quotation of Habakkuk 2:4 in Romans 1:17: "The righteous will live by faith/faithfulness." I often italicize words in the biblical text, as elsewhere, for emphasis, particularly to illustrate a literary structure, such as chiasm (for example, Romans 11:22) or sorites (for example, Romans 5:3–5). See the discussion there for a fuller explanation of these terms.

Finally, since Romans is not the simplest text in the New Testament—though it is one of the most theologically profound—I pray for you and all of my readers the same blessing Paul prayed for his: "May the God of hope fill you with all joy and peace in believing, in order that you may abound in hope through the power of the Holy Spirit" (Rom. 15:13).

ACKNOWLEDGMENTS

I am deeply grateful to Dean Martha Horne and to the Virginia Theological Seminary for providing the sabbatical year in which this book was written and to the Duke University Divinity School (especially Dean Gregory L. Jones, Academic Dean Willie J. Jennings, and the Chair of the Biblical Division, Richard B. Hays) for their gracious hospitality during that sabbatical time. Stephanie Egnotovich, Executive Editor at Westminster John Knox Press provided invaluable guidance from start to finish. Special thanks are due to my Romans Seminar students at both Virginia and Duke and to two congregations in Washington where I taught Romans—St. Stephen and the Incarnation Parish and Friends of Jesus Church—for their enthusiasm for the project and their interest in its completion. Linda Kaufman, Liane Rozzell, and Richard Hays read versions of the manuscript and made helpful suggestions for its improvement. It will be evident to scholarly readers that a few voices in particular have provided the definitive shape for this particular reading of Romans: those of Richard B. Hays, N. T. Wright, J. Louis Martyn, Leander E. Keck, and behind them, Ernst Käsemann and Karl Barth. Other dialogue partners who have guided this reading of Romans include Ed P. Sanders, Wayne A. Meeks, Luke T. Johnson, James D. G. Dunn, Beverly R. Gaventa, Charles B. Cousar, Jouette M. Bassler, Robert Morgan, Elizabeth E. Johnson,

Hans W. Frei, George A. Lindbeck, David H. Kelsey, Ellen F. Davis, Brevard S. Childs, John Howard Yoder, Robert Coles, Walter Brueggemann, Elsa Tamez, Neil Elliott, Burton H. Throckmorton, Sharon H. Ringe, Ched Myers, William Stringfellow, and Gordon Cosby. I give thanks to God for them all. This book is dedicated to Gordon and Mary Cosby who, like Abraham and Sarah, showed me that God was calling it into being back at the beginning when there was nothing there and it looked impossible.

Introduction

The universe is made of stories, not of atoms.

Muriel Rukeyser

It is most lively and productive to think of one body of literature, the Bible, representing in any time and place the testimony of the narrative stretching from Abraham to the Apostles, which can be juxtaposed to any other age by its Psalms being sung again, its letters being read again, its stories and parables being retold. Then in the juxtaposition of those stories with our stories there leaps the spark of the Spirit, illuminating parallels and contrasts, to give us the grace to see our age in God's light and God's truth in our words.

John Howard Yoder[1]

It is my claim in this book that Romans is Paul's sustained argument for the righteousness of God and that the best way to untangle Paul's complex argument is to understand it as built on a great story—the story of what God has done in Christ—that includes many other stories. These stories-within-a-story lie just below the surface of Paul's argument and are available to us as aids for understanding his letter. Paul assumes this narrative substructure throughout his argument and alludes to it so frequently that he almost "tells" it. This proposed reading of Romans—as a defense of God's righteousness with attention to its narrative substructure—would have been unthinkable during most of modern church history. The currently prevailing recommendation for reading Romans dates back to the sixteenth century and has enjoyed a long and profitable tenure.

---

1. John Howard Yoder, "The Use of the Bible in Theology," in *The Use of the Bible in Theology: Evangelical Options*, ed. Robert K. Johnston (Atlanta: John Knox, 1985) 113.

According to Philipp Melanchthon, Martin Luther's companion in the early Protestant Reformation, Romans is "a compendium of Christian doctrine,"[2] the definitive treatise on faith against works and the *locus classicus* for the doctrine of individual predestination to heaven or to hell. This approach to Paul's letter to the Romans, as powerful as it was at the time of the Protestant Reformation, appears more limited today, when the particularity, or specific situation, of Paul's entire letter is kept in focus. After all, if Romans is only, or even primarily, a theological treatise on selected topics, then we might only need to read chapters 1 through 4 (to get the doctrines of natural law, human sinfulness, and faith versus works); the first part of chapter 9 (to get the doctrine of predestination); and a few verses of chapter 13 (to get the doctrine of church and state). Most of the rest of Romans could easily go right into the trash can. This raises the following question: Is Romans really best read only or primarily as a theological treatise on selected topics of Christian doctrine?

Paul was a church planter, a missionary who set up shop as a tentmaker among city workers (according to Acts 18:2–3) and organized them into house churches, which he instructed for maybe a year, maybe less. Then he would leave and go on his way to the next city, where he would do the same thing all over again. Meanwhile he wrote letters back to the churches he had founded and to others, like the churches at Rome, that he hoped to visit soon. Paul was a man preoccupied with God. He thought deeply and wrote eloquently about the things of God in his letters. In that sense he was certainly a theologian and a fine one. But Paul was not a systematic theologian, and he has successfully resisted thousands of attempts, even very eloquent attempts like that of Melanchthon, to turn him into one. Instead, Paul was a man with a message to preach. He called it "the gospel of God."

At the beginning of his letter to the Romans, Paul describes himself as "Paul, a slave of Jesus Christ, a called apostle," that is, an apostle called by God, "set apart for the gospel of God" (1:1). Paul says this gospel of God was "promised in advance by God through the prophets in the Holy Scriptures" (1:2). He means, of course, Israel's prophets in the Holy Scriptures of Israel. These Scriptures, says Paul, are "about God's Son" (1:3). That "God's Son" and the Messiah of Israel was Jesus of Nazareth would hardly have been assumed by Paul's Jewish contemporaries, like Philo of Alexandria or Josephus,

---

2. "Luther's friend, Philipp Melanchthon, interpreted Paul's letter as a compendium of Christian doctrine in his 'Loci Communes,' which appeared for the first time in 1521; and continued to do so in his commentary on Romans from 1532. Ever since, it has been perceived to be such a compendium" (Peter Stuhlmacher, *Paul's Letter to the Romans: A Commentary*, trans. Scott J. Hafemann [Louisville, Ky.: Westminster John Knox, 1994] 2).

but it is so evident to Paul—and presumably to his audience—that he states it without argument. Paul elaborates: The Scriptures are about God's Son, "who was descended from David, according to the flesh, and was designated Son of God in power, according to the Spirit of Holiness, by resurrection from the dead" (1:3–4). God's Son is "Jesus Christ our Lord" (1:4), through whom Paul has been commissioned "to bring about the obedience of faithfulness" (1:5) among the nations, the Gentiles, including some of you Romans who are Gentiles, says Paul, who are "called to belong to Jesus Christ" (1:6).

Notice that everything Paul has said so far, in this one very long sentence in Greek, is in apposition to the name Paul. He is describing himself. Greek letters of the time typically began with a greeting: Sender (Paul) to the Receiver (the church at Rome), Greetings! But so far, this long convoluted sentence only modifies Paul. In a moment, he will address his recipients as "God's beloved in Rome, who are called to be saints," and he will send them greetings: "Grace to you and peace from God our Father and the Lord Jesus Christ." But the first thing we notice is that Paul cannot introduce himself without referencing a story. Not just any story but the story that is so central to Paul's life that it is in a sense what makes him "Paul."

The gospel of God invaded Paul's life and changed his way of seeing reality so powerfully that, in a way, he is telling his own story whenever he preaches the gospel of God. We hear him doing this particularly in Romans 9–11. This gospel has also changed the lives of the people in his largely Gentile churches, so he is telling their story, too, especially in chapter 6 when he reminds them about their baptism in Christ.[3] Moreover, since God is One, and the same Lord is God of both Jews and Gentiles, the gospel of God is also the story of Israel, as Paul insists in Romans 3. Within that story of Israel, the gospel of God is traced in the story of particular figures in the history of Israel, such as Abraham in Romans 4. But the story also goes all the way back to Adam, in Romans 5, who was "a type of the one to come"—the opposite of Jesus Christ, in fact, as Paul demonstrates.

Something else is going on in Romans, too. Paul shows us that all of these stories, which might look at first like separate stories—those of Paul, of his Gentile churches, of Israel, of Abraham, of Adam—are part of one great story: the story of what God has done in the death and resurrection of Jesus Christ, the gospel of God. And it is not over yet. Paul is writing to the Roman house churches partly to tell them of their role in the story that God is still writing.

---

3. Jouette M. Bassler comments, "The story is important to Paul and his churches not simply because it was the *kerygmatic* story but because it was *their* story" ("Paul's Theology: Whence and Whither? *Pauline Theology II: 1 and 2 Corinthians*, ed. D. M. Hay [Minneapolis: Fortress, 1993] 3–17 at 16).

In Paul's view, a great deal depends on whether they will quit fighting among themselves and rise to the occasion of being a base of operations for Paul and his coworkers in the next chapter of God's story, which is to happen in Spain once Paul delivers the funds he has been collecting for the Jerusalem church. Romans was written so that the gospel of God would have its effect on the Romans as it had had its effect on Paul. When that happens, Paul believes, the story will come out right.

Why would Paul introduce himself by telling a story? Robert Coles—psychiatrist, teacher of literature at Harvard, and chronicler of the moral lives of children—has written a book titled *The Call of Stories: Teaching and the Moral Imagination*.[4] In it, he describes the beginning of his training as a psychiatrist and mentions his wise teacher, Dr. Ludwig, who taught him to honor the stories of the people who came to see him and not rush too quickly to diagnosis, even though coming up with a diagnosis is safer for the psychiatrist. It allows distance and control; however, said Dr. Ludwig:

> The people who come to see us bring their stories. They hope they tell them well enough so that we understand the truth of their lives. They hope we know how to interpret their stories correctly. We have to remember that what we hear is *their story*.[5]

Coles goes on to say,

> He urged me to be a good listener in the special way a story requires: note the manner of presentation; the development of plot, character; the addition of new dramatic sequences; the emphasis accorded to one figure or another in the recital; and the degree of enthusiasm, of coherence, the narrator gives to his or her account.[6]

Because, as Dr. Ludwig insisted, "Their story, yours, mine—it's what we all carry with us on this trip we take, and we owe it to each other to respect our stories and learn from them."[7]

I propose that in our Christian communities we learn to do what Robert Coles learned, namely, to see people as the subjects of their stories rather than as needs they express, conditions they might have, or problems we think they might cause us. That way, as Coles suggests, we don't turn people into things, but we appreciate them as actors in a narrative that is central to their lives.

---

4. Robert Coles, *The Call of Stories: Teaching and the Moral Imagination* (Boston: Houghton Mifflin, 1993).

5. Ibid., 7.

6. Ibid., 23.

7. Ibid., 30.

Moreover, we may be able to help them locate their own stories in the larger story of what God has done in Jesus Christ. In fact, we can all help each other to see that great story more clearly by telling the small pieces of the story that we know in our own lives. By telling our own stories and listening to each others' stories, we become resources for one another to discern the ways and works of God.

What does that have to do with reading Romans? Everything! Paul pastored the Roman Christians by reminding them of God's story in such a way that they could see how their own stories might fit into what God had done and was doing. Moreover, when we read Romans, we need to learn how to read Paul—not just as the historical source of the text but as someone with a story to tell. That is, we need to be good listeners of Paul: we need to note his manner of presentation, the development of his plot and characters, and the emphasis he places at certain points. If Paul is right, the story that lies beneath his argument is not just *a* story, but *the* story: the gospel of God, which, as he says in Romans 1:16–17, is the power of God for salvation to everyone who has faith, to the Jew first and also to the Greek. For in it, the righteousness of God is being revealed, from God's faithfulness through the faithfulness of Jesus Christ, to engender faithfulness in us who hear this gospel, as it stands written in the prophet Habakkuk (2:4): "The one who is righteous through faithfulness will live."

Walter Brueggemann also helps us to appreciate why it is important to read the story in Romans. Brueggemann argues that storytelling is essential to evangelism. In fact, as he says, "The decisive clues for our practice of evangelism are found in the drama and dynamic transaction of the biblical text itself."[8] He adds,

> I assume that the biblical text is not a handbook for morality or doctrine as it is often regarded, nor on the other hand, is it an historical record, as many are wont to take it. Rather the biblical text is the articulation of imaginative models of reality in which "text-users," i.e., readers in church and synagogue, are invited to participate.[9]

The evangelical church must know its stories and be able to tell them with power, because

> evangelism means inviting people into these stories as the definitional story of our life, and thereby authorizing people to give up, abandon, and renounce other stories that have shaped their lives in false or distorting ways.[10]

---

8. Walter Brueggemann, *Biblical Perspectives on Evangelism: Living in a Three-Storied Universe* (Nashville: Abingdon, 1993) 8.

9. Ibid., 8.

10. Ibid., 10.

Storytelling, then, is not a neutral activity, for none of us lives in a world without stories. We live, instead, in a world that has many competing stories. Our imaginations are already saturated with stories to which we have made trusting, even if unwitting, commitments. Evangelism, according to Brueggemann, "is an invitation and summons to 'switch stories,' and therefore to change lives."[11]

Brueggemann also suggests that we pay attention to how people change: not as a result of achieving doctrinal clarity nor in response to a direct moral appeal. Instead, he argues, people change their hearts and minds when they are given a new model, construal, or interpretation of reality and can see how to fit their own stories into this altered way of seeing reality. So imagination is critical, poetic, and finally ethical: our present situation results from the Enlightenment's failure of imagination; therefore, our present task is to fund or authorize a counterimagination that challenges the known world. This is in fact what the Bible is already doing: it describes a world that clashes with the presumed world of our culture. Brueggemann's question to the church is, "Have we enough confidence in the biblical text to let it be our fund for counterimagination?"[12]

Again, what does this have to do with reading Romans? Again, everything! Paul, as an evangelist in his own day, intuitively understood what Brueggemann is talking about: the gospel of God is saving reality, but there are other rival interpretations of reality that God's story must displace. Paul *does* have confidence in the biblical text as the source of reality markers for himself and for his congregations. These are God's promises made ahead of time through the prophets in the Holy Scriptures of Israel. As we listen to Paul defending God's righteousness by referring to the story of what God has done in Jesus Christ, we can watch a gifted evangelist at work and we can learn to tell the gospel of God for our time and in our situation. Now back to Romans!

We have already seen how Paul begins the letter with a narrative summary of the gospel of God that links the Holy Scriptures of Israel to what God has done in Jesus Christ. It is essential for Paul to show two things: (1) it is the same God who made covenant promises to Israel who is now calling Gentiles into Paul's congregations, and (2) this does not mean that God has been unfaithful to the people of Israel. As Karl Barth saw clearly at the time of the holocaust and as Wayne Meeks has argued more recently,[13] if someone were to argue,

---

11. Ibid., 11.

12. Walter Brueggemann, *Texts Under Negotiation: The Bible and Postmodern Imagination* (Minneapolis: Fortress, 1993) 25.

13. Wayne A. Meeks, "On Trusting an Unpredictable God: A Hermeneutical Meditation on Romans 9–11," *Faith and History: Essays in Honor of Paul W. Meyer*, ed. J. T. Carroll et al. (Atlanta: Scholars, 1990) 105–124.

"Yes, God *did* make a covenant with Israel, but that was then and this is now and God has made a new covenant that excludes Israel and includes the church instead," what is to prevent God at some later date from breaking covenant with the church as well? Paul has to show that God is keeping faith with Israel *precisely* by bringing Gentiles into the covenant already made with Israel.

In fact, Romans is not a theological treatise on either faith and works or predestination. Instead it is a sweeping defense of the righteousness of God, the covenant faithfulness of God "to the Jew first and also to the Greek," a phrase Paul repeats several times at the beginning of the letter and demonstrates in the logic of his argument. Paul shows God's covenant righteousness by referencing stories, a series of stories that together comprise one great story, the gospel of God in Jesus Christ, as the following brief overview will show.

The story of God's righteousness in Jesus Christ is at once the story of (1) God's sovereign renewal of the created cosmos, (2) God's redemption of humanity from universal bondage to Sin and Death, and (3) God's reconcilation of Jews and Gentiles (which involves both God's faithfulness to Israel and the keeping of God's promise for the Gentiles). It is critical to discern the *apocalyptic* framework in which the story appears: creation groans with expectation (Rom. 8:22) as Paul and his communities live out the script of the end time; they are players in the last act of God's apocalyptic drama of salvation, a story that began with creation and the fall and continues through Israel's history up to the present moment. Then it breaks off immediately before the last chapter: Paul's next mission to the Gentiles, which is to happen in Spain with the help of the Roman Christians.

The story of what God has done in Jesus Christ, which appears just below the surface of Paul's argument for the righteousness of God in Romans, can be summarized as follows: First, it is the story of what God has done to save the lost world of creation and humanity in the sacrifice of Jesus Christ (Rom. 1–3, climaxing in 3:21–31). Then Paul underlines the story of the faithfulness of Jesus by comparing it to the earlier story of the faithfulness of Abraham in Romans 4. Paul's discussion of Abraham is followed in Romans 5–8 by a narrative flashback to the human story in Adam—to our bondage to Sin and Death through human disobedience—now contrasted with our deliverance from Sin and Death through the faithful obedience of Jesus Christ. This deliverance testifies to the gracious mercy of God, overcoming both Sin and Death on our behalf. Therefore Paul can assure us in Romans 8 that nothing can separate us from the love of God in Jesus Christ.

Nothing, he works out in Romans 9–11, means nothing. Even Israel's unbelief cannot ultimately separate Israel from the love of God in Christ. In fact, God is using this very situation to bring in the Gentiles and to make Israel jealous, so God will have both Israel and the Gentiles at the end (11:32). Then at

Romans 12:1–2, Paul applies the metaphor of sacrifice (which he had used in Rom. 3:21–31 to speak of Jesus Christ) to the whole community that belongs to Christ through baptism into his death. Their bodies are no longer their own because they are possessed by God. Their minds are no longer to be conformed to the dying age but are being transformed in the newness of resurrection life. Finally, the same metaphor of sacrifice is applied specifically to the case of Paul and to the Christian community at Rome. They are to imitate the love of God and the faithful obedience of Jesus Christ by choosing not to please themselves but to please the neighbor, as Christ did (15:1–6; that is, they are to quit fighting) and they are also to imitate Jesus the Messiah, "the one who rises to rule the Gentiles," by supporting Paul's mission to the Gentiles in Spain (15:7–13, 24).

But the story is unfinished. Its rhetorical conclusion is deliberately left open-ended: Will the members of the Roman house churches welcome one another (their brothers and sisters, who are the work of God and for whom Christ died) in imitation of God and of Christ? Will they seek to please their neighbors and to build up the community in imitation of Jesus Christ's death on the cross? Will they join with Paul in support of his mission to the Gentiles in Spain, in fulfillment of God's purposes as foretold by God's prophets in the Scriptures concerning his Son and in imitation of the Messiah whom God has sent to the Gentiles? The force of Paul's argument is increased by the technique of suspense at several points in the story, and especially at its conclusion. Paul—as defense attorney for God, storyteller, pastoral caregiver, evangelist, and moral visionary—does not hesitate to apply this pressure to the community at Rome in support of his mission and in support of their ongoing life together. He writes to them, as he says, "very boldly" (15:15) because he is a "prisoner of hope" and of the God of hope.

This book is written in thanksgiving to God for the work of Paul and in an effort to continue his ministry of evangelism in our own time. May we who read Paul's letter to the Romans also be as bold as he was to envision the gospel of God for our churches today. May we tell the story of God's love as powerfully as Paul does, though perhaps with shorter sentences and with less complexity of thought. After all, this is the story that demonstrates the righteousness of God. It is good news—the best possible news—and it should be proclaimed boldly. It is the story of the power of God for salvation to everyone who has faith. Even if it is long and complicated, it is a story worth hearing and telling again and again.

1

"Not Ashamed of the Gospel"

(Rom. 1:1–17)

Of my friendly readers I ask that they should take nothing and
believe nothing from me which they are not of themselves persuaded stands within the meaning of what Paul wrote. Of my
unfriendly readers I ask that they should not reject as an unrea-
sonable opinion of my own what, in fact, Paul himself propounded.
Karl Barth[1]

Paul has left us an extremely precious document for Jewish studies, the spiritual autobiography of a first-century Jew.
Daniel Boyarin[2]

PAUL AND THE ROMAN CHRISTIANS

In this book, I suggest that the best way into Paul's complicated argument in
Romans is to divide it into sections and to read each section as if listening to
a story. This first chapter focuses on the story of Paul's apostolic call and on
the story of how the Roman house churches came to their present situation.

Paul's letter to the Romans, like other letters, almost certainly presupposes
an actual historical situation known to the author and to his first hearers/
readers. Later readers may try to reconstruct this situation from the letter itself

---

1. Karl Barth, (Bonn, October, 1932), "The Author's Preface to the English Edition,"
The Epistle to the Romans, 6th ed., trans. Edwyn C. Hoskyns (Oxford: Oxford University Press, 1933, 1950) x.
2. Daniel Boyarin, *A Radical Jew: Paul and the Politics of Identity* (Berkeley, Ca.: University of California Press, 1994) 2.

and from whatever external evidence is available. We are fortunate to know quite a bit about Paul and about the house churches in Rome to which he wrote. Our information about Paul comes primarily from his own writings (the seven or more letters we have that were written during the fifties C.E. and were later gathered, edited, arranged, and placed in a collection of early Christian writings now called the New Testament); from a theological biography of Paul written a generation or so later (roughly the second half of the Acts of the Apostles); from other early Christian writings, both internal and external to the New Testament, that interact with Paul and Pauline theology (or with the authors' perception of those); and from other traditions about Paul that have been preserved.

Paul was an evangelist, a missionary, a church planter. When he describes himself as "a slave of Jesus Christ, a called apostle, set apart for the gospel of God" (1:1), he is explaining who he is by referencing his story, or more precisely, the story of what happened to him when God intervened powerfully in his life in order to change its direction completely. If, as seems likely, sometime around the year 30 C.E. Jesus of Nazareth was crucified by the Roman authorities in Jerusalem and raised from the dead by God three days later, the movement that would later come to be called "Christian" had its beginning then. Most scholars want to date God's "conversion" or "call" of Paul to within a few years of that event, perhaps 34 or 35 C.E. That would have given Paul enough time to build up a reputation among the Judean churches as a persecutor of Christians (Gal. 1:22–24),[3] before the amazing reversal that brought into being the church's first and perhaps most brilliant theologian.

Paul alludes to the story of his calling in three short phrases, each of which is theologically loaded. First, he describes himself as "a slave of Jesus Christ" (1:1). This says both that Paul confesses Jesus of Nazareth to be the long-awaited Messiah (*Christos* in Greek) of Israel and that Paul acknowledges him as "Lord" (1:7). In Paul's way of thinking, no one is autonomous or self-directed; all human beings serve someone or something, whether they know it or not. Paul knows that he belongs to God in Jesus Christ, which means that he is "under obligation" (1:14, a debtor) just as if he were literally a slave. Slaves are at the disposal of their Lord, and Paul often speaks of himself as a slave or even as a prisoner of Christ.

Next, he refers to himself as "a called apostle" or someone "called to be an apostle" (1:1), which tells us more of his story. Whenever Paul uses the verb "call," its subject is almost always God. Paul follows the biblical custom of referring to God without naming God by using the "divine passive": instead

3. J. Louis Martyn, *Galatians: A New Translation with Introduction and Commentary*, Anchor Bible 33A (New York: Doubleday, 1997) 182.

of saying, "God called me," he describes himself as "called," and the reader knows to supply the words "by God." Understanding this convention enables us to know what Paul's first readers would have seen: that throughout the letter, Paul is talking almost constantly about what God has done in Jesus Christ, even when he does not actually use the name "God." An "apostle" is someone who is "sent with a commission" or authorized to perform a particular action on behalf of the sender. In Paul's case, the Sender is God: God has called him to go on a mission to evangelize or "preach the gospel to" Gentiles (non-Jews) to bring about their faithful obedience, "the obedience of faith" (1:5; 16:26), to Jesus Christ.

Finally, Paul describes himself as one "set apart for the gospel of God" (1:1). The words "set apart" remind us of Paul's background as a Pharisee (see Phil. 3:5–6) because the word "Pharisees" may mean "separated ones," or those who had "separated" themselves from the world in order to be holy to God. The term may have originated around the time of the Maccabees in the middle of the second century B.C.E., when the successors of Alexander the Great were seeking to force Greek ways on Israel. Here, Paul uses the divine passive again to speak of God's action setting him apart to proclaim the gospel, or good news, of what God has done in Jesus Christ (Rom. 1:1–6). In Galatians (1:1, 11–24) Paul describes more fully how God redirected his energies from "violently persecuting the church of God and attempting to destroy it" (1:13) to "preaching the faith he once attempted to destroy" (1:23) as the result of "a revelation of Jesus Christ" (1:12). The word translated "revelation" (*apokalypsis*) in Galatians 1:12 is also important for understanding Paul's letter to the Romans. He uses the verb "is being revealed" (1:17) to speak not simply of information about God or from God but to refer to the world-changing event that has occurred in the death and resurrection of Jesus Christ. *For Paul, this event has changed everything in every place.*[4] The full weight of that statement becomes clearer as one reads his letter to the Romans. Because Jesus Christ is Lord, no aspect of human life— indeed, not even the creation itself nor the heavenly powers that try to oppose God's will (8:38–39)—falls outside of the sphere of God's gracious and merciful love, seen most clearly in the death and resurrection of Jesus Christ. Nothing in all the world can separate us from that love, which is good news indeed!

Paul had good news to tell (*euangelion theou*, "the gospel of God"). He did this by telling the story of what God had done in Jesus Christ and by founding communities committed to living out the implications of that gospel in their

---

4. On Paul's "epistemological crisis" see J. Louis Martyn, "Epistemology at the Turn of the Ages," *Theological Issues in the Letters of Paul* (Nashville: Abingdon, 1997) 89–110. See also Alexandra R. Brown, *The Cross and Human Transformation* (Minneapolis: Fortress, 1995).

life together. Paul was a church planter. As Wayne Meeks has demonstrated, Paul's pattern seems to have been to come into a strategically located urban center, often with coworkers; to recruit local leaders and found a church; to stay for a period of time to assist with instruction and organization; and then to move on to the next city to repeat the process.[5]

Inevitably, Paul was on the road a lot. In order to stay connected, he needed to write letters back to the communities he had established and to his coworkers there. From the travel itineraries described in the book of Acts alone, one scholar has calculated that Paul traveled nearly ten thousand miles during just that part of his career we know about.[6] Paul's mobility, and that of his coevangelists, may not have been unusual. Roman roads were excellent and well maintained. Trade routes around the Mediterranean meant that sailing ships were often available for passage. In fact, letters seem to have been entrusted for delivery to someone who was traveling towards the intended recipients, and, judging from the amount of correspondence that has survived from the first century, many of them reached their destination. Paul seems to have sent his letters with coworkers or other Christians who were headed to the church he was addressing. Since the early Christian churches were primarily urban and strategically located in cities along the major trade routes, this was a logical way for Paul to communicate with his fledgling communities.

We know quite a bit about the situation of the early Christians in Rome, both before and during the time Paul wrote to them. As the imperial capital and the administrative center of its political and economic policies, Rome enjoyed enormous prestige. Many wealthy and influential people lived there, but that did not mean that the daily life of Roman Christians was either easy or comfortable. As Elsa Tamez has shown, the fact that Rome was famous for its high consumption of goods from every corner of the known world did not mean that poverty had disappeared.[7] To use a contemporary analogy, the first impressions of a visitor to Washington, D.C., may reflect the elegance of its monuments, the grandeur of its hotels, or a sense of the political and economic power that shapes the fates of lesser nations. But even a casual observer will quickly see the many poor and homeless people who sleep on the park benches in the summer and on the heating grates in the winter. First-century Rome also would have had its elite, its working class, and its poor.

---

5. Wayne A. Meeks, *The First Urban Christians: The Social World of the Apostle Paul* (New Haven, Conn.: Yale University Press, 1983) 9–10.

6. Ronald F. Hock, *The Social Context of Paul's Ministry: Tentmaking and Apostleship* (Philadelphia: Fortress, 1980) 27, cited in Meeks, *The First Urban Christians*, 16.

7. Elsa Tamez, *The Amnesty of Grace: Justification by Faith from a Latin American Perspective*, trans. Sharon H. Ringe (Nashville: Abingdon, 1993) 93.

Urban life during Paul's time was overcrowded: the population density in cities of the Roman Empire was like that of industrial slums in Western cities today.[8] Most people were packed into crowded apartments, which were made bearable only by the open spaces of public facilities. Privacy was almost unknown; neighbors saw everything; news and rumors traveled quickly; and riots could spring up without warning. Daily existence was lived out, for the most part, on the streets and sidewalks, where people gathered, where teachers instructed their disciples, where workers made and sold their goods. There were ethnic ghettoes—for example, Jews in Rome were concentrated in an area called the *Transtiberinum*—and ghettoes of tradespeople who were engaged in a common craft. Areas and streets often gained their names from the artisans who traded there (e.g., Linenweavers' Quarter, Leatherworkers' Street, Portico of the Perfumers).[9] In Acts 18:2–3, Paul and his coworkers Prisca and Aquila are described as tentmakers, who came to know each other through their trade. Much early Christian evangelizing may have occurred just this way: Paul or one of his coworkers would preach the gospel, that is, tell the story of what God had done in Jesus Christ, to other artisans working in the same area.[10] Some would become interested and would be curious to know more. As interest and numbers grew, they would form a cell group, an assembly of Christians, that would meet in someone's house to worship God, receive instruction in the Scriptures and in Christian ways, and provide mutual support.

The church in Rome was probably composed of several such Christian assemblies or house churches. At least two or three of them are mentioned in Romans (16:5, 14, 15). We cannot be sure if those various house churches assembled at a common meeting place, but we are reasonably certain that the house church formed the basic unit of Christian life. This was hardly surprising, since the household was the standard social and economic unit of city life during this time.

The most important background information for reading Paul's letter is that these Roman house churches were probably composed of both Jewish Christians and Gentile Christians. This is important to know because Jews (including Jewish Christians like Paul, Prisca, and Aquila) and Gentiles (including Gentile Christians) coexisted in an uneasy relationship that often involved misunderstanding and stereotyping of the other group. If groups

---

8. Ramsay MacMullen, *Roman Social Relations* (New Haven, Conn.: Yale University Press, 1974) 63, cited by Meeks, *The First Urban Christians*, 28–29.

9. Meeks, *The First Urban Christians*, 29.

10. Hock, *The Social Context of Paul's Ministry*, 37–42, cited by Meeks, *The First Urban Christians*, 29.

of people typically interact with others according to a mental map of their social world, in Paul's time, Gentile Christians typically divided the world into two groups: *Greeks*, civilized people who spoke Greek including the Romans themselves; and "*barbarians*" (lit. "bearded") or uncivilized outsiders. At least some of the Gentile Christians among Paul's first hearers would have taken for granted his contrasting categorization (Greek/barbarian; wise/foolish) in Romans 1:14, although Paul himself seems to deconstruct it shortly, in 1:22.

For Jews, the mental mapping of the social world also involved dividing humanity into two groups: *Israel*, the people of God; and *Gentiles*, the other nations among whom they found themselves and under whose empires they had to live. Israel was further divided into Judeans, or Palestinian Jews, and Diaspora Jews, who were dispersed or scattered among the Gentiles—such as Jews and Jewish Christians living in Rome. Since the conquests of Alexander the Great in the fourth century B.C.E., Hellenization, or the widespread influence of the Greek language and civilization, was a fact of life for Jews. Greek was the common language, so, for example, Paul's letter to the Romans was written in Greek rather than Latin. And since Pompey's first-century-B.C.E. victory over the Seleucids, the Jews had been living under Roman rule.

Life for the Jews under Roman rule and in Rome itself had been difficult. The first known reference to a Jewish community in Rome dates from 139 B.C.E. when the Jews were apparently expelled by the Praetor Cornelius Hispaius for being followers of a Hellenistic-Oriental Sabazio cult, almost certainly a confusion about either *Sabaoth* (the name of God, the Lord of Hosts) or the keeping of the *Sabbath*, the most conspicuous practice of Judaism. Judaism seems to have been misunderstood from the beginning and continuously by its Gentile Roman rulers. In the first century B.C.E., Cicero described the Jewish religion as "a barbaric superstition,"[11] an opinion shared by Horace[12] during the Augustan period (after 30 B.C.E.). The Jews experienced continual shifts between periods of toleration and opposition. They were expelled again under the Emperor Tiberius in 19 C.E. In spite of this erratic persecution, there was a loosely organized group of synagogues in Rome when the Christian movement began there, sometime before 49 C.E. Rome was the first city in the western Mediterranean where this new religion took root. A later Roman historian, Suetonius, reports that the Emperor Claudius expelled

---

11. Cicero, *Pro Flacco*, 67–69, cited by Wolfgang Wiefel, "The Jewish Community in Ancient Rome and the Origins of Roman Christianity," *The Romans Debate*, rev. and exp. ed., ed. Karl P. Donfried (Peabody, Mass.: Hendrickson, 1991) 85–101.

12. Horace, *Serm.* 1.4.143, 1.5.100, cited by Wiefel, "The Jewish Community."

the Jews from Rome in 49 C.E. *impulsore Chresto* "because of riots about Chrestos."[13] This probably means that Jews who believed that Jesus was the Messiah or Christ (Christians) and Jews who did not were engaged in religious disputes that annoyed the Roman ruler, who threw them all out. This history is important background for understanding the situation in the Roman house churches to whom Paul wrote.[14]

The Edict of Claudius that expelled the Jews from Rome legally expired upon his death in 54 C.E., when Nero became emperor. Originally, the Roman Christian churches had been populated by Jewish Christians (including Prisca and Aquila; cf. Acts 18:2), but after the expulsion of the Jews, including Jewish Christians, the Christian churches must have continued under Gentile Christian leadership. In the meantime, these churches had become disconnected from the Jewish synagogues, and other factors had probably shifted. Some of the communities may have switched to Sunday worship or discontinued the dietary regulations prescribed by Torah, the Jewish law given to Moses. At Claudius's death, Jews—including Jewish Christians—probably returned to Rome in great numbers, and suddenly the Roman house churches must have experienced a merger of two rather different groups who had been divided for five years and were now learning to live together. Paul's letter to the Roman house churches was probably written in 57 or 58 C.E., when the now much-changed divided communities had been trying to work things out for three or four years. Paul's letter (Romans 14–15 especially) suggests that substantial difficulties remained. An additional complicating factor lay in the fact that Paul had not founded the church at Rome. In fact, he had never been there, although he had often wanted to visit and hoped to visit them soon, after his journey to Jerusalem (1:10; 15:22–25). The long list of names to whom Paul sends greetings in chapter 16 suggests that Paul both knew people in Rome and knew about others there. Nevertheless, there were many who did not know him, and we see Paul at his diplomatic best as he writes his letter to the Romans.

---

13. Janne, H., "Impulsore Chresto" 531–53, cited in Wiefel, "The Jewish Community." For a papyrus account of Claudius's own words, see Claudius, *Pap. Lond.* 1912.73–105, in Molly Whittaker's *Jews and Christians: Graeco-Roman Views* (Cambridge: Cambridge University Press, 1984) 99–100.

14. This paragraph follows the argument of Wolfgang Wiefel, "The Jewish Community," 85–101. For more information about first-century-C.E. Jews in Rome, see Tessa Rajak's "Inscription and Context: Reading the Jewish Catacombs of Rome," *Studies in Early Jewish Epigraphy*, ed. J. W. Van Henten and P. W. Van der Horst (Leiden: E. J. Brill, 1994) 226–41. See also Claudia Setzer's *Jewish Responses to Early Christians: History and Polemics, 30–150 C.E.* (Minneapolis: Fortress, 1994).

PAUL'S LETTER TO THE ROMANS

In Paul's time, his letter would have had great importance because it was understood to be a substitute for the personal presence of the apostle himself.[15] Paul would have composed the letter and dictated it to an *amanuensis* or scribe, who would have put it in writing. In Romans, somewhat unusually, the scribe Tertius says hello to the community at the end of the letter (16:22). Simpler letters would not need explanation and interpretation and could simply be delivered to the recipients by those who carried them for the senders. But letters as complicated as Paul's epistles would probably have required an interpreter who could not only read the letter out loud to the community but could also explain and clarify its more difficult ideas. The letter would have been read aloud in the context of the gathered community's worship, probably like a sermon.

In fact, Paul's letters, like good sermons, are constructed with great care to have the maximum rhetorical effect on his hearers. He might even have coached someone (perhaps Phoebe who is mentioned in 16:1–2) to emphasize certain phrases or words for clarity and power. As Paul composed the letter, he would have been aware of its performance at the other end as an oral and aural event taking place in the presence of God and of the community gathered to worship God. Paul seems to have had a strong understanding of the Holy Spirit, such that he could expect that God would take his words and use them to re-preach the gospel to the Roman congregation. It would have been as if Paul himself were there with them, proclaiming to them "the gospel of God" as the letter is being read.[16]

We can often understand a great deal about the context and purpose of a Pauline letter by looking closely at its opening and at its ending.[17] Ancient letters had a common form, just as ours do today, but whereas we typically begin with the name of the recipient ("Dear Mary") and end with the name of the sender ("Love, John"), the ancient Greco-Roman letter convention was more like contemporary office memos or e-mail ("John to Mary, greetings"). A polite statement wishing health or good fortune to the addressee or complimenting the person would follow, before the letter moved to its business (body). The conclusion would contain more good wishes or greetings from mutual friends.

---

15. Robert W. Funk, "The Apostolic *Parousia*: Form and Significance," *Christian History and Interpretation: Studies Presented to John Knox*, ed. W. R. Farmer, C. F. D. Moule, R. R. Niebuhr (Cambridge: Cambridge University Press, 1967) 249–268.

16. Martyn, *Galatians*, 22.

17. Paul Schubert, *The Form and Function of the Pauline Thanksgivings* (Berlin: Töpelmann, 1939). See also Ann Jervis, *The Purpose of Romans: A Comparative Letter Structure Investigation* (Sheffield: Sheffield Academic Press, 1991).

Paul's letters follow this ancient form but expand it considerably. We have already seen how he expands the name of the sender—himself—to allude to the story of his calling in 1:1. He also expands the name of the recipient (1:7) to stress that he is writing to "*all* of God's beloved in Rome, who are called to be saints," that is, people whom God is sanctifying or making holy. Romans 1:2–6 summarizes "the gospel of God," probably using a hymn or another text commonly used in worship that the Romans and Paul both knew. It tells the story of Jesus Christ in miniature. Paul makes a point of saying that God had promised to send God's Son already, in the prophetic Scriptures of Israel (our Old Testament).

Paul's diplomatic politeness is evident in his prayer of thanksgiving (1:8–15). He compliments the community with a slight *hyperbole* (exaggeration), "Your faith is proclaimed throughout the whole world" (1:8), and assures them that he prays for them constantly. At the end of his letter, he will ask for their prayers for himself and for the gracious reception of the funds collected from Gentile churches that he is carrying to Jerusalem (15:30–33). Paul is careful to stress that while he has spiritual gifts to share with them, he also expects that they will be mutually encouraged by one another. He explains that he has "a harvest to reap" among them as he does among Gentiles in general; his assignment, or vocation, from God is to proclaim the gospel to the Gentiles, including the Gentiles at Rome.[18]

"NOT ASHAMED OF THE GOSPEL"

What is "the gospel of God" (*euangelion theou*) that Paul is so eager to proclaim to them? By now, he has their full attention on that subject because he has mentioned it three times in the short span of fifteen verses. He has described himself as "set apart for the gospel of God" (1:1); he has told them that he serves God with his spirit in the work of proclaiming the gospel of God's Son (1:9); and he has expressed his eagerness to proclaim the gospel to the churches in Rome (1:15). Paul's next statement (1:16–17) could be understood as the answer to the question, What is the gospel of God? It has rightly been called the thesis or purpose statement of the letter. But Paul's thesis is so densely laden with theological terms whose meaning is not yet clearly defined that it will take Paul the rest of the letter to explain it. My translation leaves the ambiguities in place for the reader to see, because much of the discussion of Romans involves the precise translation of these complex

---

18. John Howard Schütz, *Paul and the Anatomy of Apostolic Authority*, Society for New Testament Studies 26 (Cambridge: Cambridge University Press, 1975).

theological terms. They are discussed one at a time in the rest of this chapter and will be revisited throughout the book. Paul states his thesis in 1:16–17 as follows:

> For I am not ashamed of the gospel; because it is the power of God for salvation to everyone who has faith, to the Jew first and also to the Greek. For in it the righteousness of God is being revealed through faith for faith (or from faithfulness through faithfulness); as it stands written: 'The righteous one will live by faith/faithfulness.' (or 'The one who is righteous through faith/faithfulness shall live.')

Almost every word in Paul's thematic statement is important to the rest of the letter and will become clearer by reading Romans itself again and again. However, a few words of explanation may be helpful here at the start. There are different ways to read almost every phrase in the statement, as in much of the rest of Romans. Take, for example, Paul's statement "I am not ashamed of the gospel." There are several ways to interpret his comment: (1) He could simply be using a form of rhetorical understatement (*litotes*) that means "I am proud of the gospel."[19] Then the rest of the theme would explain the gospel that Paul was eager to proclaim. (2) Paul might mean these words literally, which raises the question for us, Why should anyone think that Paul might be ashamed of the gospel of God that he is called to proclaim? (The second purpose for writing Romans listed in the next section of this chapter clarifies that issue: Paul may begin defensively because he senses that his gospel has been misunderstood.) (3) Paul might feel ashamed of the gospel because it looks like God is compromising or even abandoning the covenant promises made to Israel in favor of inclusion of the Gentiles. Paul will return to this issue in Romans 9–11. (4) A suggestive reading that encompasses aspects of all these interpretations has been put forward by Richard Hays, who shows that Paul seems to be drawing on the language of Israel's lament psalms and prophetic writings, whose authors express confidence that God will not allow them to be put to shame in the face of their enemies. This conviction is reflected, for example, in Isaiah 50:7–8: "I know that I shall not be put to shame, because the One who proves me right is near."[20]

---

19. Leander E. Keck, "The Letter of Paul to the Romans," *The HarperCollins Study Bible*, New Revised Standard Version. General Editor, Wayne A. Meeks (New York: HarperCollins, 1993) 2117. See also Ernst Käsemann, *Commentary on Romans*, trans. and ed. Geoffrey W. Bromiley (Grand Rapids: Eerdmans, 1980) 22; and Luke T. Johnson, *Reading Romans: A Literary and Theological Commentary* (New York: Crossroad, 1997) 25.

20. Richard B. Hays, *Echoes of Scripture in the Letters of Paul* (New Haven, Conn.: Yale University Press, 1989) 38–39.

Paul next insists that the gospel is "the power of God for salvation."[21] A few verses later (1:20), he will describe God's eternal power and "Godness" evident in the creation of the world. The same God who is the only one powerful enough to create the universe is also the God who has power to save the creation, including created humanity. Paul does not call the gospel a message *about* God's power. Rather, he says, it *is* God's power. The gospel is the event of God's power that has brought about salvation, namely, the death and resurrection of Jesus Christ. The Greek word for power (*dynamis*) finds a cognate in the English "dynamite," an association that helps us to think of the gospel as God's explosive world-changing power.[22]

The gospel is the power of God for salvation "to everyone who has faith" ("in God" is assumed). Here we encounter one of the three or four most important words (or word groups) in the letter and a major translation issue. "To everyone who has faith" could also be translated "to everyone who believes" or "to everyone who trusts" or "to everyone who puts trust." Any of those would be a good translation of the Greek verb "*pisteuō.*" In addition to the verb, Paul also uses the noun form "*pistis*" (which can mean "faith," "faithfulness," belief," or "trust" in English) and the adjective "*pistos*" ("faithful," "believing," "trusting," or "trustworthy," especially when applied to God). This range of possible meanings is important to the understanding of Romans, because in English there is quite a difference between someone who is "faithful" and someone who is "believing." English lacks a verb "to faith," so whenever we see the word "believe" in an English translation we must remember that it is the same Greek word that means to "trust" or to "put faith in." Because the *pistis* word group is rendered so inconsistently in English translations, I will remind my readers throughout the text of its range of meanings in Greek by using parentheses to show alternative translations. We shall return to the translation issue again and again in our discussion of Romans. What Paul probably means here (in 1:16) is "everyone who trusts or puts faith in God," which is to say, everyone who believes the promises of God about which Paul will say more later.

---

21. "Out of some eighty references to God's righteousness in the Psalter, over half are at least loosely connected with salvation. It is plausible to see in Rom. 1:16–17 an echo of Ps. 97:2 in the LXX (Hebrew and English 98:2): 'The Lord made known his salvation (*soterion*; Rom. 1:16 has *soterian*). In the presence of the Gentiles (God) revealed his righteousness' (aorist active; Paul's divine passive 'is being revealed', i.e., by God, has the present tense of the same verb)" (Robert Morgan, *Romans* [Sheffield: Sheffield Academic Press, 1997] 20–21).

22. N. T. Wright, *What Saint Paul Really Said* (Grand Rapids: Eerdmans, 1997) 61. See especially the work of Ernst Käsemann on the character of the gospel as God's invasion of the cosmos throughout his *Commentary on Romans* cited above.

The gospel is the power of God for salvation to everyone who has faith, "to the Jew first, and also to the Greek" (Gentile). Paul repeats this formula several times (e.g., 2:9, 10) in Romans. He uses it to argue both for the priority of Israel and for the impartiality (or fairness) of God towards both Jews and Gentiles. At stake in both issues is "the righteousness of God."[23]

Paul continues his thesis in 1:17: For in it (the gospel, which is the power of God for salvation) "the righteousness of God is being revealed." Let's examine this statement phrase by phrase. A more thorough discussion of "the righteousness of God" (*dikaiosynē theou*) appears in the next chapter, but it is useful to say a few words here by way of introduction to this all-important phrase in Romans. The righteousness of God is God's justice, especially for Israel, with whom God is in covenant relationship. God's justice is at issue if God has not kept the covenant promises made to the people of Israel in the Scriptures. The righteousness of God is also related to God's creation and judgment of the whole world, so God's justice is at issue if God's dealings with Gentiles are not the same as or comparable to God's dealings with Jews. The righteousness of God also refers to God's power to "right things" (to "make things right" or to "put things right").

Once again, one of the key words or word groups of Romans can be translated into words that mean very different things in English. The Greek noun *dikaiosynē* can mean "righteousness," "justice," "right dealing," and "rectitude or uprightness." The adjective *dikaios* can usually be rendered simply "righteous" or "just" with no difficulty, and it also incorporates the larger idea of "being in right relationship" with God or with neighbor. Again, the problem is in the verb: *dikaioō* can mean "to make right or put right," which is very different in meaning from our English word "justify"—except in the case of "justifying a margin." Some have proposed "rectify"[24] or the older "rightwise" to talk about how God puts things right with sinful humanity. Again, we will have occasion to refer to this important word and to its translation into English as we read Paul's letter.

The righteousness of God "is being revealed" (*apokalyptetai*), continues Paul in Romans 1:17. "Revealed" here has the sense of being disclosed or unveiled: the word is related to "apocalypse," which means a revelation or unveiling. The righteousness of God is being revealed "from faithfulness through faithfulness" or "from God's covenant faithfulness to Israel through the faithfulness of Jesus Christ which has extended God's covenant promises to Gentiles."

---

23. Jouette M. Bassler, *Divine Impartiality: Paul and a Theological Axiom*, Society of Biblical Literature Dissertation Series 59 (Chico, Calif.: Scholars, 1982).

24. Leander E. Keck, *Paul and His Letters*, rev. ed. (Philadelphia: Fortress, 1988) 112; Martyn, *Galatians*, 250.

This is the heart of Paul's apocalyptic gospel: God is revealing God's own covenant faithfulness through the gospel, which is the world-changing event of God's power for salvation, the death and resurrection of Jesus Christ.

The righteousness of God is being revealed in the gospel from faithfulness through faithfulness "as it stands written" (in the Scriptures of Israel): "The righteous one shall live by faith/faithfulness" or "The one who is righteous by faith/faithfulness shall live." Paul closes his thesis in 1:16–17 with a quotation from the prophet Habakkuk (2:4). Paul probably intends this quotation to mean more than one thing. As I list some of the ideas that are arguably implied for Paul in Habakkuk 2:4, it will help to read through these several options carefully, remembering that they are not mutually exclusive. Paul is probably quoting Habakkuk in order to say all of these things: (1) the righteous one (the person who is in right relationship with God and will therefore live) has been put into that right relationship by God's action of putting things right (God's faithfulness); (2) that action of God, which puts sinful humanity in right relationship with God once more, has been accomplished through the obedient death of Jesus on the cross (Jesus' faithfulness); (3) Jesus (the righteous one) was faithful all the way to death because he trusted God (Jesus' faith, God's faithfulness); (4) those who believe that Jesus is the Christ (trusting God who raised him from the dead) put their faith in God and imitate the faithfulness of Jesus. The term "the Righteous One" is used elsewhere in the New Testament as a title for Jesus (and in other Jewish literature as a title for the Messiah), so another possible meaning is (5) Habakkuk prophesied that God's Righteous One will live (forever, having been raised from the dead) because of his faithfulness (his trusting obedience has been vindicated by God).[25]

In a few short and densely packed lines, Paul has stated the gospel that he has longed to proclaim to the Christians at Rome (1:11, 15). To today's reader, that thesis (and the preliminary comments on it) can seem a bit overwhelming at first. It may help to remember that the gospel of God is the story of Jesus Christ. It is the story of the righteousness of God made evident in the faithfulness of Jesus Christ, which has changed everything forever. The rest of the letter to the Romans tells that story again and again from different angles, until it becomes so clear that we are willing to entrust our lives to it. The gospel is the power of God for our salvation: the same God who made us also loved us enough so that Jesus Christ died for us (5:8), and nothing in all creation can separate us from the love of God in Christ Jesus (8:39).

---

25. Richard B. Hays, "'The Righteous One' as Eschatological Deliverer: A Case Study in Paul's Apocalyptic Hermeneutics," *Apocalyptic and the New Testament: Essays in Honor of J. Louis Martyn*, ed. J. Marcus and M. Soards (Sheffield: Sheffield Academic Press, 1988) 191–215.

WHY DID PAUL WRITE ROMANS?

A contemporary Christian missionary, Steve Mosher, frames the question that has long puzzled scholars in a practical way: Why would a busy missionary like Paul write a long letter like Romans?[26] There is probably no one reason. Instead, I suggest that the following eight reasons should be kept in mind while reading Romans:

1. Paul wrote to introduce himself and his theology, especially his controversial law-free gospel for Gentile converts, to the house churches at Rome. Paul had not founded the church at Rome and had not had the opportunity to visit it yet. But the Roman Christians had heard a lot about Paul, especially that he did not require the circumcision of his (male) Gentile converts to Christianity that was the sign of covenant obedience required by Jewish law. Some of the Jewish Christians who returned to Rome after Claudius's death in 54, such as Prisca and Aquila (16:3–4) would have agreed with Paul that it was not necessary for Gentile Christians to keep the Jewish law. Other Jewish Christians, however, would have had grave doubts about Paul and his law-free gospel for Gentile converts. Gentile Christians in Rome also needed to be introduced to Paul and to understand exactly what he was and was not saying about the inclusion of the Gentiles in God's covenant promises to Israel.

2. Paul wrote to correct false impressions and misunderstandings about what he taught. Paul's letter to the Galatians has been so powerful in the history of Christian thought that it is sometimes difficult to imagine that it might not have worked well for Paul himself. In Galatians, Paul had used highly polemical language to discuss the Mosaic law and had scathingly critiqued rival missionaries who wished to impose the law on Gentile converts to Christianity. Paul was probably criticized for his apparent "disloyalty" to Judaism, both by Jews who saw him as apostate and by Jewish Christians who thought he was preaching a morally "soft" gospel. Paul could have become defensive in response to these charges. He would have insisted (Rom. 1:16) that he was "not ashamed of the gospel" he preached *when it was understood correctly*. His careful, tactful language in Romans still does not give an inch on the disputed questions, but it stands in marked contrast to the bitter and angry tone of Galatians.

3. Paul wrote to reassure the Jewish Christians at Rome of the priority of Israel and the irrevocability of God's covenant with Israel. For, it was asked, if Gentiles could be fully Christian without keeping the Mosaic law, why had God given that law to Israel in the first place? Paul's gospel seemed to undercut God's special covenant relationship with Israel, of which circumcision was

---

26. Steve Mosher, *God's Power, Jesus' Faith and World Mission: A Study in Romans* (Scottdale, Pa.: Herald, 1996) 11.

the concrete sign. Had God revoked God's covenant promises to Israel? If so, what was to prevent God from later revoking this new covenant made with the Gentiles? Jewish Christians at Rome—and they had founded this church!—would also have been increasingly anxious about the growing number of Gentile converts, especially as a result of Paul's preaching. Where were the Jewish converts? Why wasn't God's gospel reaching them or why weren't they listening to it? Had the word of God fallen or failed? Paul deals with these questions throughout Romans, and especially in chapters 9–11.

4. Paul wrote to reassure the Gentile Christians at Rome of God's impartiality and of the fact that they, too, were included in God's covenant promises to the patriarchs of Israel, even though their males were not circumcised. In his letter to the Galatians, Paul had insisted that Gentile Christians were full and equal members of the community baptized into Christ. Subsequently, Paul had been strongly criticized for this position, and he was now on his way to Jerusalem, where the opposition to his law-free gospel was strongest. Could they count on him to say now what he had said before? If they had any doubts on that score, Paul's words in Romans should have reassured them.

5. Paul wrote to urge the Roman Christians to quit fighting over nonessential matters and live together as a unity with diversity. There may have been other issues of diversity in faith and practice instead of, or in addition to, the issues between Jewish Christians and Gentile Christians. However, the work of reconciling Christians who hold different points of view lies at the heart of Paul's gospel. Chapters 14 and 15 deal with the difficulty of living out his theological vision in practice. Paul insists that welcoming one's theological "enemies" is theologically mandated by the work of God in Christ, which reconciled all of humanity while we were enemies of God (5:10). In imitation of God (14:3) and Christ (15:7), therefore, the Roman Christians are to welcome their neighbors with whom they disagree. Moreover, Paul has a practical need for the Roman house churches to resolve these issues: He needs a united church at Rome to support his mission to Spain.

6. Paul wrote to recommend Phoebe, his coworker who probably had carried his letter to Rome. Phoebe may have been independent and wealthy, and she may have been traveling to Rome on business of her own, not just to carry Paul's letter, something she probably did as a Christian leader at Cenchreae.[27] She may have been Paul's financial agent.[28] Alternatively or additionally, she may have been the one who would perform and interpret Paul's letter to the

---

27. Meeks, *The First Urban Christians*, 60.

28. Johnson, *Reading Romans*, 7: "She has served as a patron of Paul's work in the East, and he is now sending her to Rome in order to organize and prepare for Paul's expedition to Spain. Paul recommends her to the Roman church as his business agent."

Roman house churches. Moreover, Paul may have been expecting her to help them work out the implications of his letter for their life together.

7. At any rate, Paul wrote to start building the Roman house churches into the base of operations he would need for his mission to Spain. He seems to have thought that his work in the Aegean region was completed (15:23), and his eyes were on the new mission field to the west. Paul hints that he would welcome their financial support as well as their prayers (15:22–33) and invites them to invest themselves in what God is doing through his ministry: preaching the gospel of God to Gentiles far and wide.

8. Finally and above all, Paul wrote to proclaim the gospel of God to them. He was the self-described "apostle to the Gentiles" (11:13); there were Gentiles in Rome, and he needed their support to proclaim the gospel to Gentiles in Spain.

SUGGESTIONS FOR READING ROMANS

Paul's argument in Romans is admittedly challenging. Translation issues abound. The movement of the argument itself is complex. Much of Paul's time is spent in scriptural exposition of largely unfamiliar texts. Even the story-within-a-story structure that assists readers to understand Romans remains just below the surface of the argument and must be teased out. Nevertheless, Romans is the most important and theologically profound of Paul's letters. It is well worth our time and energy to engage Paul here. Because this letter is so important, I offer the following four suggestions as guidelines for readers. It may be useful to review them occasionally throughout your reading or to return to them if the argument seems overly confusing.

1. Divide and conquer. Romans logically divides itself into four major parts: 1–4, 5–8, 9–11, and 12–16. Within these major sections are smaller units of thought, many of which begin with the word "for," "therefore," or some other connective that links them to the previous unit of thought. These connectives often introduce a statement that gives the deeper theological reason for the argument Paul has just made. For example, in Romans 1:15, Paul expresses his eagerness "to proclaim the gospel to you who are in Rome." Why? He explains why in his thesis, 1:16–17, as shown by the connective "for" at the start of 1:16. Paul's first statement "*For* I am not ashamed of the gospel" is then warranted by his second (missing in the NRSV): "*for* it is the power of God for salvation to everyone who has faith," which then leads to the theological bottom line: "*for* in it the righteousness of God is being revealed. . . ."

2. Keep your eye on the main point. Paul's argument is difficult and often convoluted. Remember that, from start to finish, Romans is an argument

for the righteousness of God. This righteousness is made evident in the faithfulness of Jesus Christ, understood as his obedient death on the cross, the event that has changed everything forever.

3. Paul uses a rhetorical style called "diatribe," or direct address to an imaginary listener or "interlocutor" in the congregation, in order to advance his argument. As the argument progresses, Paul asks—and often answers—rhetorical questions to make certain that no one misunderstands his thought. These rhetorical questions are guideposts for the reader, since they serve as markers of Paul's argument. For example, in Romans 7:7 Paul asks, "What shall we say, then, that the law is sin?" He then answers his own question: "Of course not!" Paul does this because he realizes that in the verses just prior to his question he had in fact come very close to equating law and sin. Therefore, he heads off an anticipated confusion on the part of his hearers and readers.

4. Paul's argument is best understood as a great story that has within it a series of other smaller stories. The great story is that of what God has done in Jesus Christ. The many smaller stories are those of Paul and of the Roman churches (1:1–17 and 15:14–33); of how God saved the lost world (1:18–3:31); of faithful Abraham, Sarah, and Isaac (4:1–25); of disobedient Adam (and Eve) retold from Genesis 3 (Rom. 5–8, especially 5:12–21 and 7:7–11); of Jesus Christ's obedient death on the cross (throughout, but especially 5:12–21); of the Christian baptized into the death of Jesus (6:1–23 and 8:1–39); of creation and its fulfillment (8:18–30); and of Paul's missionary preaching, Gentile responsiveness, and Israel's unbelief (9–11). And there is the ongoing story of what God is doing in the Roman churches and in Paul's upcoming mission to Spain (12–16, especially 14:1–15:13) and, finally, the story of Paul's present journey to Jerusalem and his hopes to visit Rome (15:14–33).

Summary. In the first few verses of Romans, Paul signals his Roman hearers that he is going to show them how his own story and the story of the church at Rome fit into the story of God's mercy and justice to *all* people.

FOR FURTHER REFLECTION

1. Paul's description of himself as "a slave of Jesus Christ" and his use of the word "Lord" to describe the claim that God in Christ has upon him are offensive to some Christians today. Are they offensive to you or to others in your faith community? What do you think Paul means to communicate by these metaphors? If you were writing such a self-introduction, what words would you use to describe your relationship with God, Jesus Christ, and the Holy Spirit?

2. In this chapter, Washington, D.C., was used as a contemporary analogy to Rome. The *occasionality* of Paul's letters (he wrote each of his letters for a specific situation) and their *particularity* (Paul wrote each letter to a specific

community) were a problem for some in the early church and may raise questions today as well. Why should we read a letter addressed to somebody else about their issues? One helpful way to approach Paul's letters is by analogy. As you read them, it may be helpful to ask yourselves, Does anything like this ever happen in our church? Are we facing similar or comparable issues?

3. Having read about the historical background and the probable composition of the Roman house churches, you will now be able to understand better why Paul writes what he does to them. What is the social (political, ethnic, economic) history of your faith community? How is that background reflected in the recurring differences of opinion in your church?

4. Imagine receiving a letter from an evangelist like Paul in the context of your own community of faith. In what forum or context would the letter be read and heard? Who might interpret it?

5. Reread Paul's thesis (Rom. 1:16–17). Can you describe in your own words "the gospel of God" that Paul is proclaiming to the house churches at Rome?

6. I have suggested that the best way into Paul's complicated argument in Romans is to divide it into sections and to read each section as if listening to a story. This first chapter has focused on the story of Paul's apostolic call and the story of how the Roman house churches came to their present situation. Think about the importance of telling our stories and hearing each others' stories. What stories have shaped your life and your deepest convictions about reality? They may be your own story/stories or they may be stories you have read and heard.

7. When Paul alludes to his story, he is witnessing to the power of God that has changed every aspect of his life. Many contemporary Christians have also experienced "giving testimony" to God's grace through the telling of their stories. Other groups that have experienced this model are Alcoholics Anonymous (and similar twelve-step programs) as well as those who have powerful memories of a painful or difficult history, such as war veterans or cancer survivors. Sometimes, a whole generation tells its story and witnesses to the power of God for salvation and reconciliation. In the United States, those who lived through the civil rights struggle have stories to tell of God's merciful love in the face of hate and hostility. If you were to introduce yourself to a group of people who did not know you, what story or stories would you tell? If you were to describe your church to someone who had never worshipped there, what story or stories would best reflect the quality of your congregational life together?

2

"The Redemption
That Is in Christ Jesus"

(Rom. 1:18–3:31)

> The dark night is God's attack on religion. If you genuinely desire
> union with the unspeakable love of God, then you must be pre-
> pared to have your "religious" world shattered. If you think de-
> votional practices, theological insights, even charitable actions
> give you some sort of a purchase on God, you are still playing
> games.
>
> *Rowan Williams[1]*

Romans 1–3 is the first story within the larger story of Romans. It tells us three
things. First, it tells us that human unrighteousness and unfaithfulness cannot
undo God's righteousness, God's covenant faithfulness. Second, it tells the
two-part story of a world gone wrong. Part one is the universal human story,
which is applicable to both Gentiles and Jews, all descendants of Adam and
Eve. Part two is the particular story of Israel, who is meant to be God's "light
to the nations" (Isa. 49:6) but who in fact is "living in darkness" (Isa. 49:9).
Third, it tells the story of God's merciful rescue operation for the lost world—
both humanity and Israel. God's own action in the death and resurrection of
Jesus Christ was precisely the only way the world's salvation could work. God
did what humanity could not do for itself, being lost and corrupt; God did what
Israel could not do for the world, by keeping covenant faithfulness on behalf
of Israel. Therefore, the whole world and all of its people—both Jews and
Gentiles—are one, because God is One and the same God who created us all,
saves us all and loves us all.

---

1. Rowan Williams, "The Dark Night," *A Ray of Darkness: Sermons and Reflections*
(Boston: Cowley, 1995) 82.

GOD'S RIGHTEOUSNESS
AS COVENANT FAITHFULNESS

In his thesis (1:16–17) Paul declared that he was "not ashamed of the gospel of God." Why not? "Because it is the power of God for salvation to everyone who has faith, to the Jew first and also to the Greek." Why is it the power of God for salvation? "Because [in this gospel] the righteousness of God is being revealed, from faithfulness through faithfulness, as it stands written, 'The one who is righteous by faithfulness shall live.'" But what does Paul mean when he uses the expression, *dikaiosynē theou*, "the righteousness of God?"

The meaning of this phrase has been the subject of a long debate for two reasons: because of its ambiguity in Greek and because of various theological assumptions made since the Protestant Reformation. The genitive in Greek can have more than one meaning. For example, "the love of God" can mean either "God's love for us" or "our love for God." The first, "God's love for us," is called a subjective genitive because God is the subject of the phrase: it is God who is doing the action; God loves. The second, "our love for God," is called an objective genitive because God is the object of the action: we are doing the loving, and God is the object of our love. The similar phrase, "the righteousness of God," can be interpreted to mean "God's own righteousness" (subjective genitive) or "our righteousness before God" meaning "the righteousness that is effective before God" (objective genitive). What looks at first like a third possibility (genitive of origin), "the righteousness that is a gift of God," is only another way of talking about "our righteousness from God," the second option.

Since the Protestant Reformation, which itself was strongly influenced by Martin Luther's reading of Romans, scholars have tended to think of "the righteousness of God" in the second sense: our righteousness in the sight of God. Why? The argument goes like this: We have no righteousness of our own, but God imputes or imparts the righteousness of Jesus Christ to us. Then, when God looks at us, God sees not our unrighteousness but the righteousness of Christ given to us, which covers our unrighteousness. In fact, Luther spoke of our actions, even our best deeds, as "filthy rags" in the sight of God but argued that we wear the righteousness of Jesus Christ (which has become our own through baptism) before God. Luther's highly influential reading of "the righteousness of God" has been and still is powerful for Christians, but it is almost certainly not what Paul meant by the phrase, which is even more powerful once it is understood. In order to understand that original meaning, we need to examine the Jewish roots of the phrase, which has meant many things but not very often "imputed" righteousness.

"The Righteousness of God" in Israel's Scriptures

Israel's Scriptures provide the context for Paul's thought in Romans. In Jewish literature prior to Paul, "the righteousness of God" had at least three interrelated meanings: (1) God's covenant faithfulness to Israel; (2) God's justice, especially for the poor and powerless; and (3) God's eschatological (end-time) saving power to make things turn out right.[2]

God's Righteousness as God's Covenant Faithfulness to Israel

The most important and primary meaning of God's righteousness is God's covenant faithfulness to Israel. In the Septuagint (LXX), the Greek version of the Old Testament, the Greek word *dikaiosynē* translates the Hebrew word group *tzedek, tzedaqah* into "righteousness" in English. This Hebrew word group suggests the basic notion of fidelity within a relationship that guarantees order and reliability. Righteousness is understood both socially and cosmically. To say that God is "righteous" means that God is reliable and trustworthy: the sun will come up every morning; enough rain will fall; the earth that God created will be maintained by God. So, too, in social dealings, when God makes a promise, God keeps it. When Israel reads the promises of God made to Abraham, Isaac, and Jacob in the Scriptures, Israel can rely on and trust these words of God: God keeps God's word.

Action that is "righteous" or done "in righteousness" is action done "in right relationship" with one's covenant partner. It is "doing the right thing by" someone. Thus Judah's comment about Tamar in Genesis 38:26—"She is more righteous than I" ("She is more in the right than I," NRSV)—means not that she is morally better but that by her outrageous behavior she has placed both of them more in right relationship with what is covenantally right.[3] The prophets often used the analogy of marriage to describe the covenant relationship between God and Israel. The ancient world lived with a double standard whereby a wife was expected to be faithful to her husband while the

---

2. Thorough bibliographies on this subject appear in the commentaries on Romans by Cranfield, Dunn, Wilckens, and Käsemann. Surveys of the recent history of the debate are found in Manfred T. Brauch's "The Righteousness of God in Recent German Scholarship," an appendix to E. P. Sanders, *Paul and Palestinian Judaism* (Philadelphia: Fortress, 1977) 523–542 and in Marion L. Soards, "The Righteousness of God in the Writings of the Apostle Paul," *Biblical Theology Bulletin* 15 (1985) 104–109. Excellent short summaries appear in L. E. Keck, *Paul and His Letters*, rev. ed. (Philadelphia: Fortress, 1988) 110–122, J. Louis Martyn, *Galatians: A New Translation with Introduction and Commentary*, Anchor Bible 33A (New York: Doubleday, 1997) 263–280, and N. T. Wright, *The New Testament and the People of God* (Minneapolis: Fortress, 1992) 335–338.
3. Keck, *Paul and His Letters*, 112.

husband was not so limited. God, by contrast, was faithful and reliable to Israel. God could be trusted and counted on. So the first and most basic meaning of "the righteousness of God" is "God's covenant fidelity to Israel."

In this context, we can understand the logic behind what is probably the earliest biblical occurrence of the word "righteousness" in the song of Deborah (Judg. 5:11). Deborah was the first of the prophets, and many scholars believe that her song is one of the oldest fragments of Hebrew poetry. Deborah's song speaks of God's military victories over the Canaanites as God's "righteousnesses" (KJV: righteous acts; NRSV: triumphs). Not only has God's victory put things right for Israel, but in that righteous action, God "did what was right by Israel in light of God's prior covenant commitments."[4] In the same way, the poetic parallelism of Isaiah 51:4–5 closely relates God's salvation and God's righteousness (*tzedaqah*), showing that God's deliverance, which accords with "what it is right for God to bring about" for Israel, manifests God's covenant-keeping righteousness.[5]

God's Righteousness as the Justice of God, the Righteous Judge

A second important meaning of "the righteousness of God" comes out of the setting of the law court. It is sometimes called "forensic" righteousness because in a law court, things are "put right" and people are shown to "be in the right" or "justified." This legal metaphor works in at least two ways in the Jewish Scriptures that provided the context of Paul's thought in Romans. The first model pictures God as plaintiff. While Israel or a member of Israel occasionally brings charges against God (as in the book of Job), God more often has a "case" against Israel: God has been faithful, but Israel has not been faithful. In Isaiah 5:3–4, for example, God speaks as the owner of an unproductive vineyard that is about to be destroyed in judgment. Psalm 143, important in Israel's tradition, helps us to understand Romans 1–3, for Paul actually paraphrases it in 3:20.[6] The psalmist begins by admitting that God is "in the right" or "justified" in God's condemnation:

> Hear my prayer, O God,
>   listen to me in your faithfulness,
>   answer me in your righteousness;
> Do not enter into judgment with your servant,
>   for no one living is righteous in your sight.
>   (Ps. 143:1–2)

---

4. Krister Stendahl, *Final Account: Paul's Letter to the Romans* (Minneapolis: Fortress, 1995) 16. Keck, *Paul and His Letters*, 112.

5. Keck, *Paul and His Letters*, 112.

6. Richard B. Hays, "Psalm 143 and the Logic of Romans 3," *JBL* 99 (1980): 107–115.

But then the psalmist prays for God's covenant faithfulness. Even though God is right and the psalmist is wrong, God is trusted to "put things right":

> For the sake of your name, O Lord, preserve my life.
>   And in your righteousness rescue me from trouble.
>   (Ps. 143:11).

The second model of forensic righteousness pictures God as the just judge who gives justice and vindicates, or justifies, the oppressed. The legal context here is a civil action between two parties. The accusing plaintiff complains of a wrong done and insists upon being awarded damages while the defendant either denies doing the wrong or explains that it wasn't his or her fault. The judge hears the evidence on both sides fairly and impartially, then decides for the one who is "in the right." Moreover, once the judge has acted, the controversy is settled and the two parties (who were alienated from one another) are restored in relationship once more. They have been "put right" with each other.

The social aspect of God's justice is also important here: God as righteous judge acts in accordance with the law to vindicate the poor and the helpless and to punish the wicked evildoer or oppressor. So, for example, if a plaintiff brings false accusations against a helpless stranger or orphan, God takes up the side of the helpless against the powerful evildoer. The covenant between God and Israel is in the background. If Israel is acting wrongly with respect to others, God's impartiality means that God will vindicate the helpless at Israel's expense. In fact, the prophet Amos even suggests that God's special covenant relationship with Israel leads to stricter judgment of Israel than of the other nations (Amos 3:2). But if the other nations unjustly accuse Israel and their wicked prosecutors bring false charges against the people of God, God the just judge will act to save Israel from her oppressors (Dan. 7:9–12).

God's Righteousness as God's Power
to Put Things Right in the End Time

During the situation of Israel's exile in Babylon after 587 B.C.E., the saving and eschatological (end-time) aspects of God's righteous vindication of Israel against the oppressing foreign nations became especially important. In certain psalms (especially Pss. 96 and 98) and in Isaiah 40–66, the phrase "the righteousness of God" describes God's saving actions on behalf of God's captive people, Israel. As Ernst Käsemann argued, "the righteousness of God" becomes almost a technical term for God's "saving faithfulness" with respect to Israel and the nations: God will sit in judgment as the righteous judge of the whole earth.[7] Part of putting things right between Israel and the nations (the Gentiles) is restoring right relationship. God will bring about peace and justice in all the world, including peace and justice between Israel and the rest of the nations. Israel understood the Babylonian exile in the context of the story of the exodus: just as God had acted to save Israel from Pharaoh's army at the Red Sea, so God would intervene once again in human history to rescue Israel from Babylonian servitude and exile from the land promised to Israel's ancestors.

The apocalyptic writings that date from between the time of exile and the first century of the Christian era when Paul wrote Romans continued the righteousness traditions found in the Psalms and in Isaiah 40–66. These writings stress the power of the Creator who acts to save the lost creation that is threatened by hostile and oppressive powers. These hostile powers, especially Sin and Death, entered the world through the disobedience of Adam and Eve. They now oppress both the human creature and the created order, but God will act to vindicate the enslaved creation. The apocalyptic writings combine increasing despair about the possibility of any human righteousness—except in the small community of the elect—with increased longing for God's eschatological deliverance. For example, the Dead Sea Scrolls from Qumran (written shortly before the time of Paul) confess human unrighteousness or wickedness while praying for "the righteousness of God," that is, the eschatological saving power of God who will act in the last days to put things right (cf. 1QS XI, 2, 5, 14, 1QH IV, 20). In other Jewish literature of the same period, God's righteousness is understood more legally to mean that God will reward righteous deeds and punish the offenses of the unrighteous (*Pss. Sol.* 8:23–25; 9; Wis. 12:12–18, esp. 12:15).

God's Righteousness in Paul's Letter to the Romans

When Paul says in Romans 1:17 that in the gospel "the righteousness of God is being revealed from faithfulness through faithfulness" and when he quotes Habakkuk 2:4, "The one who is righteous by faithfulness shall live," he is probably drawing on all of the meanings of God's righteousness I have just described. Paul seems to have four meanings in mind: (1) God's righteousness as the Creator to the entire creation; (2) God's special covenant relationship with Israel; (3) God as the impartial judge who will put things right, especially

---

7. Ernst Käsemann, "The Righteousness of God in Paul," *New Testament Questions of Today*, trans. W. J. Montague (Philadelpia: Fortress, 1969) 168–193. "Justification and Salvation History in the Epistle to the Romans," *Perspectives on Paul*, trans. M. Kohl (London: SCM Press, 1971) 60–101. See also his *Commentary on Romans*, trans. G. W. Bromiley (Grand Rapids: Eerdmans, 1980) 23–30.

for the poor and the oppressed; and (4) God's saving faithfulness that will restore all things to right relationship at the end time. For Paul, however, the all-important shift has occurred: God has already acted in the death and resurrection of Jesus Christ "from faithfulness through faithfulness" (Rom. 1:17). God's action of covenant fidelity to Israel, all humanity, and the world was accomplished and manifested through the faithful obedience of Jesus Christ who died on the cross. God's resurrection of Jesus Christ shows that the expected end time is already upon us, since the resurrection of the dead is one of the signs of the end time. God's covenant righteousness is being revealed (*apokalyptetai*, Rom. 1:17).

What is true in the heavenly realm and in the age to come is now shown to be true in the earthly realm and in the present age: God's saving justice has been announced in Jesus Christ! God's demonstration that the crucified Jesus of Nazareth is the risen Lord was the apocalyptic event in which the veil separating heaven from earth is torn in two or pulled aside, so that God's saving justice is evident to the whole world. Jesus' faithfulness is also his righteousness by which he will live forever (Hab. 2:4). Those who trust in him trust also in God's covenant faithfulness because he is God's eschatological deliverer of Israel and of the world.

GOD'S RIGHTEOUSNESS AS WRATH AGAINST SIN
ROM. 1:18–3:20

When Romans is read as Melanchthon's "compendium of Christian doctrine," Romans 1:18–3:20 is typically seen as Paul's doctrine of universal human sinfulness: all people are sinful in the sight of God "since all have sinned and fall short of the glory of God" (Rom. 3:23); therefore all people are in need of the saving work of Jesus Christ. Although this is certainly *true* and has been preached with power since the Protestant Reformation, it misses most of what is going on in the first three chapters of Romans. In another common doctrinal reading, Romans 1 and 2 are thought to express Paul's doctrine of natural law, especially when 2:14 is (mis)read to say that Gentiles do "by nature" what the law requires. Once again, one certainly *can* derive a doctrine of natural law and/or a doctrine of general revelation from these chapters, but these concerns, as important and useful as they may be to systematic theologians, are clearly peripheral to Paul's argument.

Romans 1:18–3:20 is better understood as the story of a world gone wrong, told in two parts. Part one (1:18–32) deals with the universal human story applicable to both Gentiles and Jews, all descendants of Adam and Eve. It is told with special emphasis, however, on Gentile sinfulness, probably in order to stress the universal condition of human bondage to Sin and Death. Part two (2:1–3:20) is the story of Israel's particular sinfulness by virtue of its being God's covenant people. We see that Israel was intended to be "a light to the nations" (Isa. 49:6), God's special means of grace for the nations (Gentiles) and for the world; but instead of being God's light, Israel is itself living in the darkness of exile (Isa. 49:9), unable to be a light to anyone.[8] Both Gentiles and Jews then—all humanity—find themselves in the position of having nothing to say before God. Every mouth is silenced, and the whole world is accountable to God (3:19). In 3:20, Paul paraphrases the psalmist who spoke for all of us in confessing universal human unrighteousness:

> No human being will be found righteous in the sight of God by means of deeds prescribed by the law. (Ps. 143:2)

Rather than summarizing doctrines of Pauline theology, Romans 1:18–3:20 was probably written with the situation of Paul's upcoming visit to the house churches at Rome very much in mind. First, some people (probably Jewish Christians) may have accused Paul of preaching a gospel that is morally "soft" in order to win Gentile converts. If so, he needs to show that he can deal straightforwardly with human sinfulness. Indeed, Paul may need to show this anyway, simply in order to preach the gospel to those at Rome. Something in the human spirit makes it difficult to believe the good news of God's saving power and merciful love unless it is clear that the proclaimer of that good news is fully capable of telling the truth about Sin and Death. An evangelist who preaches only God's love without insisting also upon God's righteousness against wickedness and evil does not really preach good news.

Second, in Romans 1:18–3:20 Paul plays on stereotypical misunderstandings of Gentiles and Jews to challenge the tendencies of each group to judge and despise the another. He will discuss these prejudices directly at the end of his letter, in Romans 14 and 15. In Romans 1:18–3:20 Paul demonstrates, first for Gentiles, then for Jews, that no one has a claim against God. Then and only then are we—and Paul's readers at Rome—prepared for Romans 3:21–31, the story of God's gracious mercy to a world gone wrong and in desperate need of God's saving love. As he tells the story, Paul keeps us in suspense: in the past God has acted to save where only a few have been righteous, but what about the situation where "no one is righteous" (3:10), where "all have sinned and fall short of the glory of God" (3:23)?

Karl Barth told the story of a man who lost his way home late one night in a blinding snowstorm and subsequently realized to his horror that he had

---

8. N. T. Wright, "Romans and the Theology of Paul," *Pauline Theology, Volume Three: Romans*, ed. D. M. Hay and E. E. Johnson (Minneapolis: Fortress, 1995) 37.

walked across a lake covered only by a thin sheet of ice.[9] From his place of
safety on the other side, he looks back and gives thanks for God's merciful
deliverance from the cold waters of death. Similarly, in 1:18–3:20, Paul tells
the story of the danger of destruction, which he calls God's wrath, in the context of the gospel of the saving rescue of God in Jesus Christ. The gospel of
God's salvation is stated in Romans 1:16–17, even though it is not described
fully until 3:21–31. Because Paul's audience knows the outcome of the story,
they can look back from the safety of God's merciful love for all humanity to
the dangers of bondage to Sin and Death.

Paul begins this section by asserting in Romans 1:18 that God's wrath
is being revealed from heaven against all the ungodliness and unrighteousness (*adikia*) of those who by their unrighteousness suppress the truth. He
argues that God's eternal power and "Godness" (which are invisible) are
evident in the creation of the visible world, so humanity is "without excuse"
before God (1:20). Here he is speaking particularly of Gentile humanity, who
might try to use the excuse that they did not know God's will because they
do not have God's law. What is the unrighteousness or wickedness for
which Paul is indicting them? It is that they did not honor God as God
(1:21) but exchanged the glory of the immortal God for images of creatures
(1:23).

What does this language recall? In the distant background is the memory
of the golden calf in Exodus 32, Israel's classic story of idolatry leading to sexual immorality.[10] But in the immediate background is the story of the creation
and fall of Adam and Eve (Gen. 1–3). Paul signals in two ways that he has Genesis 1–3 in mind. First, he uses the expression "images in the likeness of" creatures (Rom. 1:23), echoing Genesis 1:26, which recalls humanity made in the
image and likeness of God. Then he speaks of "serving the creature rather than
the One who created it" (Rom. 1:25), an allusion to the serpent in Genesis 3.
God intended that Adam and Eve should image God for the world, reflecting
God's glory through their obedience to God, but instead they reflected the
lesser glory of creation back to itself.

Language about the image and likeness of God would have carried particular force for Christians living in Rome because it was the custom of Roman
emperors to demonstrate their power by erecting a statue of themselves in the
colonies under Roman rule. Although the absent emperor was literally invisible, his power was manifest in his image and likeness, which he had caused to

---

9. Karl Barth, "Saved By Grace," *Deliverance to the Captives*, trans. M. Wieser (New
York: Harper & Row, 1978) 35–42.

10. Wayne A. Meeks, "'And Rose Up to Play': Midrash and Paraenesis in 1 Cor
10:1–22," *Journal for the Study of the New Testament* 16 (1982): 64–78.

be made and which reminded the people of his rule.[11] If the people in the colony were to tear down that image and erect a statue of themselves or of someone else, that would be an act of treason. So, by analogy, argues Paul, Adam and Eve wrongfully withheld the worship and honor due to God and gave it instead to God's creatures, that is, to the serpent who told them they could become like God, and to themselves. When that happened, the order of God's good creation began to unravel. Because God's word of warning—that Death would be the consequence of their disobedience—was the truth, the serpent's word—that they would not die if they disobeyed—was a lie. Adam and Eve "exchanged the truth of God for a lie" (Rom. 1:25) and in that way the powers of Sin and Death entered the world. Humanity has been in slavery to them ever since.

During Paul's time, Jewish ethical thought linked Adam and Eve's disobedience with idolatry, assumed that sexual immorality was the logical consequence of idolatry, and held that homosexuality was the prime example of sexual immorality. So when Paul singled out homosexuality as his main example of moral decadence resulting from the fall, he was hardly an innovator. Genesis 1:27 had already described the image and likeness of God specifically as "male and female," meaning the complementarity of male and female. So the sexual bonding of women with women and men with men would have been, in Paul's view, the logical opposite of the relationship God had intended the image of God to represent. Paul's order in Romans 1:26–27 probably reflects the order of Genesis 3, namely that Eve fell before Adam. That logic is combined with the traditional Jewish argument that the first sin—idolatry—leads to all the others (cf. Wis. 14:12). Paul provides a representative laundry list of resulting vices in 1:29–31 NRSV:

> They were filled with every kind of wickedness (*adikia*), evil, covetousness, malice. Full of envy, murder, strife, deceit, craftiness, they are gossips, slanderers, God-haters [or God-hated], insolent, haughty, boastful, inventors of evil, rebellious toward parents, foolish, faithless, heartless, ruthless.

A quick review of Paul's list shows that all humanity is included here. Finally, the moral corruption is so pervasive that those committing acts of unrighteousness not only do them but even call them righteous, an indication that the last remaining memory of God's ordered righteousness is gone. Sin and Death appear to have won the game: because all humanity is implicated in the Sin that

---

11. Wisdom of Solomon (Wis. 14:17), written about 250 B.C.E. and found not in the Hebrew canon but in the Septuagint (LXX), gives this account of the origins of idolatry: "When people could not honor monarchs in their presence, since they lived at a distance, they imagined their appearance far away, and made a visible image of the king whom they honored, so that by their zeal they might flatter the absent one as though present."

now rules Adam and Eve and because "the wages of sin is Death" (Rom. 6:23), all humanity now lies helplessly imprisoned under the reign of Sin and Death.

Where is God in all this? In Romans 1:23–28, Paul describes a complex pattern where humanity three times "exchanged" God's gracious rule for one of their own devising (1:23, 25, 26) and, in response, three times "God gave them up" (1:24, 26, 28) to their own choices. This downward spiral, or moral declension, progresses from (1) the disobedient, willful decision for idolatry to (2) the less freely chosen consequences of "degrading passions" to (3) the even less freely chosen consequences of "an unfit mind" that is so unable to discern right from wrong that it approves what is wrong. Paul stops at this point in the story, interrupting the plot at its darkest hour in order to tell the matching declension story for Israel in 2:1–24. At this point, it looks as if God is willing to allow both humanity and all the rest of creation, which humanity was supposed to be guiding by its imaging of God, to dissolve into moral confusion and chaos.

Following the order of Paul's argument, we, too, will have to wait until the surprising reversal of 3:21–31 to hear how the story comes out. In the meantime, I must make some clarifying comments. Romans 1:18–32, one of the two biblical texts most clearly prohibiting homosexuality (cf. Lev. 18:22; 20:13), is sometimes tragically misread as calling for the punishment of death to those who engage in same-sex relations. There is, however, no support for that interpretation, either from Paul's vantage point or from our own. In fact, that misreading is, in Paul's words "without excuse" (Rom. 2:1). I say this for at least three reasons. First, the logic of Paul's argument is that the most dramatic sins described appear at the end of his list: the problem with idolatry is its subtlety (Gen. 3:1). In his view, sexual immorality is a warning light that signals the moral chaos to come. Second, the phrase in 1:32, "those who practice such things deserve to die," refers to *everything* in Paul's long list of vices in 1:29–31 plus *all* those things Paul did not mention of which they are representative examples (cf. "*such* things," not "*these* things" in 1:32), rather than only to homosexuality, which is, in Paul's view, a sign of more serious moral shipwreck ahead.

Third, still within the framework of Paul's argument, Romans 2:1 parallels 1:18 as the start of the corresponding argument about Israel. Paul uses stereotypical language about Gentile sexual immorality to craft a trap for those who judge the failings of others. Paul probably anticipated that some of his Jewish Christian readers would have enthusiastically joined the crusade condemning Gentile immorality. If so, they would quickly discover that Paul's rhetorical sword cuts both ways when he says "you, the judge, are doing the very same things!" (2:1). Paul describes how these "judges" are storing up wrath for themselves "on the day of wrath, when God's righteous judgment will be revealed" (2:5). "Thus," as Richard Hays notes,

Paul's warning should transform the terms of our contemporary debate about homosexuality: no one has a secure platform to stand upon in order to pronounce condemnation upon others. Anyone who presumes to have such a vantage point is living in a dangerous fantasy, oblivious to the gospel that levels all of us before a holy God."[12]

Stepping now outside the vantage point of Paul's own argument, a few more things remain to be said. While it is absolutely clear that Paul thought same-sex relations were immoral, many Jews and Christians today would not agree with him and might use the logic of his own argument to challenge him. Paul's argument is based on the apparently unquestioned assumption that hetero-sexuality is "natural" and homosexuality is "unnatural" (1:26), which is not at all clear empirically.[13] The fact that Paul has strong opinions about what is natural and unnatural does not necessarily mean that he is correct, a judgment he himself seems to invite at 1 Corinthians 11:13–15:

> Judge for yourselves: is it fitting for a woman to pray to God with her head unveiled? Does not nature itself teach you that if a man wears long hair, it dishonors him, but if a woman has long hair, it is her glory?

Paul assumes that it is unnatural for men to have long hair (presumably he would not like most portraits of Jesus) or for women to have short hair or to wear their hair uncovered. But, for example, it is the male lion that has the long mane; peacocks (male) that have the long, bright feathers. There can be honest differences of opinion about what is natural in God's created order and therefore what reflects and gives glory to God. Same-sex relationships also occur naturally throughout God's created order. Paul urges the Christians at Rome to try to *discern* God's will (Rom. 12:2). He is probably speaking ironically at Romans 2:18 when he says that Jews know it. See also Romans 10:2 where he speaks of zeal that is not enlightened: Paul himself was dead sure he was right to be persecuting the church of God—until God in Christ showed him otherwise. As Robert Morgan has argued,

> So in matters of political and sexual ethics contemporary Christians are not excused from the hard work of deciding what is right and wrong just because Paul in his day thought certain matters beyond dispute.[14]

---

12. Richard B. Hays, *The Moral Vision of the New Testament: Community, Cross, and New Creation: A Contemporary Introduction to New Testament Ethics* (San Francisco: Harper-Collins, 1996) 389.

13. Bernadette J. Brooten, *Love Between Women: Early Christian Responses to Female Homoeroticism* (Chicago: University of Chicago Press, 1996) 215–302.

14. Robert Morgan, *Romans* (Sheffield: Sheffield Academic Press, 1997) 124.

The critical questions about this issue for Christians today are both exegetical and hermeneutical: not only how to interpret such passages but also what to think about them in the light of later experience and perception.[15]

So then, both from *within* the terms of Paul's argument and from a vantage point *outside* of it, Christians are called to faithfulness to God's will as best we can discern it; to humility as we think about the judgment of God that we will all face; and to charity for those with whom we must reluctantly disagree on this admittedly complex and controversial issue. No matter what remains unclear, it is absolutely clear, as Beverly Gaventa argues, that to use Romans 1:18–32 "to justify the exclusion of persons who are homosexual would be the greatest distortion of Romans and its claims about God's radical and universal grace."[16]

Romans 2:1–16 not only springs a trap on those of us, whoever we are (2:1), who are inclined to pass judgment on others without realizing the extent of our own sinfulness before God; it also raises serious doubts about whether *anyone* will be found righteous in the sight of God. Paul insists on God's impartiality as the just judge of the world. For those who obey not the truth but unrighteousness (*adikia*) there will be wrath and fury; there will be anguish and distress for everyone who does evil, the Jew first and also the Greek. In the same way, there will be glory, honor, and peace for everyone who does good, the Jew first and also the Greek, for God shows no partiality (2:8–11). God's impartiality will be demonstrated not only when God repays all according to their deeds (2:6) but also when God judges the world in a way that respects the different moral situations of Jews and Gentiles. Jews who have the law will be judged by its provisions. Gentiles, who by nature do not have the law[17] but who do what the law requires, will be judged favorably. Here Paul holds out at least the possibility that there will be a group of Jews who keep the law and a group of Gentiles who do what the law requires. So far, however, it is only a possibility, and how that could happen remains to be spelled out.

---

15. This is a slightly altered version of a statement by Luke T. Johnson, ("The critical question for present-day Christians is not exegetical but hermeneutical—that is, what to think and do about such passages as these in the light of later experience and perception.") *Reading Romans: A Literary and Theological Commentary* (New York: Crossroad, 1997) 34. See his excellent discussion there. In my view, the exegetical question must remain central: it is not replaced by the hermeneutical task.

16. Beverly Roberts Gaventa, "Romans," *Women's Bible Commentary*, exp. ed. with Apocrypha, ed. Carol A. Newsom and Sharon H. Ringe (Louisville, Ky.: Westminster John Knox, 1998) 403–410 at 407.

17. See the discussion in C. E. B. Cranfield, *A Critical and Exegetical Commentary on the Epistle to the Romans*, ICC (Edinburgh: T&T Clark, 1975) I: 155–57 for the list of exegetical possibilities for Romans 2:14.

In Romans 2:17–24, Paul adopts the rhetorical style of diatribe, which allows a writer to anticipate objections to the argument and to overcome them within the argument itself. Paul enters into conversation with an imaginary Jewish opponent who wishes to insist on Jewish privilege as a result of God's gracious election of Israel.[18] Paul's imaginary opponent would substantially agree with Paul's argument to this point: Yes, there is a relationship between idolatry and immorality. Yes, God will judge all according to their deeds. Yes, God is impartial. At this point, however, differences arise. Paul's interlocutor notes that God has chosen Israel to be a light to the Gentiles! Paul counters, "If you are sure that you are a guide to the blind, a light to those who are in darkness" (2:19), then how do you account for sin within Israel? Why has your own light become darkness? It is important to notice that the charges Paul lists in 2:21–23 are part of Israel's *own* prophetic self-critique (Jer. 7:9; Mal. 3:8–9; Hos. 1–3; Jer. 3:8) rather than an empirical assessment of the state of Judaism in Paul's day.[19] But for Paul and, he assumes, for his imaginary opponent, the fact of Israel's ongoing exile is evidence enough of Israel's sins, especially of breaking the law that Israel claims as its special privilege:

> For, as it is written: 'The name of God is blasphemed among the Gentiles because of you.' (2:24 NRSV).

Here Paul takes a statement from the exilic prophets (Isa. 52:5; Ezek. 36:20) that originally served as a comfort and turns it into an indictment. In its original prophetic context, the saying reassured the people that God would act to rescue Israel for the sake of God's name among the nations. Paul, however, uses it as evidence of Israel's unfaithful witness to God. Israel's sins have resulted in the opposite of her call to be a light to the world (Isa. 49:6); they have only revealed the depths of her own darkness (Isa. 49:9).[20]

On that grim note, Paul once again hints that there may be a people who keep "the just requirements of the law" (*dikaiōmata*, 2:26) and that they may or may not be circumcised outwardly, since real circumcision is a matter of the heart. (See Deut. 10:16; Jer. 4:4; 9:26; Ezek. 44:9 for circumcision of the heart.)

---

18. This paragraph follows the argument of N. T. Wright, "Adam, Israel and the Messiah," in *The Climax of the Covenant: Christ and the Law in Pauline Theology*, (Minneapolis: Fortress, 1992) 18–40 and "Romans and the Theology of Paul," 30–67, especially at 33.

19. Prophetic critique of Israel is discussed by Mary C. Callaway in her "A Hammer That Breaks Rock in Pieces: Prophetic Critique in the Hebrew Bible," *Anti-Semitism and Early Christianity: Issues of Polemic and Faith*, ed. Craig A. Evans and Donald A. Hagner (Minneapolis: Fortress, 1993) 21–38.

20. Richard B. Hays, *Echoes of Scripture in the Letters of Paul* (New Haven, Conn.: Yale University Press, 1989) 45. Also Wright, "Romans and the Theology of Paul," 37.

But for Paul's imaginary opponent, this raises the next logical question: If God praises spiritual rather than literal circumcision (2:29), then what advantage is there to being a Jew? What's the point of circumcision, the sign of the covenant? Is there still a covenant between God and Israel (3:1)? These are all-important questions that Paul will take up at greater length in Romans 9–11. Here in 3:1–9 he gives only a hint of his later answer.

Then what advantage has the Jew? What is the value of circumcision? Paul's answer is surprising to anyone following his argument so far. We expect him to say, "None," and instead he says, "Much, in every way." Then as we wait for him to list a string of advantages, he mentions exactly one: The Jews have been entrusted with (*episteuthēsan*) "the oracles of God" (3:2). Again we encounter the divine passive: God has entrusted the Scriptures to Israel, given them to Israel for safekeeping. To use a contemporary example, if I entrust my money to a bank in a trust fund, that does not mean that the bankers can do whatever they want with it: it is for the benefit of the person for whom I am intending it, for my beneficiary, although the bankers use it and benefit from it as well.[21] So Paul's metaphor here is that God entrusted Israel with the Scriptures not only for Israel's own use but also in a fiduciary capacity. That is why Paul calls the Scriptures the "oracles of God": They were written down long ago for a later generation, namely, the generation of Paul and his Gentile churches. Israel is indeed called to be a light to the nations in this way: God had always planned to include the Gentiles in God's covenant mercies, and the Scriptures show this, as Paul will demonstrate in the rest of his argument in Romans.

But what about Israel's own relationship with God, apart from the fiduciary relationship for the Gentiles? Paul insists that God is true to Israel, true to the covenant relationship, true to the covenant promises. Even if some in Israel were unfaithful (*ēpistēsan*; cf. 2:21–23), their unfaithfulness (*apistia*) cannot nullify God's faithfulness (*pistin*). Even if everyone is a liar, God must still be true. Paul supports this claim by citing Psalm 51:4, the psalm David is said to have prayed after being confronted by Nathan after his adultery with Bathsheba and the murder of her husband Uriah. Tradition records that David spoke these words to God as evidence of God's justice: "so that you may be vindicated (proved righteous) in your words, and prevail in your judging" (Rom. 3:4). Indeed, the truth of our human unrighteousness (*adikia*) serves only to prove the righteousness of God, *dikaiosynē theou*, that God is right and is acting as a just judge in condemning us. Then it would be ridiculous to say

---

21. I am indebted to N. T. Wright for this analogy. It should not be pushed too far: the Scriptures are fully Israel's Scriptures while (in Paul's view at least) they are also intended by God for a future use with Paul's mixed or even primarily Gentile churches that could hardly have been foreseen in advance by anyone but God.

that God is unjust to inflict wrath upon us, for in that case how could God judge the world (3:6)?

We have already identified several stories retold or alluded to in Paul's argument in Romans 1:18–3:20. He has reminded us of the golden calf (Exod. 32) and the disobedience of Adam and Eve (Gen. 3). He has contrasted the call of Israel to be a light to the nations with the darkness of exile (Isa. 49). He has quoted Psalm 51, whose title connects it to the story of David's confession of sin. Now, in referring to the wrath of God and God's judgment of the world, Paul alludes to another story that lies submerged in his argument. It is the story of the unrighteousness of the people of Sodom and of Abraham's intercession in Genesis 18. He pleads with God for the remnant of righteous inhabitants of Sodom, that they might not be destroyed along with the wicked.[22] There the question of the righteousness of God is raised directly by Abraham, who asks, "Shall not the Judge of all the earth do what is right?" (Gen. 18:25). God agrees with Abraham's understanding and consents to spare the city, even if only ten righteous people are found there. But even with Abraham's intervention, Sodom is destroyed in God's wrath. There are not even ten righteous people to be found there.

This story underlies Paul's statement in Romans 3:9–10 that "all, both Jews and Greeks, are under the power of Sin, as it stands written, 'There is no one righteous, not even one.'" The chain (*catena*) of indicting texts from the psalms and prophets that follows in Romans 3:10–18 underlines Paul's point like a battering ram crashing through the last locked door of resistance. Finally, there is nothing to say. Those under the law are indicted by the very Scriptures with which they have been entrusted. Jews are no better off than Gentiles (3:9) when it comes to answering God's charges of unrighteousness. They are as much under the power of Sin as the Gentiles are. Every mouth is silenced and the whole world is held accountable to God. For "no human being will be found righteous" in God's sight by deeds of the law, says Paul, paraphrasing Psalm 143:2. We saw earlier that in this psalm the psalmist, like David, confesses his sin and the sins of all humanity before God, throwing himself on the covenant mercies of the Creator.

Until now Paul has told the story of the world gone wrong in two parts: first, the story of humanity as a whole represented by Gentiles, then the story of Israel in particular covenant relationship with God under Torah. Paul's story

---

22. This story is *not* interpreted by subsequent biblical writers, with the sole exception of Jude 7, to be about sexual immorality or homosexuality. See Ezekiel 16:49, "This was the guilt of your sister Sodom: she and her daughters had pride, excess of food, and prosperous ease, but did not aid the poor and needy" and the discussion of the text in Hays, *The Moral Vision of the New Testament*, at 381.

continues: Gentiles, together with all humanity, are hopelessly compromised by their participation in Adam's fall and enslaved to Sin and Death; Israel was supposed to be God's faithful servant, a light to the nations, but Israel proved unfaithful, as compromised and enslaved as the Gentiles Israel was to enlighten. The inhabitants of the world are in grave danger when suddenly God's ancient promise to Abraham is revived in the person of Jesus Christ. Here is an example of one of the "oracles of God" (3:2) in action, which Paul discovered in an earlier argument (cf. Gal. 3:16 and the singular seed of Abraham that is Jesus Christ) and to which he will return later in Romans 9:29, quoting Isaiah 1:9 LXX: "If the Lord of Hosts had not left us (a) seed, we would have become like Sodom and resembled Gomorrah."

GOD'S RIGHTEOUSNESS
AND OUR REDEMPTION IN CHRIST
ROM. 3:21–31

When Romans is read *only* as a summary of Christian doctrine, 3:21–31 is the place where you find Luther's doctrine of "justification by faith" and his supporting proof text: "For we reckon that a person is justified by faith apart from works of the law" (3:28). This reading has several consequences. First, the verses (29–31) that follow 3:28 seem totally irrelevant, even though they concern the righteousness of God as the integrity of God and the subsequent unity of Jews and Gentiles, who have the same God. As a result, older commentaries often express puzzlement at Paul's sudden jump to what seems like a completely different subject. A second consequence of this reading is that Romans 4:1–25 becomes less significant: Abraham functions solely as an example of someone who is justified by faith, with Genesis 15:6 as Paul's proof text. As we shall see, that interpretation misses most of what is going on in Romans 4, in addition to providing an inadequate reading of 3:21–31.

Romans is best read as the continuous story of what God has done in Jesus Christ and what God continues to do in the lives of those who are baptized into Christ Jesus. Romans 3:21–31 is the first rhetorical climax of the letter and the most important telling of the story of God's redemption of the lost and enslaved world through the death and resurrection of Jesus Christ. We hear the dramatic rescue story through Paul's three powerful metaphors: *justification* (What will become of the prisoners condemned to death?); *redemption* (Will the lost family members be ransomed from their kidnappers?); and *atonement* (Will the sins of the people separate them from God's forgiveness?). These three alternative descriptions of God's saving action in the death and resurrection of Jesus Christ not only served to advance Paul's argument to the Roman house churches but also continue to provide provocative analogies that help later readers of Romans to connect God's story with the stories of our lives.

The Story of Jesus Christ Told in Terms of Justification

Much of Paul's argument in 1:18–3:20 was framed in the context of the law-court model of the righteousness of God. The wrath of God the righteous judge of all the earth is being revealed against all ungodliness and unrighteousness (1:18). The evidence of creation and the created order has been used against humanity in general and Gentiles in particular so that they are "without excuse" (1:20). They are filled with every kind of unrighteousness, as Paul demonstrates in his vice list of 1:29–31. They know God's righteous verdict (*dikaiōma*) that those who do "such things" deserve to die (1:32). The story of the fall of Adam and Eve (Gen. 3) is in the background: through their disobedience, Sin and Death entered the world and now all humanity, as well as the creation itself, is enslaved to these powers that are hostile to God. The self-appointed judges, who condemn those caught in the nets of Sin and Death yet act in comparable ways themselves, forget that their own situation is equally precarious: They will not escape the judgment of God (2:3) but are storing up wrath for themselves on the day of wrath when God's righteous judgment will be revealed (2:5). God will reward or punish all people according to their deeds (2:6; cf. Ps. 61:13 LXX and Prov. 24:12), judging those under the law (Jews) according to the law and those who by nature do not have the law (Gentiles) according to whether they do what the law requires. Everyone will appear before God's bench on the day when "God through Jesus Christ will judge the secret thoughts of all people" (2:16).

Nor is Israel exempt from God's judgment by virtue of its calling to be a light to the nations. Israel has not been that light but instead has walked in darkness along with them (2:19) as Israel's own prophets have attested (2:21–24). What counts with God is not outward circumcision but the circumcision of the heart (2:29). To be sure, the Jews have been entrusted with the "oracles of God" (3:2), but these Scriptures only confirm the rightness of God's condemnation (3:4–5). The infliction of wrath is the logical corollary of God's righteous judgment of the world (3:6), for "shall not the judge of all the earth do what is right?" (Gen. 18:25). Both Jews and Greeks are under the power of Sin (3:9), and "there is no one righteous, not even one" (3:10). The defendants—all humanity, including Israel—are left without a word to say: the whole world is accountable, *hypodikos*, subject to and rightly condemned by the righteous judgment of God. The defendants deserve the death sentence.

But now apart from the law, though the law and prophets testify to it (3:21), God has acted in covenant faithfulness, answering the plea of the psalmist

(Ps. 143:11) that in spite of the fact that no one living is righteous before God, God will nevertheless save the psalmist, Israel, and the world from danger. God has acted in covenant fidelity to the covenant people Israel quite apart from their own righteousness. Even though everyone has been a liar, God has nevertheless been true (3:4). God has done for the world what Israel could not do for the world, or even for itself, by providing the one true Israelite who would act in covenant faithfulness to do and be what Israel should have done and been.[23] That one true Israelite is Jesus Christ. He is Israel's representative, as the Israelite who keeps covenant with God. He is also God's representative, since the righteousness of God is enacted through his own faithfulness, his faithful obedience unto death on the cross. Paul reminds us once more of Genesis 3 when he says "all have sinned and fallen short of the glory of God" (3:23). This verse refers to the lost glory of the image of God forfeited by Adam and Eve. God has acted as the righteous judge to put things right between Godself and the world lost to Sin and Death. The poor, helplessly enslaved world has been given an advocate; the guilty have been pardoned; they have been put right with God "by [God's] grace as a gift" (3:24).

Recall Paul's thesis statement from 1:16–17: for Paul the gospel is not a message *about* God's power; it *is* God's power, the event of God's saving power both enacted and revealed in the death and resurrection of Jesus Christ. God's *dynamis*, the explosive world-changing power of God to save, is also God's righteousness "from faithfulness to faithfulness" (1:17). The faithful obedient death of Jesus Christ on the cross was simultaneously God's own action of covenant fidelity to Israel and to all humanity. That the faithful obedient death of Jesus Christ was God's own act of righteousness is proved by God's raising him from the dead. Paul's argument for the righteousness of God in Romans stands or falls precisely here: unless the faithfulness of Jesus Christ is also the righteousness of God as shown in his resurrection from the dead, then, as Paul says elsewhere, "Our preaching has been in vain and your faith has been in vain" (1 Cor. 15:14). The faithful death and resurrection of Jesus of Nazareth whom Paul proclaims as Christ and Lord is the apocalyptic event in which the veil separating heaven and earth is removed so that God's saving justice is manifest to Israel and to all the world. The faithfulness of Jesus is both his own righteousness by which he will live forever (Hab. 2:4) and the definitive proof of the righteousness of God towards all those who trust in him and who therefore also trust in God's covenant faithfulness. Jesus Christ is God's eschatological savior of Israel and of the world.

It should now be clear why the preferred translation of *dia pisteōs Iēsou Christou* (3:22) is the most straightforward one: "the faithfulness of Jesus

---

23. Wright, "Romans and the Theology of Paul," 34.

Christ," rather than "through faith in Jesus Christ," the translation influenced by Luther's opposition between faith and works. Jesus Christ is God's own covenant righteousness shown in his faithful obedience to death on behalf of the lost world. Jesus Christ's faithfulness is also representative of the faithfulness Israel should have offered so that justice is in fact done: The honor due to God (1:21) and not given by the other inhabitants of the world has in fact been given by the faithful obedience of Jesus.

It should now also be clear that in the same verse (3:22), *dikaiosynē theou*, should also be translated in its most straightforward way as "the righteousness of God" and not "the righteousness that is from God" or "the righteousness that avails before God" or anything that implies that this is righteousness that has been imputed or imparted to the human defendants in the law court. God has acted in covenant righteousness in the death of Jesus Christ precisely in order to put things back in right relationship with Israel and, through Israel, with the world. The eschatological vindication that Israel expected at the end of history, God has done now; the verdict of the last day, the dreaded day of God's wrath, has been brought forward with *mercy* the hoped for but unexpected outcome. How does Paul know that this is the verdict of the end time? Because God raised Jesus from the dead, which shows that the last days have come. God has done what the postexilic prophets promised God would do then: God has acted according to the just requirements of the law; God has judged impartially between Israel and the nations, vindicating the poor and those oppressed by Sin and Death. God has also dealt with Sin, although Paul leaves this unstated here (see 5:6–9 and 8:3).

The Story of Jesus Christ Told in Terms of Redemption

The law-court model of God's saving action in Jesus Christ is the most familiar to us and the one most developed by Paul in Romans 1–3, but he also uses a second equally powerful metaphor (redemption) to describe what God has done in Jesus Christ. The language of redemption (*apolytrōsis*) is about buying back a family member (or family property) that is in danger. When redemption deals with the recovery of family property (Lev. 25:25; 27:19), the stress is on who has the right and the responsibility to redeem (see Ruth 4:1–6); when redemption pertains to the rescue of a relative (Lev. 25:47–55), the context is often the slave market where the impoverished family member has been forced to sell him/herself into servitude because of heavy debt or poverty. In addition, this metaphor includes the idea of "the redeemer of the blood," that is, the relative who has the right under law to avenge a murder (Num. 35:9–28; Deut. 19:6–13; Josh. 20:2–9). Israel had already used this legal concept metaphorically to describe God's action as Redeemer in bringing Israel out of slavery in

Egypt (cf. Exod. 15:13, "You led in your steadfast love the people whom you redeemed"). God was also spoken of as the Redeemer of the poor and the orphaned: those who had no family member to redeem them or whose family members had failed them called to God for help (cf. Job 19:14, "My relatives have failed, and my close friends have forgotten me"). A person without friend or family to act the part of redeemer could languish forgotten in prison forever. Israel's king was expected to act the part of redeemer for the poor and oppressed (cf. Ps. 72), but above all, God, as Israel's true king, played the part of Redeemer for the people of God.[24]

This metaphor is familiar to Christians today in a number of settings. We actually use the language of redemption and redeeming in the context of a pawn shop, where an object of value is temporarily placed into the custody of another to raise money for some emergency. When the rent must be paid, a man may have to pawn his guitar to raise money. At that point, the guitar is in danger: If the person who pawned it fails to show up with the borrowed money at the agreed-upon time, the guitar will be sold: the treasured family possession will be lost forever. Similarly, if a woman's dog is lost and the dogcatcher picks it up, we speak of redeeming the dog from the pound. Again, the beloved possession is in danger: if the dog is left there unredeemed, it will be sold or put to death. Bail bond brokers are also redeemers in the sense that they will lend money to get a family member out of jail. Finally, travelers in some countries need to worry about kidnappers who capture tourists and threaten to kill them unless their family members raise the necessary ransom money. All of these contemporary analogies can help us to understand Paul's point in Romans 3:24. Humanity was captive, enslaved by Sin and Death, just as Israel had been enslaved by Pharaoh in Egypt. God's redemption in Jesus Christ rescued them from prison, redeemed them from slavery, ransomed them from the kidnappers, brought them home from the pound or the pawn shop, welcomed them home as beloved members of the family.

The Story of Jesus Christ Told in Terms of Atonement

Paul has already told the story of what God has done in Jesus Christ by means of two powerful metaphors; now he adds one more version of the story, told this time in the context of Israel's sacrificial traditions. In Romans 3:25 Paul describes "Christ Jesus" as the one "whom God put forward as a sacrifice of

---

24. This paragraph summarizes pages 104–110 of A. Katherine Grieb, "Affiliation with Jesus Christ in His Sacrifice: Some Uses of Scripture to Define the Identity of Jesus Christ in Romans," (Ph.D. diss., Yale University, 1997) where a fuller treatment of all three of Paul's soteriological metaphors in Romans 3:21–26 may be found.

atonement," or as "a place of atonement," through his blood. The phrases "sacrifice of atonement" and "place of atonement" are both translations of the word *hilastērion*, which has a special meaning in Israel's history. It is the term used to describe the *kapporeth*, or "mercy seat," that is, the lid of the ark of the covenant that rested in the "holy of holies" of the tabernacle of God. This holiest of all places was where God and Israel met symbolically, one day a year, on *Yom Kippur*, or the Day of Atonement, when the high priest of Israel, after fasting and praying all night, went into the holy of holies and poured the blood of bulls and goats as an offering for the sins of his people and himself.

So *hilastērion*, the word Paul uses to describe Jesus Christ, can mean either the place where sins are forgiven or the means by which sins are forgiven. Scholars have argued about whether to call this act of God "propitiation,"[25] which focuses on the appeasement of someone who is angry (God's wrath), or "expiation,"[26] which focuses on the sin that is staining the people of Israel and needs to be purified. It seems simplest to use instead the language of reconciliation and the coined word "at-one-ment," or atonement, to refer to the place where and the means by which God deals with the sins of Israel.

It was a bold move theologically for Paul and other early Christians to describe the death of Jesus as *a sacrifice for sin* and to speak of his *blood* as the means by which the sins of the people were forgiven. After all, Jesus did not die bound on an altar dedicated to Israel's God, as Isaac almost did and as Jepthah's unnamed daughter did. Instead, he was put to death by the Roman authorities on a cross, as Paul knows very well. Romans 6:6 is one of many references to the crucifixion of Jesus throughout the Pauline letters. Crucifixion is not a bloody death. It is more like drowning or suffocating in that it leaves the victim gasping for air because of the body's weight upon the lungs. But for Paul and other early Christians this horrible death, which was the shameful execution of a condemned criminal, has been metaphorically transformed into the means by which the sins of Israel were forgiven by God. Jesus' death is reinterpreted as the death of the paschal lamb (1 Cor 5:7), as Israel's sin offering (Rom. 4:25; 8:3; 1 Cor. 15:3ff.), and as the ceremony for the renewal of the covenant (1 Cor. 11:25), which involved the pouring out of blood (cf. Exod. 24:3–8).[27]

When Paul uses this language to speak of Jesus' death in Romans 3:25, he is saying that God put Jesus Christ forward as a way of dealing with the sins

---

25. Leon Morris, "The Meaning of ἱλαστήριον in Rom III,25," *New Testament Studies* 2 (1955/56): 33–34.

26. C. H. Dodd, "Atonement," *The Bible and the Greeks* (London: Hodder & Stoughton, 1935) 82–95.

27. See Grieb, "Affiliation with Jesus Christ in His Sacrifice," 110–111.

of Israel committed in breach of the covenant and with the sins of the world that resulted from the disobedience of Adam and Eve. Jesus Christ represents Israel and therefore also represents the world for which Israel was chosen to be God's servant. As the Anointed One, the Messiah, he is the designated representative of Israel (like the high priest; see Hebrews for a corresponding argument). Like the mercy seat, he is the place where God will deal with the covenant violations of Israel. Moreover, he is himself the sacrifice for sin. So Jesus Christ is the person who offers the sacrifice, the place where the sacrifice is performed, and the sacrifice itself. Because the death of Jesus Christ is God's action ("whom God put forward," 3:25) the faithful death of Jesus on the cross is also the manifestation (3:21) of God's covenant righteousness. The death and resurrection of Jesus Christ is the proof or demonstration both that God is righteous and that God puts right "those who share in the faithfulness of Jesus" (3:26) or "those who put their trust in Jesus" (here the genitive could go either way). Jesus' sacrificial death is God's own act of covenant righteousness, which reveals God's love for Israel and for the whole world.

The result of God's action in Christ is once more the silencing of the world (3:19) and particularly of any who are tempted to boast of their own righteousness before God (3:27). Paul may have in mind Israel's boast of their possession of the law or their vocation as light to the nations testified to in the law and the prophets, for he probably alludes to the law in the same verse: "Where then the boasting? It is excluded. By means of what law? That of works? No, but by means of the law of faith/faithfulness" (3:27). The word *nomos* here is often translated "principle," so that Paul is read to say that boasting (*kauchēsis*) is excluded by the principle of faith as opposed to the principle of works. The more natural referent of the term, however, is the Mosaic law,[28] which also fits better with Paul's concluding statement in Romans 3:31 that he does not overthrow the law by this emphasis on the faithfulness of Jesus Christ; rather he establishes and upholds the law. God had always intended to include Gentiles in the covenant promises made to Israel's ancestors. Once the death of Jesus Christ is understood as God's righteous saving action, testified to by the law and the prophets (3:21), on behalf of Israel, the nations, and the whole world, it is also seen to be fully compatible with the law entrusted to Israel.

Finally, the righteousness of God is described in terms of God's integrity: it is one and the same God who rescues both Jews and Gentiles from the powers of Sin and Death. God is *not* the God of the Jews only, of course, so Paul's rhetorical question has an obvious negative answer. God is the God of the

---

28. James D. G. Dunn, *Romans*, 2 vols. Word Bible Commentary 38. (Dallas: Word, 1988) I:186.

Gentiles as well (cf. Amos 9:7, 11–12). Because God is One (the most basic article of Israel's belief; cf. the *Shema*, Deut.: 6:4, "Hear, O Israel, the Lord Our God, the Lord is One"), Jews and Gentiles are also really one, in spite of their differences and in spite of their tendencies to stereotype and caricature one another. Those who live "by the faithfulness of Jesus Christ" (3:26) or who trust the God whose covenant righteousness was demonstrated in the faithful death of Jesus (3:22, 25) are one people of God, put back in right relationship with God (justification); redeemed from slavery to Sin and Death (redemption); and set free from the consequences of their sins (atonement). Because God is One, God has chosen one means of dealing with Sin and Death—Jesus Christ—for both Jews and Gentiles. From that time forward, they are no longer divided by the law and the practices of Torah observance that Jews do and Gentiles do not; but they are one people of God in Christ.[29]

Summary. In Romans 1:18–3:20 Paul has told the story of a world lost and enslaved to the powers of Sin and Death. In 3:21–31 he has told the story of God's dramatic rescue of the world using the metaphors of justification, redemption, and atoning sacrifice for sin. Because Jews and Gentiles are loved and saved by the same God (God is One), Jewish Christians and Gentile Christians are really one people in Christ.

FOR FURTHER REFLECTION

1. Romans 1:18–3:20 introduces several different ways of thinking about Sin and Death as enemies of God and enslavers of God's people. Paul suggests that the story of Israel's apostasy (the golden calf in Exod. 32), the story of the fall of Adam and Eve (Gen. 3), and the story of Abraham's plea for Sodom (Gen. 18) are useful for reflecting on our own tendencies to sell ourselves into slavery. Which of these stories best connects with your own experience of the power of Sin? Similarly, Romans 3:21–26 provides three different ways of thinking about God's dramatic rescue of the lost world. Paul uses the metaphor of the law court (defendants acquitted from the death penalty), the slave market (lost family members redeemed from slavery), and Israel's sacrificial system (forgiveness of sins and renewed covenant with God). Which of Paul's metaphors best connects with your own experience of God's mercy?

---

29. Their oneness in Christ is not to be sabotaged by an overemphasis on the different prepositions Paul uses to describe them in Romans 3:30. Paul may use the different language to preserve the memory of their past distinctiveness, before the work of God in Christ, or it may simply be a stylistic variation.

2. Romans 1–3 also invites contemporary readers to think about differences between people and about stereotyping those who are different. For Paul, stereotyping was a major problem for Jews and Gentiles, and therefore for Jewish Christians and Gentile Christians in the house churches in Rome. What are the contemporary analogies in our churches and in the world around us? How does Paul's use of the *Shema* (Deut. 6:4 "Hear, O Israel, the Lord our God is One Lord") function in his argument to unite this divided community into one people of God in Jesus Christ?

3. Not many of us today would choose to begin a letter of self-introduction to a church that did not know us with a discussion of same-sex relationships, one of the most controversial topics in the church today and one about which many parts of the church are completely unable to reach agreement. One of the dangers of our discussion today is that many Christians refuse to recognize those whose views on this subject differ from their own as truly Christian. How is your faith community dealing with this topic, or is it dealing with it? Is Romans 1:18–32 part of your discussion?

4. Many people have seen contemporary analogies to the exodus—God's redemption of Israel from slavery in Egypt—in the civil rights movement of the United States and in the anti-apartheid movement in South Africa. An important part of both these movements was the stress on "black and white together" and the hope for "reconcilation" (understood in a variety of ways). In the context of the Truth and Reconciliation Commission, Archbishop Desmond Tutu urged all those on either side of the conflict in South Africa to confess their sins, seek forgiveness, and accept the freedom and pardon offered by God. How does the "reconciliation" model of salvation (Rom. 5:11; see also 2 Cor. 5:18–21) fit with the models of justification, redemption, and atoning sacrifice for sins that Paul uses in Romans 3:21–26 to describe God's liberating action in Jesus Christ?

3

"Abraham, for He Is the Father of Us All"

(Rom. 4:1–25)

I do not demand a reason from Christ. If I am convinced by reason, I deny faith. Abraham believed God. Let us also believe, so that we who are the heirs of his race may likewise be heirs of his faith.

Ambrose, on the death of his brother[1]

Without naming Abraham directly, Paul has already introduced him into the story of God's covenant righteousness in Romans 1–3, in his allusion to the story of Abraham's intercession for the righteous in Genesis 18:25: "Shall not the Judge of all the world do what is right?" In Romans 4, Paul tells the story of Abraham and Sarah as they learn to trust God in the history of the birth of Isaac, the child of God's promise. Not far in the background is another story: the story of Abraham's near sacrifice of Isaac and God's timely rescue of the beloved son (Gen. 22).[2] The story of Abraham, especially, is a concrete instance of the righteousness of God that is being revealed in the gospel: the

---

1. Ambrose, *On the Death of His Brother Satyrus* 2.89, in *Fathers of the Church: A New Translation*, ed. R. J. Deferrari (Washington: Catholic University of America Press, 1947) 22:236, cited in *Ancient Christian Commentary on Scripture: New Testament VI: Romans*, ed. Gerald Bray (Downers Grove, Ill.: InterVarsity, 1998) 111.

2. Perhaps the wonderful and terrible story of Genesis 22 is never very far in the background of either the Old Testament or the New. See Erich Auerbach, *Mimesis: The Representation of Reality in Western Literature*, trans. Willard Trask (Princeton: Princeton University Press, 1953) 3–23; Shalom Spiegel, *The Last Trial: On the Legends and Lore of the Command to Abraham to Offer Isaac as a Sacrifice: The Akedah*, trans. Judah Goldin (New York: Pantheon, 1967); and Jon D. Levenson, *The Death and Resurrection of the Beloved Son: The Transformation of Child Sacrifice in Judaism and Christianity* (New Haven, Conn.: Yale University Press, 1993).

power of God for salvation to everyone who trusts in God, to the Jew first and also to the Greek (1:16–17).

ABRAHAM AND THE UNITY OF JEWS AND GENTILES

Now that we have heard the story of how God saved a lost world through the faithfulness of Jesus Christ (3:21–26), which is the foundational story of God's covenant righteousness in Romans, it is logical to ask, How is that story connected with the rest of Paul's argument? Specifically, how is it connected both to his concern to show that God has kept faith with Israel in the process of including Gentiles in the covenant promises given to Israel's ancestors and to his concern for the unity of Jewish Christians and Gentile Christians in the house churches at Rome? We will see Paul answering that question one step at a time throughout the letter, as he finds ways to talk about God's covenant faithfulness to Israel, God's mercy shown to Gentiles, and the unity of Jewish Christians and Gentile Christians in Jesus Christ.

In Romans 1:16–17, his thesis, Paul has already named both the social distinctiveness of Jews and Gentiles ("the Jew first and also the Greek") and the unity of God's powerful salvation-creating righteous purpose ("salvation to everyone who has faith"). While not ignoring the distinctive situations of those who by nature have the law and those who by nature do not (2:12–14), he has also shown that "there is no distinction" (3:22) between their situations with respect to God's righteousness. Seen in relation to God, they are united in a variety of ways. Paul has shown (3:9–18) their unity in deserving condemnation at the hands of God. To be sure, this is not the way that they would choose to see themselves as united, but Paul insists that neither group can judge the other without also indicting itself (2:1–3).

They are further united in the way that they will be judged by God, according to their deeds. To everyone who does evil, whether Jew or Greek, there will be anguish and distress; to everyone who does good, whether Jew or Greek, there will be glory, honor, and peace. God shows no partiality (2:6–11). They are united in their common situation of being "under the power of Sin" (3:9) and therefore subject to Death. They are also united in their silence, their recognition that no one has a claim against God's just judgment of the world: the mouths of both Jews and Gentiles are stopped in the presence of the Judge of the whole world (3:19). Most importantly they are united as the "all" who have sinned and fall short of the glory of God (3:23) and who have therefore received God's gracious mercy (justification, redemption, atoning sacrifice for sin) as a gift (3:21–26). Finally, they are united because "God is one." Therefore, the same God is necessarily God of both the Jews and the Gentiles (3:29–31).

The unity of Jews and Gentiles in God's salvation-creating purpose is also one of the major themes of Romans 4:1–25 as Paul continues to tell the story of God's righteousness in connection with Abraham. When Romans is read only or primarily as a collection of doctrinal *loci*, Abraham's major function is to serve as an example of "justification through faith," and Genesis 15:6 functions primarily as Paul's supporting proof text, since it is one of only two Scriptures that combine the words "righteousness" and "faith" or "faithfulness." (The other is Hab. 2:4, already cited in Paul's thesis in 1:16–17). But such a doctrinal reading causes us to miss most of what Paul is actually doing in Romans 4, which is much more interesting and important to his argument in Romans as a whole. The story of Abraham is the story of "the gospel of God" (Rom 1:1) in miniature: God's faithfulness bringing forth human faithfulness (1:17).

As readers of Romans, we are alerted to the importance of the story of Abraham for Paul by the rhetorical question he asks at the beginning of the chapter: "Have we found Abraham to be our ancestor *according to the flesh*?" (4:1). Because the Greek in this verse is difficult, the translation in your Bible may differ from this one substantially.[3] Rhetorical questions like this were used by Paul, and other ancient writers, to move an argument along and to keep it on track. A question is raised, usually one that must be answered "yes" or "no," just at a point of possible misunderstanding. Then the question is either answered, often emphatically, by the author or it is left to be answered by the reader/hearer to indicate the right way that the argument should be directed. Rhetorical questions are gifts to us later readers as well: they help us to track the important turning points in Paul's argument, like markers left on a wilderness trail.

"Have we found Abraham to be our ancestor *according to the flesh*?" The implied answer is "No! Of course not. Abraham is our ancestor in a much more important way than merely according to the flesh." Paul has already used the expression "according to the flesh" (*kata sarka*) at the beginning of his letter (1:3–4) to describe Jesus, who was descended from David "according to the flesh" or "humanly speaking." This was immediately contrasted with the more important information that he was designated or appointed "Son of God" in power "according to the Spirit of Holiness," that is, from God's side. Later, in Romans 9:3, Paul will use the same expression to describe his relationship with his fellow Jews who do not believe that Jesus is the Christ: they are related in a human way (by race or nationality) but not at the level that matters most. Two verses later (9:5) he will speak again of Jesus who was of Israel "according to the flesh," but who is not recognized as Messiah by unbelieving Israel.

---

3. Richard B. Hays, "'Have We Found Abraham to Be Our Forefather According to the Flesh?': A Reconsideration of Rom. 4:1," *Novum Testamentum* 27 (1985), 76–98 and *Echoes of Scripture in the Letters of Paul* (New Haven, Conn.: Yale University Press, 1989) 54–55.

It is clear from these other uses in Romans and elsewhere that the words "according to the flesh" already mean more than human origin: in Romans 1:3–4 Jesus' descent from David according to the flesh is contrasted with his designation according to the Spirit of Holiness in power. In Romans 9:5, Jesus' descent from Israel "according to the flesh" has not helped the Jews to whom Paul is preaching to recognize him as their Messiah. Descent from the flesh, then, doesn't seem to accomplish much. Moreover, in Romans 8:4–9 and 12–13, Paul contrasts living according to the flesh to living according to the Spirit. This strategy shows that he has another understanding of what it means to be "according to the flesh": that is the way people think, not the way God thinks (cf. to "set the mind" on things of the flesh, 8:5–6). So, by means of his rhetorical question in 4:1, Paul is anticipating the common human tendency in his hearers to think of Abraham as our ancestor according to the flesh and correcting that potential misunderstanding on the spot.

If Abraham were "*our*" ancestor according to the flesh, then the word "our" would include Paul and other Jewish Christians but not Gentile Christians, because Abraham is only the ancestor of those born Jewish or those who have become Jews by conversion. This argument will be familiar to readers of Galatians as the one Paul opposed in that earlier letter. Raising the issue again here, he draws on some of his earlier argument and expresses it now more simply. Paul had preached a law-free gospel to the Galatians, arguing that Gentiles who became Christians did not have to become Jewish and take on the requirements of the Jewish law symbolized by male circumcision.[4] In opposition to Paul's law-free gospel, rival evangelists, Jewish Christian "Teachers," insisted that Gentile converts to Christianity must imitate Abraham, the paradigm of Gentile conversion, by doing what Abraham did. They must become circumcised and keep the Torah or Jewish law. To become a Christian, then, was to become a Jewish Christian, by taking on the requirements of the covenant.

Paul argued, on the other hand, that when Scripture says the covenant promises of God were given "to Abraham *and to his seed*" (Gen. 17:8), the word "seed" (*sperma*) is singular and refers to Jesus Christ, the rightful seed of Abraham (Gal. 3:16).[5] Therefore, those "in Christ"—including those Gentile converts baptized into Jesus Christ—are part of "Abraham's seed" and inheritors of the covenant blessings that God promised to Abraham, even though they are not circumcised.

It is reasonable to assume that the Christians of the house churches in Rome might have heard about Paul's letter to the Galatians and the obvious

---

4. J. Louis Martyn, *Galatians: A New Translation With Introduction and Commentary*, Anchor Bible 33A (New York: Doubleday, 1997) on "The Teachers," 117–126.

5. Beverly Roberts Gaventa, "The Singularity of the Gospel," *Pauline Theology*, vol. 1, ed. Jouette M. Bassler (Minneapolis: Fortress, 1991) 147–159.

response to Paul's argument: "Wait a minute, Paul: in the very chapter you quote regarding the promises given to Abraham and to his seed (Gen. 17:8), Abraham gets circumcised and circumcises his son Ishmael (Gen. 17:23–27). Later, when Isaac is born, he circumcises Isaac, too (Gen. 21:4)!" The argument about circumcision raises the question Paul addresses directly in Romans 4: How is someone—Abraham or anyone else—"put right" with God? (The English "justified" in most translations of Rom. 4:2 translates the verb form of *dikaiosynē*, righteousness.) If Abraham is "put in the right" by his works (like circumcision), then he has something to boast about—but not before God! (4:2)

Paul's readers will remember that "boasting" (*kauchēsis*) in oneself or in one's own achievements was just excluded in Romans 3:27, as a result of God's own action of covenant righteousness in the death and resurrection of Jesus Christ. God "puts right" those who share in the faithfulness of Jesus (or those who put their trust, believe, in Jesus). Boasting in the presence of God, then, given everything Paul said from 1:18–3:20, is shown to be a human (fleshly) way of thinking—hardly an appropriate behavior to attribute to Abraham, the great ancestor of Israel.

According to Genesis 15:6, "Abraham put faith in God, and it was reckoned to him as righteousness." Paul quotes Genesis 15:6 three times in Romans 4: in verses 3, 9, and 22. The first time, he quotes it to make the point that is clearly stated in 4:5, that God "puts right" (puts in right relationship with God) the *ungodly* (those who have nothing to boast about) as a gift, not as something they have earned (4:4). That this blessing comes to the *ungodly* is underlined by a quotation from Psalm 32:1–2:

> Blessed are those whose unlawful acts are forgiven and whose sins are covered; blessed is the one against whom the Lord will not reckon sin.

Psalm 32 is identified both in Psalms and by Paul in Romans 4:6 as "a psalm of David." We remember David from Romans 3:4, where he was confessing sin before God. Here it is the ungodly David who now, forgiven, pronounces a blessing on "the one against whom the Lord will not *reckon* sin" (Ps. 32:2).[6] The catchword "reckon," which appears in both Psalm 32:2 and in Genesis 15:6, is an accounting term, and its use underlines Paul's statement that God's mercy is a gift, not something that has been earned. The alternative way of thinking—the human way, "according to the flesh" (*kata sarka*)—would land Abraham, and all of us, squarely back in the predicament of all the ungodly described in 1:18–3:20.

---

6. Hays, *Echoes of Scripture in the Letters of Paul*, 48–49.

Paul alters the quotation from Genesis 15:6 slightly when he quotes it the second time, in 4:9, in order to make a different point: "Faith was reckoned to Abraham as righteousness." First Paul asks another rhetorical question:

> Was this blessing [from David] pronounced *only* on the circumcised or *also* on the uncircumcised?" (4:8)

In Romans 4:2–5 Paul has just questioned the whole notion of earning any blessing from God, so the reader's instinctive response to Paul's rhetorical question is to guess what the relationship is between "trusting God" and either circumcision or uncircumcision. That's exactly what Paul wants, and before the reader has quite recovered balance, Paul fires off another rhetorical question and this time, answers it himself.

> How then was [trust in God] reckoned? In the situation of circumcision or of uncircumcision? It was not *after* but *before* he was circumcised. So he received the sign of circumcision as a seal of the righteousness of faith he had while he was still uncircumcised. (4:10–11)

Paul argues that the reckoning of righteousness to Abraham in Genesis 15:6 (and God's promise in Gen 17:8 to Abraham and his seed) comes *before* the description of Abraham's circumcision in Genesis 17:23–27 by the design of God specifically to teach us.

> The purpose was to make him the father of all who have faith without being circumcised and so have righteousness reckoned to them, and also the father of the circumcised who are not only circumcised but who also follow the example of trust [in God] that our father Abraham had before he was circumcised. (4:11–12)

Now, as the result of Paul's argument, the "*our*" in "our ancestor" is shown to be the common "our" of Jewish (circumcised) Christians and of Gentile (uncircumcised) Christians. Abraham is the common ancestor of all of us who put our trust in God's covenant promises.

THOSE WHO SHARE THE FAITH OF ABRAHAM

Paul now shifts first to the content of the promise to the seed of Abraham "that he (the seed) would inherit the world" (4:13),[7] and then to the way in which the inheritance would come: emphatically *not* through the law but through "the righteousness of faithfulness" (4:13). This phrase, together with its twin

---

7. The original promise to Abraham and to his seed involved inheritance of the *land*. Paul restates the promise "that he (the seed) would inherit the *world*, but this interpretive shift had already been made in Jewish tradition before Paul (cf. Sir. 44:19–21).

in 4:11, is a reference back to Romans 3:21–26 where Paul argued that God's righteousness was both accomplished and demonstrated through the faithfulness of Jesus Christ. The promise depends on faithfulness (4:16) so that it may rest on God's grace and be guaranteed to *all* of Abraham's seed—not just to those of the law but also to those like faithful (or trusting) Abraham, for he is the father of us all, just as it stands written (in Gen. 17:5), "I have made you the father of many nations." (This sentence could also be translated "I have made you the father of many Gentiles, for in Greek as in Hebrew, the same word means both nations and Gentiles).

The promise to Abraham's seed (first, the singular seed Jesus Christ, but now the many Gentiles who have become the seed of Abraham by trusting God in Jesus Christ) is being fulfilled in the presence of the God in whom Abraham trusted, "who gives life to the dead and calls into existence the things that do not exist" (4:17). This last phrase may be a hymnic or a creedal fragment, perhaps one known both to Paul and to the churches at Rome, that speaks generally of God's powers of resurrection and either creation or newly created resurrection life. In the present context of Paul's argument, it suggests not only God's act of raising Jesus from the dead and God's ability to create life where there was none, but also the rescue of Isaac and the incredible birth of Isaac in the first place.

This suggestion is made more definite in the following verses (Rom. 4:18–20). Hoping against hope, Abraham trusted that he would become "the father of many nations," for God had promised in Genesis 15:5 that if he could count the stars in heaven, so numerous would his seed be. He "did not weaken in faith" (his trust of God) when he considered his own one-hundred-year-old body, which was "as good as dead," or when he considered the barrenness (lit. "deadness") of Sarah's womb. No lack of trust made him waver concerning the promise of God, "but he grew powerful in his faith as he gave glory to God, being fully convinced that what God had promised, God was also able to do" (4:20–21).

At this point Paul's alternative to understanding Abraham as our ancestor according to the flesh becomes clear: Abraham is, instead, our ancestor *according to the Spirit*,[8] a model of life in the Spirit of Jesus, whose faithfulness,

---

8. Since Paul does not actually use this language about Abraham, the opposite to being our ancestor, *kata sarka*, must be supplied by the reader. An alternative reading is suggested by N. T. Wright in "Romans and the Theology of Paul," *Pauline Theology, Volume Three: Romans*, ed. D. M. Hay and E. E. Johnson (Minneapolis: Fortress, 1995) 40. Wright argues that Abraham is our ancestor "according to grace" reading the *kata charin* of 4:16 as answering the question about *kata sarka* posed in 4:1. This is also possible and would pick up resonances of the word *charis* (grace) throughout Romans. My preference for "according to the Spirit" (which also appears in 1:4; 8:4; 8:5) reflects Paul's tendency to oppose "Spirit" and "flesh," whereas in Romans at least, "grace" is usually opposed to "sin" (5:20; 6:1), "law" (6:14–15), and "works" (11:5–6). Either way, it is *God's* grace and Spirit that are in view, as opposed to the human way of thinking, *kata sarka*.

demonstrated by his faithful death on the cross, was at the same time the act of God's own covenant faithfulness. Therefore, he is also a model for all the numerous seed of Abraham who share in the faithfulness of Jesus and in the trusting faith of Abraham. For Paul, the word "hope" is consistently linked with the Holy Spirit in Romans (cf. 5:5 in the next section; 8:22–25; 15:13).

Paul focuses on Abraham more than on Sarah for several reasons. First, Genesis already does, and Paul is retelling the story found there. Second, Abraham had long been used as the paradigm for Gentile converts, which is the issue in question here as well. Third, Paul wants to talk about circumcision in particular, which applies to Abraham and his sons. Fourth, central to his argument is the definition of trusting God as believing God's promises, and those promises were actually given to Abraham. Fifth, Abraham was involved in both Isaac stories (his birth and his near death on Mount Moriah), while the absence of Sarah in the second story (and subsequently) is striking.[9] Sixth, Paul had already used Abraham in Galatians to make a similar argument, and he could build on something he had at hand. In fact, he may be correcting the argument in Galatians 3 that focused on Abraham, using this letter as a chance to answer his critics. Seventh, Abraham, as one representative figure, stands more cleanly as a positive antitype to Jesus Christ, just as Adam (Adam and Eve conflated into Adam alone) will stand as a negative antitype in Romans 5. But the final and perhaps the most important reason is that Abraham's name is actually the content of the promise that came true. Abram's name is changed to Ab/raham, "the father of many" (Gen. 17:5), and this is the promise that is now the inheritance of Paul's rapidly growing Gentile churches. Thus, what God had already laid out in the story of Abraham sums up the blessing that is now being experienced by Paul's Gentile-filled congregations.

Paul makes this connection watertight in Romans 4:23–25, where he quotes Genesis 15:6 for the third and last time:

> 'It was reckoned to him as righteousness.' Now the words 'it was reckoned' were not written only for his sake, *but for ours also*. It will be reckoned to us who put our faith in the One [God] who raised Jesus our Lord from the dead,—who was handed over to death for our trespasses and was raised in order to put us right [with God].

Once more, Paul may be quoting early Christian tradition—a hymn or part of a creed—as he brings his story of Abraham to a climactic finish by insisting that it is our story as well.

---

9. The silence of the narrative of Genesis 22 about Sarah, the failure of the narrative to report the return of Abraham and Isaac to the place where the two servants were left behind, and the death of Sarah in Genesis 23 were already linked in various ways in rabbinic thought. See Katheryn Pfisterer Darr, *Far More Precious Than Jewels: Perspectives on Biblical Women* (Louisville, Ky.: Westminster John Knox, 1991) 107–112.

At this point it is useful to ask: What has Paul accomplished in his argument by telling the story of Abraham? Just as the phrase "God is One" implies the unity of Jews and Gentiles, who both have the same God (3:27–31), so Abraham is the common ancestor of us all, both Jews and Gentiles together. This is an important point for Paul's argument later in Romans 14–15 that Jewish Christians and Gentile Christians fighting in house churches in Rome should make peace with each other so that together they can support Paul's mission to Gentiles in Spain. Abraham is the father of the circumcised, Jewish Christians, because although he was circumcised, he trusted not in his circumcision but in God's covenant promises. Abraham is also the father of the uncircumcised, Gentile Christians, because he received those covenant promises without being circumcised, thereby showing that Paul's Gentile converts to Christianity can also receive the covenant promises made to Abraham and to his seed without being circumcised. Abraham trusted in the One who gives life to the dead (a reference to Isaac's own near sacrifice and to the resurrection of Jesus) and who calls into existence things that do not exist (both the creation of the world and the birth of Isaac).

Once more, as in Romans 1, Paul reasons that we can know something about the invisible God by seeing what God has done: God is known in God's acts. In Romans 1, the power of God and the "Godness" of God were evident through the creation. Now, in Romans 4, not just God's *power* is known but something of God's own *character*. We see the righteousness or covenant faithfulness of God in God's promise keeping, justice, and salvation-creating power to rescue from Death. Paul is arguing that God's reliability and trustworthiness are known because of three observable facts. First, God keeps God's promises (there may be a hint here of the creation covenant with Noah after the flood as well as the obvious allusion to the birth of Isaac). Second, God rescues the poor and the one that has no helper (young Isaac, the beloved son in danger). Third, God makes the story come out right in the end (God does indeed "provide" the ram to replace Isaac; Jesus is vindicated by being raised from the dead). We remember that these were the three ways in which "the righteousness of God" was explained in chapter two: covenant fidelity/reliability, judgment for the poor and oppressed, and putting things right at the end (eschatological vindication of the faithful).

Another connection back to Romans 1 is seen in Paul's use of language: Abraham, by his trusting obedience precisely when what God had promised to do seemed impossible, "gave glory to God" (4:20). This is precisely what fallen humanity in Romans 1:21ff. failed to do: they did not honor God as God and exchanged the glory of God for images. Paul will return to this same contrast later in the letter, saying that in spite of the forfeited glory that was lost to humanity in the fall of Adam (and Eve), we rejoice or boast in our hope of sharing the glory of God through God's grace (5:2). Paul expects the Roman house churches together to glorify God with one voice (15:6).

Paul also connects the covenant faithfulness of God to Abraham with the later faithfulness of God to Jesus Christ, who went to his death on the cross trusting God. God kept faith with Jesus, just as God had kept faith with Abraham and Sarah. So the church is to live in hope like trusting Abraham and obedient Jesus. Jim Wallis of *Sojourners* defines hope as "trusting God in spite of all the evidence, then watching the evidence change." This is also a good working definition of faith (trust in God) and of faithfulness (obedience to God in spite of all cost). "No lack of trust made him waver," says Paul, holding up Abraham as the model of the one who trusts God, "but he grew powerful in his faith as he gave glory to God" (4:20).

We learn from the phrase "he grew powerful in his faith" that faithfulness is not only a gift from God but also a skill or even a virtue that can become stronger with use: we learn how to be faithful in the process of trusting God. This means that even if we think we have very little faith in God, by living into the faith we *do* have, we can watch God increasing our faith and ourselves growing stronger in faith. Abraham and Sarah had to learn to trust God: when they first heard the promise of God's gift of a child to them in their old age, they laughed (Gen. 17:17; 18:12–15). For Paul, this very human assessment of the impossibility of the promise does not represent "lack of trust," or perhaps Paul's generous account of Abraham's unswerving faith causes him to overlook a few faults in Abraham and Sarah along the way.

At any rate, Paul's point is that these words about Abraham's faith from Genesis 15:6—"Therefore his faith was reckoned to him as righteousness"— were written for us later readers. Christians who are joined to the seed of Abraham, Jesus Christ, through baptism into his death, hear about themselves in the story of Abraham and Sarah. These words in Scripture (Gen. 15:6) were written not only for Abraham's sake but also for ours. Paul insists that righteousness will be reckoned to *all* who believe in God, who raised Jesus our Lord from the dead, "who was handed over to death for our trespasses and was raised to make us righteous" (4:25). God is acting through these words of Scripture spoken about Abraham to make us faithful, the way that God and Jesus Christ are faithful, and to make us trusting of God's promises, the way that Abraham and Sarah learned to be.

Summary. Paul's discussion in Romans 4 shows Abraham to be the common ancestor of both Jewish Christians and Gentile Christians because he is "our ancestor" not "according to the flesh" but according to the Spirit of Jesus Christ, for he trusted in God's promises even when they seemed impossible. God's word in fact came true, and Abraham became the promise associated with his name: "the father of many nations" (Gentiles). Paul insists, however, that this story about God's dealing with Abraham was also written for us. Moreover, it shows us two things: first, that God had always intended to include the Gentiles in his covenant promises to Israel; and second, that righteousness will be reckoned to us as we learn to trust God the way Abraham and Sarah did, the way Jesus Christ did. Their trust in God was justified because God is trustworthy and powerful to create out of nothing and to raise from the dead. The first few verses of Romans 5 (which follow) encourage us to trust in God's love for us, even in suffering, because the sign of God's grace, the Holy Spirit poured into our hearts, assures us that God will also be gracious on the day of judgment.

FOR FURTHER REFLECTION

1. Paul has provided several examples of faithfulness for our consideration. In what ways are the faithfulness of Abraham, of God, and of Jesus Christ alike? In what ways are they different? How is that faithfulness demonstrated in action?

2. In Romans 4, Paul has suggested that it may be more difficult to trust God in a situation when there seems to be no ground for hope. What were those situations for Abraham? Can you retell in your own words the biblical stories to which Paul refers? Did they involve any suffering? Do you agree with Paul's argument that Christians can rejoice even in their sufferings, knowing that God is faithful and that God loves us?

3. Robert Coles tells the story of Ruby Bridges, the young African-American girl who successfully integrated a southern school system in the 1950s by her courage and her willingness to walk through two lines of people calling her ugly names every morning and evening to get to school. She and her family and the members of her church prayed every day for her enemies, for the very people who were causing her suffering. How did God keep faith with her, and how did she keep faith with God? Do you think she learned to trust God?

4. The church has often taught that thinking about the lives of saints helps us to understand both the Bible and our own lives better. Does that seem true to you? Why? How? Can we learn about faithfulness in our time from others who have been faithful to God in their own generations? Whom would you choose as a contemporary example of faithfulness in an apparently "hopeless" situation?

5. This discussion leads almost inevitably into the deeper question of sorting out reality and illusion, one of the topics of the next chapter. There is no virtue in misplaced faith or the sort of simple trust that makes one a victim of

scams, a common problem especially for the poor and for the elderly. It is not because "faith" in itself is valuable, but because God is righteous and faithful or trustworthy (worthy of our faith), that we learn to put our trust in God, where it belongs, and not in the improbable promises of crooks and shysters.

6. The theologian Søren Kierkegaard (following Tertullian) spoke of believing "because it is absurd," that is, because it makes no sense to trust God. In what ways, if any, does the story of Abraham call that idea into question? In what ways, if any, does the story of Abraham support that idea? Are faith and reason inevitably opposed? What about faith and experience?

4

"The Free Gift
Is Not Like the Trespass"

(Rom. 5:1–8:39)

The Gospel . . . does not say to us, let go the hope of social justice
and peace, of liberation from oppression, of overcoming the world
of the war danger, the madness of armaments and world-hunger,
and hope, only for yourselves, for eternal life! The Gospel says to
us on the contrary, "You are called to a hope that will never put you
to shame". . . . It is Jesus who brings us into trust and thereby into
shalom. Through him, now already, the door is open into grace, to
God's life for us. . . . In addition there comes to us a new relationship to the great pressure to which we are exposed. We no longer
complain about it, we are proud of it. For this is clear to us that
from this pressure, from these troubles comes endurance, from
endurance comes character, and from our character comes fresh
hope. But hope does not disappoint us, it holds us up and will not
let us go to pieces. For now already God's Spirit is at work in us,
and through him the love of God which fills our hearts, our wills,
and our thoughts, and sets them in motion.

Helmut Gollwitzer[1]

Romans 5–8 is the next major unit of Paul's letter to the Romans, and the
contrasting stories of Christ and Adam comprise the next major story-within-
a-story of Romans. In addition, other stories are submerged in these chapters
that help us to understand Paul's argument better. That argument is tightly

---

1. Helmut Gollwitzer, *The Way to Life: Sermons in a Time of World Crisis*, trans. David
Cairns (Edinburgh: T&T Clark, 1981) 102–105.

constructed throughout Romans 5–8, within which are smaller subsections that make up the building blocks of Paul's argument.[2]

GENESIS 3: THE STORY BEHIND ROMANS 5–8

> O, Adam, what have you done? For though it was you who sinned, the fall was not yours alone, but ours also who are your descendants. For what good is it to us, if an immortal time has been promised to us, but we have done deeds which bring death? And what good is it that an everlasting hope has been promised to us, but we have miserably failed? (4 Ezra 7:118–120 NRSV)

These words, roughly contemporary with Paul's letter to the Romans, illustrate the way Adam was understood during the first century of the Christian era. When Paul sets up his contrasting story of Christ and Adam in Romans 5:12–21 (the key to Rom. 5–8 in general), he could expect that his readers would immediately associate the name "Adam" with the story of the creation and fall of humanity told in Genesis 1–3. In fact, the story of Adam's disobedience in Genesis 3 is the most helpful background reading for these chapters of Romans.[3] There are two further things readers need to know before engaging Romans 5–8.

First, Paul speaks only of "Adam" as the representative of disobedient humanity. He has probably conflated Adam and Eve into Adam for three reasons. First, the account in Genesis 2–3 entails six distinct scenes, which open and close with God and Adam as follows: (1) God and Adam; (2) the serpent with Eve (and perhaps Adam); (3) Eve and Adam; (4) God and Adam; (5) God plus serpent, Eve, and Adam; and, finally, (6) God and Adam. Adam is the common denominator of the series, for he probably appears in every scene.

---

2. These smaller units can be identified by Paul's almost formulaic or liturgical use of a phrase that refers to the work of God in Jesus Christ (for example, 5:11, "through our Lord Jesus Christ"; 5:21, "through Jesus Christ our Lord"; 6:11, "in Christ Jesus"; 6:23, "in Christ Jesus our Lord"; 7:25, "through Jesus Christ our Lord"; 8:17, "joint heirs with Christ . . . glorified with him"; and 8:39, "the love of God in Christ Jesus our Lord"). These concluding refrains; the word "therefore" or "then," which signals the beginning of a new thought (5:1, 12, 18; 6:1, 12, 15; 7:7; 8:1, 12, 18, 31); and Paul's rhetorical questions (6:1, 15; 7:1, 7, 13, 24; 8:24, 31, 32, 33, perhaps 34, and 35) all serve as useful markers for following the track of his argument.

3. C. K. Barrett, *From First Adam to Last: A Study in Pauline Theology* (New York: Charles Scribner's Sons, 1962); Morna D. Hooker, *From Adam to Christ: Essays on Paul* (Cambridge: Cambridge University Press, 1990).

Second, in addition to following the narrative of Genesis, Paul has presumably focused on Adam alone in order to set up a clearer contrast with Jesus Christ. Third, the name "Adam," which means "ground" or "dust" and so also "the human creature made of dust," refers us back to the story of the creation of humanity in Genesis 2:7, where Adam is the common ancestor of us all.

We have already been introduced to the idea of a common ancestor whose name is shorthand for his story in Abraham, the "father of many." Just as Abraham's name focuses on God's promise to Abraham (Gen. 17:5), which was so difficult to believe, so Adam's name focuses on his origin and his destiny as a result of disobedience: "You are dust and to dust you shall return" (Gen. 3:19). Just as Abraham is the common ancestor of God's covenant people (and, as Paul argues, "the father of all of us" who trust God's promises and become faithful like him, whether circumcised or uncircumcised), so Adam is the common ancestor of all humanity everywhere, who are ungodly (disobedient to the commandments) and deserving of death (Rom. 1:32). So, whenever Paul says "Adam" we can assume that he means both Adam and Eve and that, in one way or another, he is also talking about all of humanity, since Genesis 5:1–32 and subsequent genealogies in Genesis tell us that we are all descended from Adam.

Second, Paul also follows the reading convention, suggested by Genesis itself, that Genesis 1–11 is a unit of primeval prehistory or saga, a great tale describing God's good creation, human disobedience, and the effects of the fall upon both humanity as a whole and the rest of creation. Those effects are seen in the stories of the first murder (Cain and Abel, Gen. 4:1–16); the multiplication of violence (the song of Lamech in Gen. 4:23–24); the wickedness of the "sons of God" (Gen. 6:1–8, perhaps the Nephilim referred to in the same passage, whose name may be derived from the word "to fall"); God's decision to destroy "all flesh, for the earth is filled with violence on account of them" (Gen. 6:13); the great flooding of the earth in which only Noah, his family, and the animals in the ark were saved (Gen. 6:11–8:19); the sin of Noah's son, Ham, identified with the later Canaanites (Gen. 9:18–28); and, finally, the building of the infamous tower of Babel, an act of aggression towards God that leads to the confusion of languages (Gen. 11:1–9).

The complex set of narratives in Genesis 1–11 is both summarized and epitomized by Genesis 3, the story of the temptation and fall of Adam and Eve, and the consequences of their actions, including their expulsion from the garden of Eden. The fall of Adam is therefore representative of the human tendency to disobey God's commandments, just as the story of the golden calf (Exod. 32) is representative of the human tendency to commit idolatry, to "worship and serve the creature rather than the One who created it," as we saw in Rom 1:25. Indeed, we already noticed a probable reference to the serpent of Genesis 3:1 in that language of Romans 1:25. Not all of the details of the Genesis story are relevant to Paul's argument in Romans and, because of its character as ancient mythic saga, most of the details of the story ought not to be pressed as if it were a historical account that had to agree with Paul's version at every point. However, because certain features of the story in Genesis 3 lie behind Paul's argument in Romans 5–8, a quick review of those features of the story in Genesis 3 makes it easier to follow the story line that lies beneath Paul's argument in these chapters. The key words of the Genesis account that reappear in Romans 5–8 are italicized for emphasis.

God placed Adam in the beautiful and fruitful garden of Eden "to till it and keep it" (Gen. 2:15). God gave him one *commandment:*

> You may freely eat of every tree of the garden; but of the tree of the knowledge of good and evil you shall not eat, for in the day that you eat of it you shall die." (2:16–17 NRSV)

The serpent in Genesis 3:1 draws attention to that commandment, which is the only restriction placed on humanity, by asking the woman about it. Her answer mentions that *death* is the penalty for violating the commandment. The serpent *deceives* her, reassuring her, "You will not die," and invites her to *covet* the knowledge of good and evil ("for God knows that when you eat of it your eyes will be opened and you will be like God knowing good and evil" 3:5 NRSV).

The woman and the man *disobey* God's commandment and eat of the forbidden fruit. Their eyes are opened, they realize they are naked, and they try to cover themselves and to hide from God (3:6–8). God calls to the man, Adam, whose answer unwittingly reveals that he has eaten of the fruit of the tree. When God asks whether or not the commandment has been broken, the man blames the woman (and God for giving her to him); the woman blames the serpent: "He *tricked* me"; and God proceeds to deal with the serpent, the woman, and the man in succession (3:14–19). The serpent is cursed, condemned to crawl and eat dust, and put in enmity with the woman (3:14–15). God promises to cause the woman to bear children in *labor pains* and predicts that nevertheless she will desire her husband and that he will *rule over* her (3:16). God tells the man that the earth is "cursed because of you" ("thorns and thistles" shall it sprout for you) . . . "until you return to the ground, for out of it you were taken; you are dust and to dust you shall return" (3:17–19, a prediction of *death*). Moreover, God acts to prevent Adam from eating of the tree of life (and thus escaping death) by driving him out of the garden "to till the ground from which he was taken" (3:23 NRSV) in a formal *inclusio* with 2:15. There is a profound heaviness now implied in Adam's labor: he tills the ground to which he will return in death. The last sight Adam sees as he leaves the beautiful garden of Eden is the combination of fierce cherubim and "a sword flaming and turning" that God has placed at the east of the garden "to guard the way to the tree of life" (3:24 NRSV).

Romans 5–8 has as its theme the Christian life. The people of God who benefit by the saving work of God in Christ, described in Romans 3:21–31, are members of the covenant family headed by trusting and faithful Abraham. This covenant family (the circumcised and uncircumcised who trust God's promises) comprises the real humanity that God had wanted to create in Adam and has now created in Jesus Christ, the seed of Abraham and the opposite of Adam's disobedience. Genesis itself is structured so that Genesis 12, the call of Abraham, is God's antidote to the pattern of human disobedience of Genesis 1–11, which is epitomized by Adam's disobedience in Genesis 3. Abraham is God's answer to Adam.

For Paul, creation and covenant are as tightly interwoven as they are in Genesis (see also 2 Cor. 3–5 and Gal. 6), and he recognizes God's new creation and new covenant in the death and resurrection of the obedient representative of created humanity, Jesus Christ. As the seed of Abraham and as "Messiah," he is also the covenant representative of Israel.[4] Therefore the Christian family of those who are "in Christ" described in Romans 5–8 is at the same time both the family of Abraham—that is, the family of covenant, of faith and faithfulness—and the opposite of the family of Adam—that is, the family of bondage to Sin and Death, of distrust and disobedience. In addition Romans 5–8 emphasizes the work of the Holy Spirit of God (and Christ), which was not true of chapters 1–4 (1:4 and perhaps 2:29 being exceptions). Romans 5–8 deals with life in the Spirit of Jesus Christ.

When Romans is read primarily as a textbook of Christian doctrine, chapters 1–4 or 1–5, depending on the scholar, deal with justification—how you get saved: not by works but by faith—and 5–8 or 6–8, treat sanctification—now that you are saved, how you should behave. While it is certainly possible to abstract such a schema from Romans 1–8 for dogmatic or pastoral purposes, when that same structure is then imposed on particular passages in Romans as a grid to govern their exegesis, all sorts of problems and confusions result. Romans 7, in particular, becomes an exegetical disaster when it is read as a description of the life of the sanctified Christian. It is much more helpful to read 7:1–8:17 as an extension of Paul's powerful contrast between the disobedience of Adam and the obedience of Christ, a contrast that is set up in 5:12–21. Paul does have a great deal to say about holiness of life in these chapters, and Romans 6:22 contains one of his rare uses of the

---

4. N. T. Wright, "Romans and the Theology of Paul," *Pauline Theology, Volume Three: Romans*, ed. D. M. Hay and E. E. Johnson (Minneapolis: Fortress, 1995) 34, 47.

word "sanctification." But what we generally think of as "sanctification" is for Paul only *part* of the process by which God through the Holy Spirit brings the people of God to glory (8:29–30). In Romans 5–8, Paul is making good on the hint he threw out in 2:25–29: that there might somehow be a people of God who were fulfilling the just requirements of the law, who might or might not be circumcised, and that this people of God would be "the real Jews" who were Jews inwardly, having their hearts circumcised (as in Deut. 10:16) and the law written on their hearts (Jer. 31:31–34) through the power of the Spirit of God.

CHRIST'S DEATH FOR THE UNGODLY (ROM. 5:1–11)

Chapter and verse divisions were added to Paul's text many centuries after he wrote the letter to the Romans, and we must remember that his argument needs to be considered as a whole rather than broken up into the discrete units characteristic of later critical scholarship. Nevertheless, the present chapter divisions do seem to reflect, for the most part, the most natural breaks and logical turning points of Paul's argument. While some of the older commentaries treated the first five chapters of the letter as a unit, beginning the next phase of Paul's argument with his discussion of baptism in chapter 6, Romans seems to divide more naturally between chapters 4 and 5. At the same time, the break is not a sharp one: much of the vocabulary and many of the themes of the first four chapters are carried into Romans 5. And Romans 5 itself also seems to divide logically into two halves: 5:1–11 and 5:12–21.

Paul uses the literary marking device of *inclusio* (using words, phrases, or themes as bookends to define a unit of text) to identify verses 5:1–11 as a unit of his argument. The word translated either "boast" or "rejoice" (*kauchasthai*) appears in 5:2 and 5:11 while the phrase "through our Lord Jesus Christ" appears in 5:1 and 5:11, the first and last verses of the passage. Moreover, the unit 5:1–11 also forms an *inclusio* with 8:31–39, the unit at the end of Paul's larger section, Romans 5–8. A major theme in both sections is the powerful love of God in Christ our Lord. In both sections also, Paul deals with the issues of suffering and hope. Furthermore, Paul uses the same literary style of argument in each place: both in 5:3–5 and in 8:28–30 (immediately before the concluding unit, 8:31–39) he builds to a rhetorical climax by means of the device of a "stair-step argument" (*sorites*) where one thing (virtue or action of God) leads logically to another and finally to the entire series.

Paul begins, "Therefore, since we are put in right relationship to God by faithfulness, we have peace [or "let us have peace," as in some ancient texts] with

God." Paul's combination of righteousness and peace here would have been familiar to his readers from the Psalms (cf. 72:7, "In his days may righteousness flourish and peace abound," and 85:10, "Righteousness and peace will kiss each other") and from Isaiah 32:17: "The effect of righteousness will be peace." Peace is God's gift to Israel and therefore to all the "seed of Abraham" as part of the covenant relationship (cf. Isa. 54:10, "My covenant of peace shall not be removed"). Peace was also part of the prophetic hope for the age to come (cf. Ezek. 34:25–31 and 37:26, "I will make with them a covenant of peace"). Paul claims that "through our Lord Jesus Christ"—having been put right with God through Jesus' faithfulness—we have peace with God, a peace that is now possible because of the access to God's grace in which we stand.

We rejoice (or boast) in our hope of sharing the glory of God (5:2). That glory was forfeited by Adam and Eve and would have been lost to humanity forever except for God's gracious restoration of the image of God in Jesus Christ. Moreover, says Paul in 5:3, we even rejoice (or boast) in our sufferings. He might have been thinking here of the end-time sufferings that were believed to be signs of the dawning of the new age—eschatological "birth pangs" of the new creation that God was bringing about. The Holy Spirit was also seen as the first sign, or firstfruits, of that new creation, which is why it serves as the logical climax to Paul's stair-step argument in 5:3–5:

> We rejoice in our sufferings,
> knowing that *suffering* produces *patience*,
> and *patience* produces *character*,
> and *character* produces *hope*,
> and *hope* does not disappoint us,
> because God's love has been poured into our hearts through the Holy
>   Spirit that has been given to us.

The outpouring of the Spirit was widely seen as a sign of the last days, the end time in which Paul believed himself and his churches to be living (cf. Joel 2:28–29).

God's love is linked for Paul with his statement in 5:1 that we are "put right" with God through "faithfulness," or more specifically by "the righteousness of God through the faithfulness of Jesus Christ" (3:22). The extravagance of God's loving action in Christ is punctuated by Paul's insistent repetition of the idea that "Christ died for the *ungodly*" (5:6; see 4:5). Paul invites his readers to reflect on the outrageous generosity of God in Christ by engaging in a brief discussion about for what or for whom people are generally willing to die: "For only in unusual circumstances will anyone die for a *righteous* person" (5:7), though maybe for a good person or a good thing someone might actually dare to die. But God proves God's love for us in that while we were still *sinners* Christ died for us (5:8).[5]

God's extravagant action for sinners in the death and resurrection of Jesus Christ rightly induces hope and confidence in those same sinners, now put right with God, as they wait for the judgment that was expected to accompany the end of time. Arguing from the greater to the lesser, Paul reasons: since we have been put right with God by the sacrifice of Jesus ("made right by his blood," 3:25), how much more certain it is that we will be saved through him from the wrath (of righteous judgment against all unrighteousness, cf. 1:18ff.). The correlation between God's past gracious action, with its results in the present, and what we can expect from the future verdict of God as just Judge reflects once again Paul's belief that God is known in God's actions: God's character as gracious and merciful to the point of extravagance, even with sinners, leads us to believe that God will also be gracious on the day of judgment. Since while we were still enemies, we were reconciled to God (once more Paul uses the divine passive: God reconciled us) through the *death* of God's Son, how much more certain it is that we will be saved by his *life*, that is, by the resurrection life of Jesus Christ in which we, too, hope to participate through our baptism. Paul concludes by encouraging his readers to think even more boldly: "We even rejoice (or boast) in *God* through our Lord Jesus Christ, through whom we have now received reconciliation" (5:11).

God's righteousness in Christ, then, leads not only to peace with God (reconciliation) and access to God's gracious mercy, but also to hope and rejoicing, even in the midst of sufferings. That hope is not empty: it has been given to us by the God who loved us even while we were ungodly sinners and enemies—God who loved us enough to give God's Son as a sacrifice for our sins—God who has shown us this love by pouring out into our hearts the eschatological gift of the Holy Spirit, a present promise that we can trust God to be gracious on the future day of judgment. No wonder we can rejoice in God, even in God as righteous Judge.

---

5. Origen commented about 5:7, "How can Paul say this when the Bible is full of martyrs? What were they doing? In fact, the martyrs were not dying for other people, but for God, and for him anyone would dare to die. But every other death is much harder to endure, even if it is just and in accordance with the law of nature." *Commentary on the Epistle to the Romans* 2:284, 286, cited in *Ancient Christian Commentary on Scripture New Testament VI: Romans*, ed. Gerald Bray (Downers Grove, Ill.: InterVarsity, 1998) 131. Paul may well be thinking of the righteous martyrs whether *hyper gar tou agathou* in 5:7 is translated "for a good person" or "for a good thing." He may also be alluding to the story that was presumably well known to his hearers (though less familiar today) of Alcestis, the heroine of Euripides's play, who willingly dies for her husband after his parents and friends have refused to do so, thus proving her great love for him.

THE FREE GIFT IS NOT LIKE THE TRESPASS
(ROM. 5:12–21)

As we saw above, Genesis shows that God called Abraham to address Adam's disobedience. God called a people to be in covenant with God and to be a light to the world in order to deal with the effects of Sin and Death brought on by Adam's disobedience.[6] But, as we saw in Romans 1–3, Israel was too compromised by its own disobedience to be a light to anyone, even to itself. So God had to do on Israel's behalf what Israel could not do for itself or for the world. God accomplished this work by putting forward Jesus Christ as an atoning sacrifice (3:25) to deal with Sin and to redeem the lost world from slavery to Sin and Death. Now, in Romans 5–8, Paul wants to speak of the life of those who have been redeemed. But before he can do that, he must return to the situation out of which they have come.

He begins in mid-story: "Therefore, just as Sin entered the world through one man, and Death entered through Sin, and so Death spread to all because all have sinned—" then he breaks off in the middle of his sentence. (This is called *anacoluthon*, a frequent rhetorical device in Paul's letters). Perhaps he breaks his train of thought because he senses that the Roman Christians need a fuller explanation before he continues. So Paul shares with them a rough historical outline of key figures: Adam, Abraham (implicitly here), Moses, and finally Jesus Christ,[7] whom he refers to here as "Christ," probably emphasizing his role as "Messiah," the covenant representative of Israel.[8]

The question "How is God dealing with the disobedience of Adam?" could be answered more than one way. Most of Paul's Jewish contemporaries would have looked to Moses. Through Moses God gave the law to Israel as a remedy for the sin of Adam. Israel could obey the law given through Moses and thus escape Adam's sin and its effects, exile from the garden and death. The law itself seems to suggest this: "Do this and live" is the message of Leviticus 18:5, a text to which Paul will return in Romans 10:5. But Paul sees it differ-

---

6. N. T. Wright, "Romans and the Theology of Paul," 33.

7. Note C. K. Barrett's helpful comment: "Paul sees history gathering at nodal points, and crystalizing upon outstanding figures . . . who are notable in themselves as individual persons, but even more notable as representative figures. These . . . , as it were, incorporate the human race or sections of it, within themselves, and the dealings they have with God they have representatively on behalf of their [constituency]. . . .They make up a dialectical pattern which provides the clue to Paul's understanding of mankind and of its history" (*From First Adam to Last: A Study in Pauline Theology* [New York: Charles Scribner's Sons, 1962] 5).

8. Here and in much of this chapter, I am following the argument of N. T. Wright, as it appears in "Romans and the Theology of Paul," 30–67.

ently, as he explains in 5:13–14, because Sin and Death are already in the world and the law given by Moses cannot do anything about that. All the law can do is to make Sin evident, not provide an escape from it.

How does the law make sin evident or "reckon" sin? As a general term, "sin" just means going astray or missing the mark. The law, however, has specific "commandments" that are like lines drawn on the ground. A trespass or transgression (literally, going across the line), is therefore evident and measurable; you can see how far over the line the person has gone. Remember that Paul tends to personify Sin and Death, thinking of them as active powers. So, says Paul, Sin was in the world already. We know that because Sin leads to Death and Death ruled over people from Adam to Moses (and also after Moses, of course). Sin and Death even ruled over those whose sins were general and not like Adam's transgression against a specific commandment, a line he was not to cross. Adam, says Paul, was a "type" of the One to come (5:14), namely, the Messiah who would be his opposite and would deal definitively with Sin and Death.

Paul continues, "The free gift is not like the trespass" (5:15). Paul wants us to appreciate the nature of the great imbalance between Adam and Christ.[9] In the first place, Christ did not begin where Adam began, in a fresh new creation without Sin or Death, but came instead into a world full of Sin and Death. Moreover, Christ's costly obedience—it cost him his life—is grossly disproportionate to Adam's disobedience. All Adam had to do was not eat of the fruit of one tree. Finally, Israel had been called to be the obedient opposite of Adam for the sake of the world now under the reign of Sin and Death, but Israel had failed in that task. As a result, Christ had to do not only what Adam should have done but now also what Israel should have done as well.[10]

"The free gift is not like the trespass" as Paul shows us in 5:15–19. His argument plays with the well-known platonic opposites of the one and the many: many died through one man's trespass, how much more have God's grace and the free gift of grace in that one man, Jesus Christ, abounded for many. The effects are also disproportionate: the judgment (exile and death) came after one

---

9. This was one of the points of dispute between Barth and Bultmann as they read Romans 5:12–21. I follow Barth's view as modified by Käsemann (Rudolf Bultmann, "Adam and Christ in Romans 5," *Current Issues in New Testament Interpretation*, ed. W. Klassen and G. F. Snyder [London: SCM Press, 1959] 143–165; Karl Barth, *Christ and Adam: Man and Humanity in Romans 5*, trans. T. A. Smail [New York: Collier, 1956, 1957]; Ernst Käsemann, *Commentary on Romans*, trans. G. W. Bromiley [Grand Rapids: Eerdmans, 1980]). For a fuller discussion of this debate, see A. Katherine Grieb, "Affiliation with Jesus Christ in His Sacrifice: Some Uses of Scripture to Define the Identity of Jesus Christ in Romans" (Ph.D. diss., Yale University, 1997).

10. N. T. Wright, "Romans and the Theology of Paul," 46.

trespass, but the free gift after so many subsequent trespasses brings God's action of "putting things right" in covenant relationship. Death ruled as the result of one man's trespass; how much more will those many who are given the free gift of righteousness rule in life through Jesus Christ. One man's act of disobedience led to condemnation for all; however, one man's act of righteousness leads to "putting things right" and life for all. One man's disobedience made many to be sinners; but one man's obedience will make many righteous.

Now, to get back to the law, says Paul in 5:20, the law came in and the result was that the trespass multiplied. Sin "increased" because the law specifies transgressions (see 3:20; 4:15); with the law, it became evident that there was more sin. Later (in 7:7–25) Paul will argue that the law cannot control sin; all it can do is count sin. With the coming of the law, the human situation was seen to be even worse than before, but God's grace abounded even more, so that just as Sin ruled through Death, grace might rule through righteousness (God's putting things right), and this would lead to eternal life through Jesus Christ our Lord. As the quotation from Helmut Gollwitzer at the beginning of this chapter shows, "eternal life" for Paul means much more than just going to heaven when you die; it means sharing in the life to come, the age of the Spirit that will be consummated when Christ returns to renew the world.

BAPTIZED INTO HIS DEATH
(ROM. 6:1–23)

The rhetorical question in 6:1 with which Paul begins this new section of his argument is initially puzzling: "Shall we remain (*epimenōmen*) in Sin, in order that God's grace may abound?" Paul seems to think of Sin as an area or, more precisely, a power that rules over people within its jurisdiction or sphere of influence, namely, people who can be said to be in solidarity with Sin or part of the family of Sin. That means Paul's interlocutor (his imaginary conversation partner in the diatribe style we mentioned in earlier chapters) would be asking something like this: "Given that there is an Adam-family and a Christ-family, which one am I in? If I'm still 'in Adam' and if God's grace has been shown so powerfully to those who are still stuck in the Adam-family, shouldn't I stay where I am so that God will continue to bless me here?" Paul's answer is an emphatic "no!" He says, "You and I are no longer in Adam," or literally, "How can we who have died to Sin still go on living in it?" (6:2).

The Christian baptism of which Paul speaks in 6:1–11 was rightly seen by the early church to be the act of God that ended the claims of one ruler, the jurisdiction of Sin, and subjected the Christian to another Lord, Jesus Christ.

The baptized Christian is taken out of the territory of Sin and placed in the territory of God's grace as a result of being buried symbolically with Christ in the deep waters of death,[11] only to be raised from the dead with Christ "by the glory of the Father, so that we too might walk in newness of life" (6:4). This "walking" (*halakah*) is the ethical behavior appropriate to membership in the new family of Jesus Christ.

This communal way of thinking is sometimes hard for Western post-Enlightenment people to understand, with our sense of ourselves as autonomous individuals, but most of the world both then and now still thinks in terms of a family solidarity that determines who you are, how you think, and what you do. Paul is saying that those baptized into the death of Christ have died to the power of Sin over them because they have a new family head, a new ruler or Lord. This may or may not be something they can feel or even realize, but it is true of them anyway, whether they can feel it or not, whether they know it or not. Paul, however, wants them to know it: they are no longer enslaved to Sin (6:6). They no longer have to act like part of that family because they no longer belong to it.

Since they are no longer in solidarity with Sin but now are in solidarity with Christ, and since Christ, having been raised from the dead, is free from the dominion of Death, so they too are to consider (or reckon, *logizesthe*) themselves "dead to Sin and alive to God in Christ Jesus" (6:11). What is true of Jesus Christ is also true of the people of God of whom he is the representative, the covenant family who are in solidarity with him because they have been baptized into his death.[12] Therefore Paul can tell them to act like what they really are—"in Christ"—instead of what they used to be—"in Adam." Paul now reverses the metaphor: Since they are no longer "in Sin," they should no longer let Sin into them!

Once more Paul is thinking territorially, only now the body of the Christian is the disputed territory that will be occupied by one power or the other, but not both. "There's a war going on," says Paul, "and Sin wants to regain this lost territory. Don't you let Sin get a toehold in your body, which is now Christ's territory!" When Paul speaks of "your members" in 6:13, he is talking about members of the Christian's physical body that are opportunities for

---

11. See Marianne H. Micks, *Deep Waters: An Introduction to Baptism* (Cambridge, Mass.: Cowley, 1996) for a theological reflection on the significance of Christian Baptism.

12. Dorothy W. Martyn has shown how Paul's logic speaks both to the macrocosmic world of international violence and to the microcosmic world of autistic children in "A Child and Adam: A Parable of the Two Ages," *Apocalyptic and the New Testament: Essays in Honor of J. Louis Martyn*, ed. J. Marcus and M. L. Soards (Sheffield: Sheffield Academic Press, 1989) 317–333.

Sin to invade and enslave. He thinks of the parts of the body as weapons that Christians can offer either to Sin or to Christ. The good news is that we no longer have to give ourselves to Sin; we are no longer "in Adam." Because we have died to Sin in baptism, Sin no longer has a rightful claim over us, so we are free to give ourselves to God in Christ.

In 6:14 Paul makes a surprising statement: Sin will have no dominion over you because you are not under *law* but under grace. Where does the word "law" come from, since Paul hasn't mentioned law and grace in this section of his argument (6:1–14)? Robert Morgan thinks this is a "Freudian slip"[13] by which Paul shows that mentally he equates "law" and "sin," but more likely it is a reminder of the argument in 5:12–21 and an anticipation of his later argument in 7:7–25. In 5:20 Paul argued that the Mosaic law intensifies sin by "reckoning" or counting it, so those who are under the law (who will therefore be judged by the law as he showed in 2:12) would have found that Sin had been so intensified that it did indeed have dominion over them.

This leads to Paul's next rhetorical question in 6:15: "What then? Shall we sin because we are not under the power of law but under the power of grace? Of course not!" It looks like a stupid question at first, but some people seemed to be thinking that Paul himself taught "let us do evil in order that good may come" (3:8). This is his opportunity to clear up that misunderstanding once and for all. No, we should not sin because we are not under law but under grace! Paul has identified the covenant people of God as those who are "in Christ" not "in Adam" but also not "in Moses," which could legitimately lead to the fear of antinomianism, the state of being under no law at all. Paul counters this charge by using the analogy of a slave who has changed masters, an illustration that would have been familiar to his Roman hearers, who were part of a slave economy, but that also has roots in the Old Testament. He says, Once you were slaves of Sin, which leads to Death, but now you are slaves of Obedience, which leads to Righteousness. Just as you once presented the members of your body to Impurity and to greater and greater lawlessness, so now that you are territory occupied by Jesus Christ and not by Sin, present the members of your bodies as slaves to Righteousness for sanctification. Slavery to Sin (life in Adam) leads to Death "for the wages of Sin is Death" (6:23) but for those who are free from Sin and enslaved to God (note the parallel with "dead to Sin and alive to God" in 6:11) there is the free gift of God: eternal life in Christ Jesus our Lord (6:23).

To summarize briefly Paul's argument in chapters 5 and 6: he has described the present reality of having been put right with God and its results—peace, the hope of sharing in God's glory, the ability to rejoice even in suffering, God's

13. Robert Morgan, *Romans* (Sheffield: Sheffield Academic Press, 1997) 40.

love that has been poured into our hearts through the Holy Spirit. He has stressed the costly generosity of God's free gift in Christ, who died for the ungodly, for sinners. That rightly gives us confidence as we wait for the future judgment at the last day (5:1–11). Paul has then retold the story of Adam's disobedience by contrasting it to the story of Christ's obedience. What the two stories have in common is that the action of one family head affected the situations of the many who were "in Adam" and also the many who are now "in Christ." However, these actions were greatly disproportionate, and so were the results, which show (again) the extravagance of God's grace (5:12–21). Christians who have been baptized into the death of Christ are raised "to walk in newness of life" (6:4). Just as Death no longer has power to rule over Christ, so Christians ought to consider themselves dead to Sin and alive to God in Christ Jesus. Sin no longer has power over them, so they ought not to let Sin use their bodily members as if Sin still had power over them (6:1–14). They are no longer enslaved to Sin, but instead they have become slaves of Righteousness and slaves of Obedience because they are in Christ. Instead of Death, the wages of Sin, they can look forward to eternal life, the free gift of God, in Christ Jesus their Lord (6:15–23).

AN ANALOGY FROM MARRIAGE LAW
(ROM. 7:1–6)

Many commentators have found the first six verses of Romans 7 difficult to untangle. In order to explain the difference between the Adamic situation and the new situation of those who are in Christ, Paul uses another legal analogy from the field of marriage law (comparable to the example of the slave who changes masters in 6:15–23). The law is binding on a person only during the person's lifetime (7:1). Paul had said something very close to that about Sin in 6:7: "For whoever has died has been made righteous (*dedikaiōtai*) from Sin." There, however, the idea of being "put right" seems closer to rescue or redemption from slavery than to the law-court situation. One would expect from that beginning an analogy about someone whose legal obligations are dissolved by his or her *own* death.

Instead, Paul invites us to consider the example of a married woman. He uses the term *hypandros* (lit., subject to a man) to suggest that the situation of a married woman is comparable to that of a slave. The married woman is bound by the law to her husband as long as he lives, but if her husband dies, she is free from the law of the husband (or perhaps the law *concerning* the husband). Accordingly, if she lives with another man while her husband is alive, she will be called an adulteress (for which the penalty is death, Lev. 20:10). But if her husband dies, she is free from that law, and if she marries another man, she is not an adulteress (7:3). Again, Paul had said something very close to that about Sin in his slave analogy: "But now you have been set free from Sin and enslaved to God" (6:22).

In the same way, says Paul, "You have died to the law through the body of Christ, so that you may belong to another, to him who has been raised from the dead . . ." (7:4). Paul has now given us yet a third angle on this analogy: one would have expected the *law* to die rather than the Christian, but since that doesn't work, many commentators have seen here a general illustration that should not be pressed too hard in the details. That may be the case, but N. T. Wright has suggested a way that the analogy almost hangs together, acknowledging that Paul may not be entirely consistent here.[14] Wright suggests that it works better to see the law as the thing that joins the woman to the husband, so that when he dies, the law has no claim on her either. In the same way, the "old self" is the combination of the woman and the husband who represents Adamic existence, the two of which are bound together by the law. In baptism (6:6) the "old self" dies with Christ at the same time that the Christian dies to the law. (For a comparable move, see the triple crucifixion of Christ, Paul, and the world at Gal. 6:14, which lends support to the attempt to find Pauline consistency here.) When the Adamic self-identification dies, so does the obligation to the law that was binding the community to Adamic solidarity (see 5:20 again).

Now Paul adds another component to this already complicated analogy: the Christian who has died to the law in order to belong to Christ can now bear fruit for God (7:4). By contrast, in 7:5, "while we were living in the *flesh*, our sinful passions, aroused by the law, were at work in our members to bear fruit for Death." This sentence is something of a teaser: Paul drops the word "flesh" into the mix, a word that he will pick up again at 7:14, 7:25b, and finally at length in 8:1–17. Within the analogy, "living in the flesh" must refer also to the old Adamic existence, where "the end of those things is Death" (6:21) and "the wages of Sin is Death" (6:23). He will show us how that relates to sinful passions aroused by the law shortly in 7:7–13. What Paul tells us by way of transition into that section is, "But now we are discharged from the law, dead to that which held us captive, so that we are slaves not in oldness of letter but in newness of Spirit" (7:6). Paul had contrasted "letter" and "Spirit/spirit" in 2:29 when he spoke of the circumcision of the heart of the (real) Jew, who might or might not be circumcised outwardly. Here that contrast will serve as a springboard to the contrast of "flesh" and "Spirit" in chapter 8. But, lest any-

---

14. N. T. Wright, *The Climax of the Covenant: Christ and the Law in Pauline Theology* (Minneapolis: Fortress, 1991) 196.

one should then be tempted to make a simple equation between "flesh" and "letter" or "law," Paul makes a preemptive strike against that in 7:14 by contrasting the "spiritual law" with the "fleshly I" of the discourse of 7:7–25, which we shall now take up.

LAW, SIN, THE SPIRIT, AND RIGHTEOUSNESS (ROM. 7:7–8:17)

Paul has come so close to saying that the law is sin that he frames his next rhetorical question in 7:7 in order to head off that idea: "What should we say then? That the law is sin? Of course not!" "Yet," he continues, "had it not been for the law, I would not have known sin."

Who is the "I" of Romans 7:7–25? Various solutions have been proposed. Is it the voice of present Christian existence, as Nygren and others have suggested?[15] But many of the verses are in the past tense, and 7:14 describes the "I" as "fleshly" and "sold into slavery under sin." Is it Paul himself, in his pre-Christian life as an adolescent, struggling with sinful desires like Augustine, as Dodd proposed?[16] But this interpretation is refuted by Philippians 3:6 where Paul describes himself as being "blameless" as to righteousness under the law. Perhaps it is Paul or someone else who, in his pre-Christian life, came to realize that his life under the law, however blameless, was a form of "inauthentic existence," as in Bultmann's reading?[17] This interpretation owes much to modern existentialism and seems logically impossible for Paul. The most helpful readings avoid the assumption that Paul is incoherent and therefore also avoid autobiographical and psychological approaches designed to explain his incoherency. Paul's words in Romans 7:7–25 are certainly not a transcript of how it felt at the time. Nor are they an account of present experience. But then we are back where we started, it seems.

Werner G. Kümmel[18] helpfully suggested that Romans 7:7–25 is an analysis of *some* pre-Christian experience, not as it was perceived at the time or remembered later, but as it has been reconstructed theologically from a

---

15. Anders Nygren, *Commentary on Romans*, trans. Carl C. Rasmussen (Philadelphia: Muhlenberg Press, 1949).

16. C. H. Dodd, *The Epistle of Paul to the Romans* (New York: Harper, 1932) and *The Meaning of Paul for Today* (London: G. Allen & Unwin, 1958) 76ff.

17. Rudolf Bultmann, "Romans 7 and the Anthropology of Paul," in *Existence and Faith* (1932, reprint, London: Hodder & Stoughton, 1960) 173–185.

18. Werner G. Kümmel, *Römer 7 und die Bekehrung des Paulus* (Leipzig: Hinrichs, 1929); reissued as *Römer 7 und das Bild des Menschen im Neuen Testament* (Munich: Kaiser, 1974).

Christian point of view. In addition, many have noticed frequent allusions to the story of Adam's fall in Genesis 3 (see the introduction to this chapter). In fact, the story line of the "I" in Romans 7:7–25 seems remarkably parallel to the story line of Genesis 3, and the whole section makes sense if the "I" who speaks is "Adam," now telling his story from a Christian point of view. As Ernst Käsemann summarized it, "There is nothing in the passage which does not fit Adam, and everything fits Adam alone."[19] In Paul's retelling of the story of Genesis 3 through Adam's eyes, Adam can say, "I would not have known what coveting is if the law had not said, 'You shall not covet'" (7:7) by redescribing the commandment given in the garden (not to eat of the one tree) in terms of the Mosaic law "You shall not covet." Adam can also speak of how Sin seized an opportunity in the commandment (7:8) because the serpent in the garden was able to begin the fatal conversation by referring to the commandment God had given.

Romans 7:8, "Apart from the law, Sin lies dead," is more difficult to place in Paul's retelling of Genesis 3, but if "dead" is understood metaphorically as "inactive" or "unable to act" (as in Abraham's old body and Sarah's dead womb, 4:19), it could describe the situation that existed before God gave the specific commandment, when the serpent had nothing to work with. Similarly the statement "At one time I was alive apart from the law" (7:9), which Paul could never have said about himself, refers to Adam during this same situation. And the sentence "But then when the commandment came, Sin revived and I died" (7:9) means that the serpent saw an opportunity and sprang into action. The result for Adam and Eve was death: "For Sin, exploiting an opportunity in the commandment, deceived me and through it killed me" (7:10). As Paul recounts the story of the fall, this is Eve's word ("The serpent deceived me and I ate") now spoken by Adam. This retelling of the story in Genesis 3 through the eyes of Adam allows Paul to say the most important thing: "So the law is holy, and the commandment is holy, righteous, and good" (7:12). His rhetorical question, "So, then, did what is good bring death to me?" can now clearly be answered with a resounding "No!" It was Sin, using the good law to trick Adam (humanity) into slavery and Death, Sin thus showing itself to be sinful beyond measure (7:13).

James Dunn[20] has argued persuasively that the Adam story of Genesis 3 has also been conflated with the story of Israel and particularly the story of Israel's great apostasy, the golden calf in Exodus 32. If this is right, then when Paul uses the "I" in 7:7–25, he is telling both Adam's story in Genesis 3 and Israel's story

---

19. Käsemann, *Commentary on Romans*, 196.
20. Dunn, James D. G., *Romans*, 2 vols. Word Bible Commentary (Dallas: Word, 1988) I:379, 400.

in Exodus 32. He tells Israel's story in the first-person singular as a way of identifying with it and showing himself to be part of Israel's need for redemption. Even though this story doesn't match Paul's own experience of being "blameless" as to "righteousness under the law" reported in Philippians 3:6, in another sense this *is* his story; he lived there without knowing it, seen from a later Christian point of view. So, in 7:7–11, the passage we just looked at through the lens of Genesis 3, Paul is also describing the story of the arrival of the Mosaic law in Israel as the recapitulation, or reenactment, of the sin of Adam. A brief review of the story in Exodus 32 will help us to see how it works here.

Exodus 31 ends with God's giving of the law to Moses on Mount Sinai. Moses receives the two tablets of stone that contain the words of the law written with the finger of God. Exodus 32 begins by telling us what was happening "meanwhile back at the camp." Since Moses had been gone forty days, the people were restless and said to Aaron, "Get up, make gods for us . . . as for this Moses, we don't know what has become of him." Aaron collected their gold jewelry, formed it in a mold, and cast it in the image of a calf, which the people accepted as their god. So Aaron built an altar and the people held a festive celebration with burnt sacrifices to their new god, the golden calf. Being up on the mountain, Moses knows nothing of this, but God informs him of the situation and of God's plan to destroy the people. Moses pleads for the people and changes God's mind. Then Moses comes down the mountain with the two stone tablets of the law, rejoining his assistant Joshua, who had waited for him on the way back to the camp of the Israelites. Joshua hears the loud sounds coming from the camp and says, "There is a noise of war in the camp!" But Moses knows better: "It is not the sound made by winners or the sound made by losers, but the noise of singing that I hear."

When he draws near the camp, Moses' anger burns so hot that he throws the stone tablets of the law to the ground and breaks them at the foot of the mountain. He takes the calf and grinds it into powder; then he mixes the powder with water and makes the Israelites drink it. Moses confronts Aaron, who sounds like Adam and Eve, as he blames the people. He also minimizes his own role in the story dramatically when he says of the people's gold, "They gave it to me, I tossed it into the fire, and out came this calf!" Moses orders a slaughter of the three thousand evildoers but begs the Lord to spare the rest, even to kill him instead of them. God promises to withhold their punishment—for a time but not forever—and meanwhile sends a plague on the people. These results show the terrible seriousness with which God, and therefore Moses, took this incident in Israel's history.

By the time of Paul much later, the people of Israel remembered this story with horror. Just as they read the story of Adam and Eve in Genesis 3 as the story of the fall of all humanity, so they read the story of the golden calf in

Exodus 32 as the story of "the fall of Israel."[21] How does the golden calf story work itself out in Paul's argument? The arrival of the law in Israel functions as a parallel to the giving of the commandment in the story of the fall of Adam. The law itself is not sin, but through the law "I" (Israel speaks here) discovered sin. Sin uses the law (the occasion of the giving of the law to Moses on Mount Sinai) as a base of operations for suggesting idolatry, which is the worst kind of coveting—coveting another god. Sin finds opportunity in the event of giving the commandment and deceives the people. When Moses goes "offstage" up the mountain to receive the law, he is like God who walks "offstage" in Genesis 3, giving opportunity to the serpent.

The next event in Paul's retelling of the parallel stories of Adam's fall and Israel's apostasy is the arrival of the commandments. Paul's words in Romans 7:9 link the coming of the commandment to death. So, in the golden calf story, when Moses came down the mountain with the two tablets of the law, "I" (Israel) died. When the Mosaic law arrived in Israel, the first word it spoke was a word of judgment against Israel. Thus, the law arrived with the announcement that Israel had already broken it![22] The immediate penalty was the violent death of three thousand people, recalling Genesis 2:17: "For in the day you eat of it you shall surely die." The longer-range penalty, however, was, as it was for Adam and Eve, exile and death. The people of Israel who fell for the golden calf were the generation that perished in the wilderness and never reached the promised land.

To summarize Romans 7:1–13: by a series of analogies (from marriage law, from Gen. 3, and from Exod. 32), Paul has described Israel's situation under the law as a state of slavery under the power of Sin, which uses God's good law to deceive the people of God and kill them. Drawing on interpretive traditions that relate Adam's fall to the whole of humanity and the golden calf incident as Israel's particular fall, Paul has retold the two stories in parallel to underline the argument he had framed earlier in Romans 1–3 that all people, Jews and Gentiles alike, were trapped in Sin and rescued by God in Christ. In Romans 7:14–25, Paul will continue his description of humanity in general and especially Israel living the Adamic existence under Sin's power.

If the "I" of Romans 7:7–25 has puzzled commentators, Paul's sudden switch in 7:14 from the past tense to the present tense only increases the confusion surrounding this notoriously difficult passage. What clearly does *not* work is to identify this present-tense language with the present experience of the church or to equate it with the work of sanctification. This reading fails

---

21. I am indebted to N. T. Wright for this provocative reading of Exodus 32 in the context of Romans.

22. N. T. Wright, *The Climax of the Covenant*, 197.

because in 7:14 the "I" speaks of being "fleshly" and "sold into slavery under sin" and, in the following verses, the "I" describes the wretched condition of doing the opposite of what I want to do.

Some commentators, determined to find a point of Christian doctrine in Romans 7, have landed on 7:14–21 as a proof text for the doctrine of total depravity, focusing especially on 7:18, which is usually translated incorrectly something like "For I know that nothing good dwells within me, that is, in my flesh." What the verse says literally is, "For I know that *the good* does not dwell within me."[23] Perhaps Paul is referring to the platonic form of the Good or to the "good impulse" that, implanted in the self along with the "evil impulse," struggles to control the will of the self as the Dead Sea Scrolls and other contemporary Jewish writings attest. But more probably, he is referring to the "holy, righteous, and good" law (7:12) that "does not dwell within me" (7:18). If so, then Paul would have Israel saying, "Sin is the occupying power that has controlled my existence since Adam; the law, holy as it was, was powerless to prevent Sin from ruling over me and killing me." It is clear, then, that 7:14 continues the description of humanity in general and Israel in particular under the power of Sin, that is, still "in Adam."

Paul's logic here is like Karl Barth's in the sermon described in chapter 2.[24] From the safety of home, the man in Barth's story realized, to his horror, that he had crossed a lake of thin ice during the storm at night and could have died a terrible death. So, having announced the situation of our peace and reconciliation with God through Jesus Christ in 5:1–11, having shown how much more extravagant God's loving action in the obedience of Jesus Christ was than Adam's act of disobedience in 5:12–21, and having shown us that in baptism we are no longer under the power of Sin and no longer have to obey Sin in 6:1–23, Paul now forces us in 7:1–25 to look unflinchingly at the old situation from which we were rescued. Throughout the argument, Paul has exonerated the law from blame (Sin that uses the law causes the problem) and, at the same time, he has exonerated Israel whose "I" can say, "It was Sin's fault" (Sin dwelling within me). But this raises another, even deeper problem, with which Paul will have to deal: What was God doing, giving a law that would be used by Sin in order to deceive and kill humanity and the people of God? Paul will deal with this question specifically in the powerful language of 8:1–17.

---

23. As Leander E. Keck helpfully underlines in his commentary on "Romans" in *The HarperCollins Study Bible*, NRSV, General Editor Wayne A. Meeks (New York: HarperCollins, 1993) 2125. See also his "The Absent Good: The Significance of Rom 7:18a," in *Text und Geschichte* (Marburg: N. G. Elwert, 1999) 66–75.

24. Karl Barth, "Saved By Grace," *Deliverance to the Captives*, trans. M. Wieser (New York: Harper & Row, 1978) 35–42.

It is tempting to jump directly to Romans 8:1–17 without talking about 7:21–25, a difficult section. No wonder commentators on 7:21–25 have had great difficulty understanding Paul's attitude towards the Mosaic law: Paul himself puzzled about the place of the law, both in God's redemptive plan—to keep covenant faithfulness with Israel and to save a lost creation—and in his own experience. Paul seems to have experienced the law as a dual or double reality. On the one hand he, like all Jews, would delight in God's law given to Israel (see Pss. 19 and 119 for hymns of delight in the law of the Lord). On the other hand, Paul also sees another law, a shadow law, the law taken over by Sin in his flesh, that is, in the members of his physical body. This law somehow functions to bind Israel to that old Adamic existence, like the married woman in 7:1–6 who is still bound to her husband under the law. The lament of the "wretched person" in 7:25, who sees that the law is both a good gift to delight in and an opportunity for Sin to deceive and kill, is thus the lament of Israel under law that needs to be rescued from the body of this death. Thanks be to God it is done through Jesus Christ our Lord (7:25a)! Yet Paul cannot walk away from "his flesh" (9:3), his family members in Israel who are not "in Christ" and have not known this liberation. Even though Paul can give thanks personally ("I, of myself") that he serves the law of God, it is as if some part of himself is not free as long as Israel is not free. "But *with my flesh*, I am enslaved to the law of Sin," he says in 7:25b.[25] The sorrow hinted at here becomes explicit in Romans 9:1–5.

Paul turns a corner in his argument with words of reassurance for his hearers. "Therefore, there is now no condemnation for those who are in Christ Jesus. For the law of the Spirit of life in Christ Jesus has set you [or me] free from the law of Sin and of Death" (8:1–2). After Paul's long, complex description of the Adamic past in Romans 7, he returns here to the present and to the present work of the Spirit in those who are "in Christ." In one complex sentence, he describes the work of God in Christ as the definitive condemnation of Sin in the flesh: "For God has done what the law, weak on account of the flesh, could not do." By sending God's Son "in the likeness of sinful flesh, and to address Sin," God condemned Sin in the flesh, "in order that the just requirement of the law might be fulfilled in us, who walk not according to the flesh but according to the Spirit" (8:3–4).

Romans 8:3–4 is one of the most beautiful and powerful statements of Paul's atonement theology found anywhere in his letters. There is no condemnation for us because God has broken the power of the law that bound us to existence in Adam, in slavery to Sin and Death. The law was good, but weak. So God

---

25. This suggestive reading comes from N. T. Wright. While it does not fully resolve the notorious difficulty of 7:25 (finally even Käsemann wondered if it were a gloss, see *Commentary on Romans*, 212), it has the virtue of focusing our attention on the argumentative links between Romans 5–8 and 9–11.

dealt with Sin in the flesh by becoming flesh, that is, by sending God's Son in the likeness of sinful flesh to address the problem of Sin. God's Son (God's second self) condemned Sin in the flesh. As the seed of Abraham, he rightly was God's response to the sin of Adam. As the Messiah, he rightly was the representative of Israel who did the work of redemption that Israel was supposed to do. In order to deal with Sin, the Son became a sin offering (the offering for sins done unwillingly or in ignorance, appropriate for the situation of Israel described in 7:15–20) and in the process condemned Sin in the flesh, so that the just requirement of the law might be fulfilled in us who walk not according to the flesh but according to the Spirit.

That, for Paul, this "walking" is *halakah*, or the ethical pattern of life prescribed by the law, is clear from the contrasting language of the next several verses. The "Spirit" and the "flesh" (like Christ and Adam) are two opposing spheres of action or families of solidarity, so that to be a member of one or the other is to have one's thoughts and actions shaped by that allegiance. The mind that is set on the flesh is hostile to God and does not, cannot!, submit to God's law (8:7). Instead it submits to the law of Sin and of Death, the law that binds to Adamic existence and disobedience to God; those in the flesh cannot please God (8:8). For Paul, this absolute and opposing division between the realms of Christ/Spirit and Adam/flesh is a given.

As we saw in Romans 6, there is a war going on, and the bodies of those baptized represent territory once wrongfully held by Sin that has now been reclaimed by their rightful owner, the God who created them. This vivid apocalyptic language comes out of Israel's "holy war" tradition. Two stories from that holy war tradition, although they are not alluded to by Paul, may nevertheless be helpful to clarify the logic of his argument in Romans 8. The first is the story of David and Goliath, which, like Paul's argument, assumes the idea of *representative combat*. The second is the story of Gideon, which, like Paul's argument, stresses the *personal holiness* with which one must resist the enemies, Sin and Death.

The idea of representative combat is that instead of two armies slaughtering each other, each army picks one warrior, a representative champion, who will face the opposing champion that the other army has chosen. The two champions do battle on behalf of the armies they represent, and whichever champion prevails, that army has won the war. The story of David and Goliath in 1 Samuel 17 illustrates representative combat. Israel is at war with the Philistines, and the two armies meet for battle at the valley of Elah. The Philistines send out their champion, Goliath, who is described in great detail: about seven feet tall and strong enough to carry heavy armor, an experienced warrior who has been fighting for many years. He calls out to Israel to send their champion to meet him, but seeing him, Saul and his army are greatly dismayed. You remember the story: young David, who isn't even part of Saul's army, volunteers to fight Goliath and finally persuades Saul to let him do it. Saul tries to dress David in his own armor, but it is much too heavy for the boy, and he leaves it behind. David takes only his slingshot and five smooth stones. As Goliath approaches, he puts one stone in the sling and aims at the one place on Goliath's body not protected by heavy armor—his forehead. The stone strikes the Philistine champion's forehead, and he falls face down dead. Israel has won the battle against the Philistines.

The story of David's representative combat with Goliath provides an analogy for the spiritual warfare that Paul describes in Romans 8. Because Jesus Christ condemned Sin in the flesh, we who are "in Christ" also share in his victory. The logic of Paul's argument is that what God in Christ has won, those "in Christ" have also won:

> Since the Spirit of the One who raised Jesus from the dead dwells in you, the One who raised Christ from the dead will give life to your mortal bodies also through [God's] Spirit that dwells in you. (8:11, see also 5:9–11)

Paul's argument in Romans 8 also assumes the importance of personal holiness as a weapon against Sin and Death. Another story from Israel's holy war tradition sheds light on the way personal holiness functions as a weapon against unrighteousness in a situation of holy war. The story of Gideon's victory over the Midianites is told in Judges 7. Once again the power of the opponents is described dramatically:

> The Midianites and the Amalekites and all the people of the east lay along the valley as thick as locusts; and their camels were without number, countless as the sand on the seashore. (Judg. 7:12 NRSV)

But God says to Gideon, who had only 32,000 men, "'The troops with you are too many for me to give the Midianites into their hand. Israel would only take the credit away from me, saying, "My own hand has delivered me"'" (Judg. 7:2 NRSV). Gideon is ordered to proclaim in the hearing of the troops, "'Whoever is fearful and trembling, let him return home'" (Judges 7:3 NRSV). After this, 22,000 men departed, leaving Gideon with only 10,000 to fight the vast armies of the Midianites (7:2–3). Nonetheless, God again says to Gideon, "'The troops are still too many; take them down to the water,'" (7:4 NRSV). Gideon's troops had presumably not had water and were thirsty, but they were also in enemy territory and needed to be watchful in case of an attack. There God devises a test: those that get down on all fours to drink water are to be sent back; only those who carry water up to their mouths with their hands (so they can also keep watch) may remain to fight. Of the 10,000 men remaining to Gideon, all but 300 get down on all fours and drink. So 9,700 are sent home, yet Gideon wins the battle against the Midianites with only 300 men. This story is important background to Romans 8 for at least two reasons. First, God is the champion of Israel in whose victory Gideon and his now tiny army are included. Second, it points to the virtues (in the Gideon story, first courage, then watchfulness) that accompany the victory of God in the believer. In a similar way, Paul exhorts the Christians at Rome to live according to the Spirit and not according to the flesh (8:12–13).

We have seen how Paul uses the ideas of representative combat and personal holiness, important components of Israel's holy war tradition. In addition to these two features of Paul's argument in Romans 8, Sylvia Keesmaat has shown that Paul draws on the most important example of holy war tradition in Israel's history—the exodus from Egypt.[26] That the well-known story of the exodus lies behind Paul's argument in Romans 8:12–17 is clear from Romans 8:14: "As many as are led by the Spirit of God are children of God." Those led by the Spirit are the sons and daughters of Israel who sing the victory songs of Miriam and Moses at the Red Sea (Exod. 15:1–21). "For you did not receive a spirit of slavery [as in Egypt] to fall back into fear; instead, you have received a spirit of adoption" (8:15). Indeed, the cry "Abba, Father" associated with adoption into Christ at baptism characterizes Christians as children of God for whom there will be an inheritance. Just as Israel comes out of slavery in Egypt, receives the law at Sinai, and is given an inheritance (the promised land), so those joined to Israel's Messiah, those "in Christ," come out of slavery to Sin and Death. They go down into the waters that separate them from slavery to Sin, dying and rising with Christ in baptism. Through the power of the resurrection of Christ, they are given the Spirit (8:9–11) of Christ and become "heirs of God and joint heirs of Christ" (8:17), if in fact they suffer with him. Suffering with him is a sign of their affiliation with Christ and, as a consequence, of their participation in the birth pangs of the new creation inaugurated by his death and resurrection.

PRESENT SUFFERINGS AND HOPED-FOR GLORY
(ROM. 8:18–39)

The concluding section of Romans 5–8 contains some of the most powerful language in Paul's entire letter: "I account the sufferings of this present time as not worth comparing with the glory which is about to be revealed (*apokalyphthēnai*) to us" (8:18). Once more, Paul locates his conversation with the Roman

---

26. Sylvia C. Keesmaat, *Paul and His Story: (Re)Interpreting the Exodus Tradition*, Journal for the Study of the New Testament Supplement Series 181 (Sheffield: Sheffield Academic Press, 1999).

house churches in the context of apocalyptic (1:17, 18). God's revelation of reality and, indeed, God's new creation of reality has occurred in the gospel, the event of the death and resurrection of Jesus Christ. As a complement to God's revelation, "the eager longing of the creation waits expectantly for the revelation of the children of God" (Rom. 8:19). The sufferings Paul alludes to, in 8:18 as in 5:3, are the "eschatological woes" expected at the end time, the birth pangs (labor pains) of the new age. Once more the Genesis 3 story lies behind Paul's argument—this time the end of the story, where "the creation itself was subjected to futility" (Rom. 8:20; Gen. 3:17) and where it is said that the process of giving birth will be accompanied by labor pains (Gen. 3:16). Creation waits to be set free from the "bondage" to which it was subjected as a result of Adam's fall and to obtain the glorious "freedom" of the children of God (Rom. 8:21).

Just as the creation, groaning in labor pains, waits for the new creation to be born (8:22), so those "in Christ" who have the firstfruits of the Spirit also groan inwardly "as we wait for adoption, the redemption of our bodies" (8:23). And, just as Christians are within the creation, groaning from within its groaning, so the Spirit within us also groans from within our groaning (8:26). This threefold pattern is obscured in most English translations (cf. "sighs too deep for words" in RSV and NRSV), but some form of the same Greek word *stenazein* appears in all three verses. Paul associates the groaning of the Spirit of God with the prayers of Christians: "For we do not know how to pray as we should, but that very Spirit intercedes for us with groans not spoken in words" (8:26). Paul's pattern of argument assumes that the church will be present in the place of the world's deepest need and that God will be present in the midst of the church in the world: God participates in the sufferings of the new creation from within them[27]: "And the One who searches the heart, knows the mind of the Spirit which intercedes for the saints according to God" (8:27).

The stair-step argument (*sorites*) of 8:28–30 constitutes the second half of the *inclusio* that began with 5:1–5 and signals that this section of Paul's argument (chapters 5–8) is drawing to a close. "All things work together for good for those who love God, who are called according to [God's] purpose" (8:28). Here Paul writes to reassure the Christians in Rome who are "called to be saints" (1:7) according to the purpose of God:

---

27. Charles B. Cousar states this powerfully: "Even in their prayers, which might seem to offer moments of escape, the Spirit provokes an intercessory litany of groaning, joining the Christians' voices with the moans of the terminally ill who long for death, with the angry raging of the oppressed who seek freedom, with the whimpers of the hopeless who have no strength left to cry. In fact, so deeply enmeshed are the Christians' prayers with the world's pained pleas for freedom that Paul has to assure the readers that God is able amid the confusing clamor to discern the mind of the Spirit" (*A Theology of the Cross: The Death of Jesus in the Pauline Letters* [Minneapolis: Fortress, 1990] 173).

For those whom God *foreknew* God also *predestined* (to be conformed to the
image of the Son, in order that he might be the firstborn among many);
And those whom God *predestined* God also *called*;
And those whom God *called* God also *justified*;
And those whom God *justified* God also *glorified*.

(Rom. 8:29–30 paraphrased)

Paul's ringing affirmation in Romans 8:31–39 provides a fitting conclusion
to the whole section and a powerful restatement of the covenant faithfulness
of God in Christ, which is the major theme of the letter as a whole. Rhetorically, the section functions as a *peroratio* or summing up of the argument. Theologically, it frames the issues of suffering and hope raised at the beginning of
the section (5:1–11) in the assurance of God's love in Christ Jesus our Lord. In
a series of rhetorical questions, Paul lists all imaginable powers and principal-
ities that could defeat God's purpose. Paul has just described this purpose in
his *sorites:* to bring those whom God has chosen in love (foreknown, predestined, called) to the place of righteousness and glory appropriate to those conformed to the image of Jesus Christ, the Son destined to become the firstborn
of many brothers and sisters. Paul's confident trust in God's love is matched
only by his realism, already shown, about the fact of present sufferings and the
continued opposition of Sin and Death, whose rule is over and whose days are
numbered, to the inevitable triumphant victory of God in Christ.

"What then shall we say about these things?" asks Paul in Romans 8:31. "If
God is for us, who is against us?" "No one that matters" is the implied answer
to Paul's question, as he will show in greater detail in the following verses.
After all, he points out, God did not "spare" God's own Son, "but gave him up
for us all" (8:32). Paul meditates on the extravagant generosity of God in
Christ by alluding to the story of the near sacrifice of Isaac in Genesis 22 as
the catchword "spare" shows.[28] Will not that same God, who was willing to
give up the beloved only Son, "also give us all other things along with him?"
(8:32). Since God has been generous at that point of greatest costliness to God,
cannot we also hope for God's continued generosity at other points? (We saw
a parallel argument in Rom. 5:6–11.) Paul invites us to imagine the day of
God's judgment with the question "Who will press any charges against God's
elect?" (8:33). When it is God who is the just Judge declaring us righteous,
vindicating us against our adversaries, who is there to condemn? Moreover,
Christ Jesus, who died and was raised from the dead and now sits at the right
hand of God, the place of power and authority, intercedes for us, arguing our
case (8:34). No matter what opponents we can imagine who might accuse us

---

28. Nils Alstrup Dahl, "The Atonement—An Adequate Reward for the Akedah?" in
The Crucified Messiah and Other Essays (Minneapolis: Augsburg, 1974) 146–160.

in court, with God as our Judge and Jesus Christ as our lawyer for the defense, we do not need to fear the outcome.

Paul has been speaking of God's covenant faithfulness in the language of the law-court model of atonement. Now he changes the metaphor to speak of God's victory in holy war: "Who (or what) will separate us from the love of Christ? Will suffering, or distress, or persecution, or famine, or nakedness, or danger, or the sword? As it stands written, 'For your sake we are being killed all day long; we are accounted as sheep to be slaughtered'" (Rom. 8:35–36). Paul's realism is striking, especially when we notice that of the seven threats he lists, he personally has experienced six of them.[29] His quotation of Psalm 44:22 (see also Jer. 11:19; 12:3) shows that Paul does not expect any magical protection of Christians from the normal hardships of life and expects rather that the very status of being a Christian may subject believers to additional hardships and persecutions. Paul asks if anything can separate us from God's love in Christ. But, since the answer to his rhetorical question is an emphatic "No," listing the possible opponents only serves to deepen his conviction that the final victory belongs to God in Christ, and therefore also to those baptized into the death and resurrection of Christ. "No, in all these things we are more than conquerors through the One who loved us. For I am convinced that neither death, nor life, nor angels, nor rulers, nor things present, nor things to come, nor powers, nor height, nor depth, nor *anything else in all creation*, will be able to separate us from the love of God in Christ Jesus our Lord" (8:37–39).

Summary. The first eleven verses of Romans 5 encourage us to trust in God's love for us, even in the midst of suffering, because the sign of God's grace, the Holy Spirit poured into our hearts, assures us that God will also be gracious on the day of judgment. The Christ/Adam contrast is set up clearly in 5:12–21, but the Adam story (already there in Rom. 1) reappears in 7–8, once you know what to look for. For example, when Paul talks about the present suffering and the "glory" to be revealed, he is almost certainly thinking of the lost glory of Adam and Eve, which would be recovered in the last days when Messiah came. For Paul, Messiah *has* come: Jesus is the Messiah in whom the lost glory has been regained, not just for himself but for all humanity. His victory is assured but not yet fully realized. All creation, humanity, and even God's Spirit groan

---

29. I am indebted to Robert Morgan for this observation (*Romans*, 151): "Paul speaks of a God who has not spared his own Son (Rom. 8:32) and the evil powers which crucified him (1 Cor. 2:8). The reality of the cross is stamped upon the apostle's own body too (cf. Gal. 6:17). When Paul writes of 'affliction, hardship, persecution, hunger, nakedness, danger, or sword' (Rom. 8:35) it is six down and one to go for him personally (cf. 2 Cor. 11:23–27)."

waiting for the great day when the effects of the fall described in Genesis 3 will be undone and God's new creation will be visible to all.

Another submerged story line in Romans 5–8 concerns the Christian who has become one with Christ in baptism. Just as Jesus' baptism resulted in his assault by Satan in the wilderness, so the believer who is identified with Christ in baptism experiences the attack of Sin and Death. Drawing on Israel's holy war tradition, Paul describes the body of the believer as occupied territory in the middle of a war between God, who made the body as part of God's good creation, and Sin, an occupying power that has wrongfully taken possession and now, in baptism, has been evicted. Paul describes the Christian as caught between rival powers (Adam/flesh and Christ/Spirit) and having to discern which is the real world. But Paul proclaims the good news of God's faithfulness: nothing can separate us from the love of God that is in Christ Jesus. He considers and rejects a long list of things that might seem more powerful than God's love and calls on his hearers to trust the reality of God over against the illusions of the enemy.

FOR FURTHER REFLECTION

1. Paul's description of Christians' being caught up in God's war against Sin and Death and having to decide for one side or the other is not unlike the situation of many civilians and refugees in war-ravaged countries who get caught up in the conflict of opposing armies, "like sheep to be slaughtered" (Ps. 44:22; Rom. 8:36). What contemporary situations come to mind when you think about people experiencing the conflict of hostile powers and having to throw their lot in with one side or the other?

2. Paul further develops the holy war metaphor by describing the bodies of Christians as occupied territory that is being fought over by God (who created the body and is its rightful owner) and by Sin and Death (who have wrongfully occupied it to destroy it). Many Christians who have experienced the attack of Sin and Death on their bodies in the forms of drugs and alcohol have found Paul's metaphor helpful. Can you say in your own words how this works?

3. Some churches speak of "prayer warriors" to refer to one of the disciplines needed to participate in God's holy war against Sin and Death. What other disciplines or character traits are needed to prevail against these enemies? Are there any hints about these in the stories of David's victory over Goliath in 1 Samuel 17 or Gideon's victory over the Amalekites in Judges 7?

4. How does Paul compare the disobedience and unfaithfulness of Adam with the obedience and faithfulness of Jesus Christ in Romans 5:12–21? How many reasons can you list why God's free gift in Jesus Christ is not like Adam's trespass?

5. Dorothy Martyn, a psychotherapist who works with violent children and whose work was cited in this chapter, has suggested that the most important part of their healing is their ability to see themselves as members of a new family where violence is not the way of life. How is Christian baptism about becoming a member of this new family?

6. Often the violence and hatred that surround us seem more powerful and real than the love of God in Christ that Paul describes in Romans 8:31–39. Yet Paul, like Abraham in Romans 4, is confident that God keeps God's promises and that nothing in all creation will be able to separate us from the love of God in Christ. In what ways are we presented with conflicting views of reality? How do we go about deciding what is real and what is illusory?

7. Sometimes it is difficult to know where we are in the story. For example, historians now describe the Montgomery bus boycott as the turning point of the civil rights movement. The victory was really achieved there, even though there were still many long hard years to live through before that victory could be fully realized, and even though the struggle to end racism is still far from over. How do Christians go on in the face of opposition and hardship? Does Paul have any suggestions that may help?

5

"Has God Rejected His People?"

(Rom. 9:1–11:36)

The city authorities of Göttingen have erected a small memorial to the murdered Jews of the city, and the memorial is one of the stops on the walking tour. The inscription on the memorial quotes one of the psalms of lament, which complains to God about the persecution of Israel:

> All this has come upon us,
> though we have not forgotten you,
> or been false to your covenant. . . .
> Because of you we are being killed all day long,
> and accounted as sheep for the slaughter. (Psalm 44:17, 22)
>
> *Joel Marcus[1]*

The greatest influence on me when I was a nun was probably the Catholic Worker movement, which was saying, "The teachings of the church have to be realized. They have to be brought about and lived." Here was Dorothy Day in the movement—and she was not even a born Roman Catholic. She joined the church after being a Communist—or when she was a Communist. She worked on the *Daily Worker*. I guess she became a Catholic because she discovered the gospel, and she saw in the gospel a liberation theology that needed to be lived and brought out: a concern for poor people, the rights of individuals and that sort of thing. Do you know that to her dying day she prayed that she would meet Marx in Heaven?

Jeanne Morin Buell[2]

---

1. Joel Marcus, *Jesus and the Holocaust: Reflections on Suffering and Hope* (New York: Doubleday, 1997) 110.
2. Jeanne Morin Buell, quoted in Judith Porter Adams, *Peacework: Oral Histories of Women Peace Activists* (Boston: Twayne, 1991) 24.

THE PLACE OF ROMANS 9–11 IN THE LETTER

At first glance, Paul seems to shift both the tone and the subject matter of his letter dramatically here at the beginning of Romans 9. His confident rejoicing in the triumph of God's love gives way to sorrow and lament. Moreover, having just affirmed in Romans 8:39 that nothing in all creation "will be able to separate us from God's love in Christ Jesus our Lord," Paul now affirms that *he* would be willing to be separated from God's love—if his separation would mean inclusion for his brothers and sisters of the flesh, Israel.[3] If nothing can separate *us* from God's love in Christ, does *us* include unbelieving Israel? Or is "unbelief" perhaps the one thing that *can* separate someone, perhaps an entire people, perhaps even God's own people Israel, from God's love in Jesus Christ?[4]

When Romans is read as a textbook of Christian doctrine, Romans 9–11 is often seen as an appendix to the argument, as if it were set off in square brackets. Since the Protestant Reformation, commentators have had a hard time seeing how these chapters belong to Paul's letter because they don't fit into the standard progression of doctrinal topics: Doctrine of God, Creation and Fall, Sin and Need for Salvation, Justification, Sanctification and Christian Life. Although he was critical of the Reformation perspective, C. H. Dodd[5] wrote an enormously influential commentary on Romans in which he suggested that Romans 9–11 was extraneous—perhaps a leftover sermon from another time that Paul stuck in—because the argument flows perfectly well without it from the end of Romans 8 to the beginning of Romans 12. And if Paul's theological argument is reduced to the dimensions of a set of topics in systematic theology, then it seems to work without Romans 9–11, especially if it is also argued that Israel's problem is not our problem and Israel's story is not our story.[6] But when we read Romans 1–8 (and later 12–16) with care, we see that

---

3. David L. Bartlett, *Romans* (Louisville, Ky.: Westminster John Knox, 1995) 83.

4. Richard B. Hays, *Echoes of Scripture in the Letters of Paul* (New Haven, Conn.: Yale University Press, 1989), 63–64; and idem, *The Moral Vision of the New Testament: Community, Cross, and New Creation: A Contemporary Introduction to New Testament Ethics* (San Francisco: HarperCollins, 1996) 412.

5. C. H. Dodd, *The Epistle of Paul to the Romans* (New York: Harper, 1932).

6. For example, Rudolph Bultmann understood the Old Testament as expressing impossible moral demands, the background for the grace of the gospel, but not part of Christian revelation. The Old Testament was somebody else's story. See his "The Significance of the Old Testament for Christian Faith," *The Old Testament and Christian Faith*, ed. B. W. Anderson (New York: Harper & Row, 1963) 8–55. Incredibly, this view or something like it is often attributed to Paul himself; cf. Adolf Harnack's comment,

God's plan to redeem the world from Adamic existence was through Abraham and Israel. God's salvation-creating righteousness is for the Jew first and also the Greek. Then it becomes clear that Paul's long discussion in 9–11 of the place of Israel in God's providential plan to include the Gentiles stands at the very center of his argument.

Paul hinted at the importance of God's dealings with Israel earlier, in Romans 3:1–6, where he spoke of how God had entrusted "the oracles of God" (the sacred Scriptures) to Israel (3:2). Is there perhaps a hint in these texts that will explain what God is doing now with Israel? At the same place, Paul had questioned whether God's covenant faithfulness could be destroyed by Israel's unfaithfulness? He then answered with a resounding "No!" Even if every human is a liar, God will be proved true (3:3–4). Paul even dared to ask in Romans 3:5–6 whether God is unrighteous to inflict wrath on unrighteous humanity. No! Of course not, for then how could God judge the world? At that point in his argument, Paul set up the questions and gave only the briefest of answers—not because the questions were unimportant, but because they were so important that he needed to defer their discussion until after he had laid out major building blocks of his argument in Romans 4 (on Abraham) and 5–8 (on Christ and Spirit versus Adam and flesh).

Specifically, Paul showed in Romans 4 that God's covenant faithfulness is not revealed in Abraham as an ancestor according to the flesh (genealogy) or as an ancestor who kept the Mosaic law (represented by circumcision) but rather in Abraham as an ancestor who trusted God's promises that he would be the father of many nations. Those words from Genesis 15:6, "Therefore his faith was reckoned to him as righteousness," were also written for those who trust in the God who raised Jesus from the dead, whether they are circumcised or not, since Abraham is the father of us all.

In Romans 5–8, Paul showed that the effects of the Adamic fall were too powerful to be remedied by the Mosaic law. Indeed, the law only complicated the situation. Paul can indeed speak of the law as something in which to

"It is Paul who delivered the Christian religion from Judaism," in his *What Is Christianity?* (1901; reprint, New York: Harper, 1957) 176. Occasionally, Paul is even accused of being anti-Jewish and laying the groundwork for the tragic anti-Semitism that has characterized much of Christian theology through the ages. A careful reading of Romans 9–11 should allay any suspicion that Paul sees God replacing the people of Israel with the church of Jesus Christ. See Charles Cousar's excellent summary in *The Letters of Paul* (Nashville: Abingdon, 1996) 114–115. Nor has God proven fickle or unfaithful to Israel in Paul's account. As Richard Hays has shown, "Romans 9–11 is an extended demonstration of the congruity between God's word in Scripture and God's word in Paul's gospel" (*Echoes of Scripture in the Letters of Paul*, 64).

delight when he refers to the law of the Spirit in the new Christian life "in Christ." Over against that law, however, is another law, operative in the flesh, part of the Adamic existence under the law, subject to Sin and Death. If Israel trusts in the law to remedy the Adamic situation or if Israel insists that only those under the law are the seed of Abraham, Israel has not understood its own story, according to Paul. By reminding Israel of the golden calf incident (Exod. 32), Paul is showing that the arrival of the law does not protect against Sin but only demonstrates the power of Sin. By retelling the story of Isaac's birth to Abraham and Sarah, Paul stresses that it is not physical descent from Abraham that matters but sharing the faith of Abraham, trusting that God keeps God's promises. With those pieces securely in place, Paul is now ready to take up the question of his own failed mission to Israel and its place in God's plan.

PAUL'S LAMENT IN ROMANS 9:1-5

Romans 9:1–5 is Paul's own introduction to this major section of his letter. Paul's anguished grief [7] at the unbelief of his own people, Israel, is heightened by the fact that his argument in Romans 4–8 has in one way or another made over to the people of God in Jesus Christ all the privileges and prerogatives of Israel that he lists here. [8] But it is *not* the case that Paul simply takes these privileges from Israel and gives them to the Gentiles. Rather, he shows that they were entrusted to Israel for the purpose of Israel's God-given mission for the lost world, the work that has now been accomplished in the one true Israelite

---

7. James D. G. Dunn, "The doubling of *lypē* ('grief, sorrow, pain of mind and spirit') and *odynē* ('mental pain') . . . intensifies the already strong emotive force of the affidavit. It will be no accident that the only places in biblical Greek where the two words are associated are Isa 35:10 and 51:11: 'The ransomed of the Lord shall return, and come to Zion with singing; they shall obtain joy and gladness, and sorrow and sighing shall flee away.' In both verses LXX renders 'sorrow' (*yagōn*) by the double expression, *odynē kai lypē*. . . . Such lament over Israel is a well-established motif in Jewish and apocalyptic literature, particularly in reference to the destruction of Jerusalem (Jer 4:19; 14:17; Lam; Dan 9:3, etc.)" (*Romans 9–16*, Word Bible Commentary 38B [Dallas: Word, 1988] 523–524).

8. Dunn, speaking about the nature of Paul's argument so far: "that it is precisely the righteousness of God testified to by the law and the prophets (3:21), the promise of God to and through Abraham (chap. 4) into which the nations have entered; that it is the business of the law (2:15), the circumcision of the heart (2:29), the law of the Spirit of life (8:2) which has been realized and come to fulfilled expression in the nations' obedience to the gospel. The nations have begun to experience the grace and faithfulness of God which was once Israel's special privilege." (*Romans 9–16*, 530). See also his extended comments on Romans 9:4–5 (ibid., 533–535).

who is both the seed of Abraham and the Messiah of the covenant people.[9] As Paul showed in Romans 4:13, "The promise that he (the seed) would inherit the world did not come through the law but through the righteousness of faithfulness," that is, God's righteousness shown in Jesus' faithfulness at his death (3:21–26). Therefore, the inheritance of the promise now belongs to all the seed of Abraham who are "in Christ," whether Jew or Gentile. This inheritance is spelled out in 9:4 where Paul lists "adoption" (8:15–17); "the glory" (5:2; 8:18, 28–30); "the covenants" (4:6–8, 17–18, 22–25); "the giving of the law" (7:12, 22; 8:3–8); "the worship" (5:2 "access to [God's] grace" and 8:15–16, 26–27); "the promises" (4:13–16); and above all "the Messiah" himself, the greatest gift of God, who belongs to Israel according to the flesh (1:3; 9:5) but whom Israel has rejected twice, first in rejecting Jesus himself and now in rejecting Paul's preaching of the Messiah.[10]

At least two more comments are needed by way of introduction to Romans 9–11 as a whole and 9:1–5 in particular. The first concerns Paul's own place in the argument: four times during this section, at each of the major turning points of the discussion (9:1–5; 10:1–4; 11:1–6; 11:13–14) Paul interjects himself and his story into the argument. Here in 9:1–5, he speaks of himself to stress how strongly God's mercy to Israel matters to him—enough that he would be willing to be cut off for the sake of his people. At 10:1–4 he bears witness on behalf of Israel that their intentions are good: they have a zeal for God; it just is not according to knowledge. At 11:1–6 he testifies to God's

---

9. N. T. Wright, "Paul and the Theology of Romans," *Pauline Theology, Volume Three: Romans*, ed. D. M. Hay and E. E. Johnson (Minneapolis: Fortress, 1995) 30–67. For his own treatment of Romans 9–11, which is very different from the reading given here, see Wright, *The Climax of the Covenant: Christ and the Law in Pauline Theology* (Minneapolis: Fortress, 1991) esp. chap. 13.

10. The arguments over the much-debated ending of Romans 9:5 (summarized in Dunn, *Romans 9–16*, 528–529) are far from conclusive, with respect to either punctuation or interpretation. Paul wrote the words in this order: "They are Israelites . . . and from whom the Christ according to the flesh the one who is over all things God blessed into the ages. Amen." As Dunn suggests, there are two main options: (1) (the NRSV's choice) to read everything after "according to the flesh" as a relative clause modifying the Christ, which is stylistically the more natural reading but would result in one of the very few places in the New Testament and perhaps the only place in Paul's letters where Jesus is called "God"; or (2) (Dunn's choice) to put a full stop after the words "according to the flesh," which would make the rest of 9:5 a concluding doxology to God, which, according to Dunn, is the more natural reading given the rest of Paul's theology. I am not as certain as he is about that. However, assuming his view, I also wonder whether the break is in the right place. Paul might have intended to say that the Messiah is over all things (at present, see 1 Cor. 15:27–28) and to bless God forever for that. Fortunately, a decision on the matter does not directly affect the interpretation of Paul's argument in Romans 9 itself, so one can consign it to the list of things to ask Paul about someday.

faithfulness: God has in fact called a remnant of Israel in Paul himself. Finally, at 11:13–14 he describes how he glorifies his ministry as apostle to the Gentiles as part of God's plan to make Israel jealous.

So the first major "story" behind the argument of Romans 9–11 is the story of God's intervention in Paul's life, calling him to faith in Jesus as the Messiah, commissioning him as an apostle to the Gentiles. As we saw in chapter 1, Paul does not actually tell this story in Romans (as he does in Gal. 1–2 and Phil. 3), but it is clearly on his mind as he puzzles about why he has heard and responded to the good news of what God has done in Christ while his brothers and sisters in Israel continue not to respond in faith.

The second important "story" behind Romans 9–11 is the story of every Israelite who has ever prayed to God in time of trouble. Paul began Romans with the assertion that he was "not ashamed" of the gospel of God (1:16–17). There, as we saw, he seemed to be drawing on the language of Israel's psalms, especially psalms of the misunderstood or suffering righteous ones in need of God's justice, as in Psalm 25:3 (24:2 LXX): "Let no one who waits for you be put to shame."[11] As Richard Hays has shown, Romans 9–11 is structured as a lament psalm.[12] One could almost say that Paul, in writing his own lament psalm in Romans 9–11, writes representatively on behalf of all Israel, appealing to God from the language of Israel's own Scriptures, the same "oracles of God" (3:2) entrusted to Israel by God. Romans 9–11 is saturated with scriptural quotations, allusions, and echoes, far too many to discuss here. But it is clear from 9:1–5, the beginning of the section 9–11, that "the righteousness of God," the subject of the entire letter, is nowhere more at stake than it is in the question of God's dealings with God's own people, Israel. Paul begins as if he were praying to God that God would indeed show, in these same Scriptures which contain the promises to Israel's ancestors, some way through the problem of God's *apparent* unrighteousness to Israel—apparent but not real, for Paul knows that unrighteousness cannot be the case with God (3:5–6).

So, to summarize, Romans 9:1–5 is at least four things. First, it is a flashback to Romans 3:1–6, revisiting the questions raised and answered much too summarily there, and placing those questions on the table here at the proper place in Paul's argument. Second, it is a summary of the privileges and prerogatives of Israel that Paul has shown to be properly the inheritance of the seed of Abraham, now redefined in Jesus the Messiah. Third, it is a personal statement from Paul of his own investment in the argument he will be unfolding and a confession of the mystery of God's call in his own life. Finally, it is a prayer/psalm that Paul speaks representatively on behalf of those who have not

---

11. Hays, *Echoes of Scripture in the Letters of Paul*, 38.
12. Ibid., 64.

heard and responded as he has. In the rest of Romans 9–11, Paul will have to show that the same God who spoke covenant promises to Israel has not now abandoned Israel by opening those covenant promises to Gentiles—who have become part of Israel's Messiah and therefore heirs of the covenant inheritance promised to the seed of Abraham.

"GOD'S WORD HAS NOT FALLEN"
(ROM. 9:6–29)

Paul has already signaled in 9:1–5 his concern to understand God's present dealings with Israel through the words of God spoken in promises given to Israel in the past. Paul is retelling the story of Israel with the particular question of *theodicy* (God's justice) in mind. Retellings of Israel's story were common in Jewish literature of this period. *Jubilees*, for example, is a retelling of Genesis. Christian writings, such as Acts 7 and Hebrews 11, fit into this Jewish pattern. In Romans 9:6–29, Paul summarizes in a rough way the history of Israel as he understands it, treating the patriarchs in 9:7–13, the exodus from Egypt and the wilderness wanderings in 9:14–18, the exile and return of the remnant in 9:24–28, and the coming of the Messiah in 9:29.

At each point in Israel's history Paul shows that God chooses one person or group and not another, and he stresses the gracious and merciful character of God's election. Each of these examples is a story within the story of God's righteous dealing with Israel. Paul moves from Abraham, Isaac, and Jacob to the exodus, to the exile and restoration, and finally to the renewal of the covenant, the coming of the Messiah, and the ingathering of the Gentiles. But the question that is driving his retelling of the story is this: What happens to Israel—ethnic Israel according to the flesh, Paul's own flesh—after the covenant has been renewed for the benefit of the fallen world?

So Paul's retelling of the Abraham and Isaac story here stresses not Abraham's trust or his becoming the father of many (as in Rom. 4) but the choosing of Isaac over Ishmael. "Not all of Israel are Israel" and not all of the descendants of Abraham are his "seed" because, as Genesis 21:12 says, "In *Isaac* shall be named (lit. called) for you a seed." All the descendants of Abraham are children "of the flesh," but just as what is important about Abraham is not that he is our ancestor according to the flesh but that he believed the promise, so these children of the flesh are not the seed of Abraham, but only the child of promise, Isaac. Not only that, but God's pattern of choosing continues into the next generation of children born to Isaac and Rebecca. This time the choice is between twins before they had even been born. Rebecca is told "the elder will serve the younger" (Gen. 25:23), and Paul cites a text from

Malachi (1:2–3) which seems to clinch the argument: "Jacob I loved, but Esau I hated."

Malachi 1:2–3 immediately raises the question of the injustice or unrighteousness of God, for Paul, as it does for many readers of Romans today. He asks the question point blank in 9:14: "What then shall we say? That there is injustice (unrighteousness, *adikia*) on God's part?" This is especially painful since Paul has made such a point of identifying Israel with "flesh" in 9:3 and since the "promises" of 9:4 are part of the privileges of Israel that now belong to the people of the Messiah in which Israel of the flesh does not believe. Similarly, the "elder" recipients of God's covenant promises seem to have been preserving them so that the "younger" heirs might receive them. Are we then forced to draw the conclusion to which Malachi seems to be pointing, that God "loves" the Gentile Christians in Paul's churches and "hates" unbelieving Israel?

It is important to see what Paul is and is not doing here. He is *not* mustering a list of proof texts to make a point that he already has in mind. People who read Paul's argument that way often conclude that he is anti-Jewish. In fact, just the opposite is true, as will become clearer in Romans 11. Paul is arguing with God like Job; he is praying a lament psalm, begging God to show him why the conclusions he does not want to reach are wrong. When Paul tries to understand what is going on with Israel, terrible thoughts come to him, which he lifts up to God for correction. We can imagine Paul saying, "It looks like you love one group and hate the other, is that right? Is Malachi the text I should use to understand this situation? And if so, how is that fair?" Christians can learn from Paul here (as also from the Psalms and from Job) how to bring the hard questions of our lives before God, trusting that with God's direction we will be shown a way through. We can see in Paul's argument that every time he gets to one of these terrifying places, God gives him a clue, usually a biblical text, suggesting that there is another way to see it. The text from Malachi that Paul has thought of may not apply to Paul's situation after all. Instead, perhaps the more helpful text is Exodus 33:19. What brought it to Paul's mind at this point? It seems to have been God's answer given to him in time of great need. Indeed, we can read all of Romans 9–11 as a record of Paul's thought process as he works his way through the painful question of God's justice to Israel in dialogue with God—and also with the churches in Rome whom he allows to overhear the transcript of his prayer journal.

The text that suddenly came to Paul's mind as he pondered Malachi 1:2–3 was Exodus 33:19: "I will have mercy on whom I will have mercy, and I will have compassion on whom I will have compassion." The story Paul remembers here takes place immediately after the golden calf incident in Exodus 32, when God has every reason to hate Israel. Indeed, at the beginning of Exodus 33, *God initially refuses to go with Israel in the wilderness* for fear of consuming them in anger (33:3–6). The people strip themselves of their ornaments in mourning and as a sign of humiliation from Mount Horeb onward. Nevertheless, God *does* go on with them. The passage that immediately follows, Exodus 33:7–11, is an account of the tent of meeting that Moses sets up outside the camp. Moses is clear that if God's presence is not with them, they should not go. He receives God's reassurance that God's presence will be among them, that God does "know" them by name. (Later prophets treated the word "know" as synonymous with "elect," cf. Jer. 1:5; Hos. 13:5; this is important for Paul's argument in Romans.) Then, just as in the story of the call of Moses in Exodus 3, after it is clear that God knows his name, Moses asks to know God's name, hereby asking to be shown God's "glory" (33:18).

In the Exodus 3 story, God's answer to Moses was "I am who I am" or "I will be who I will be" (Exod. 3:14), which says several things at once, but says at least that God acts in freedom. It says little, however, about how God will act or what the character of God is. In Exodus 33, God's answer to Moses makes it clear that God understands that Moses wants to know something of God's very self. Granted that God *will be* with Israel, given Israel's sinfulness, is that good news or bad news? Will God be among them only to consume them in anger? God answers, "I will make all my goodness pass before you, and will proclaim before you the name, 'The Lord'; and I will be gracious to whom I will be gracious, and will show mercy on whom I will show mercy" (Exod. 33:19 NRSV). God's name or self-description is recognizably the same as the one in Exodus 3: "I will be who I will be." God's sovereign freedom is still protected in Exodus 33. But what has been added is the reference to God's goodness and the stress on God's sovereign freedom to be merciful and gracious to whomever God wills, *whether they deserve it or not!*

When Paul reflects in Romans 9 on the possibility that God may hate Israel, just as the prophet Malachi said God hated Esau (Mal. 1:2–3 at Rom. 9:13), he returns to the point in Israel's story when God would have had the most reason to hate Israel. There he finds an account of God's self-description to Moses as the one who acts in sovereign freedom to be gracious and to show mercy. It is no accident that Paul has just expressed willingness to be cut off from God's love in Christ for the sake of his people (Rom. 9:3), almost the very thing Moses had offered after the incident of the golden calf when he asks God to destroy him rather than to wipe out the people (Exod. 32:32). Paul is prepared, then, to identify with Moses at the point of fear of God's hatred for his people and, like Moses, is given a word about God's mercy instead. So, concludes Paul, "it depends not on human will or effort but on the mercy of God" (Rom. 9:16).

Perhaps it is the similarity of the name of God in Exodus 33 to the name of God in Exodus 3, when God called Moses to oppose Pharaoh, that takes Paul to the next sequence of thought. Or maybe it is just the general association of

Moses with the story of the exodus of Israel from Egypt in spite of Pharaoh's hardness of heart. God does not always show mercy, as Paul knows well. He has already said in Romans 2 to those who presume to pass judgment on others that by their hard and impenitent hearts they are storing up wrath for themselves on the day of wrath when God's righteous judgment will be revealed (2:5). He has also referred to the circumcision of the heart (2:29). For the postexilic writers (cf. Deut. 10:16; Jer. 4:4; 9:26; Ezek. 44:9), circumcision of the heart had been a reference to God's sign of covenant renewal after the sins of Israel had led the people into exile. Not surprisingly, Paul also thinks of this inner circumcision as the sign of the true Jew, the one upon whose heart God's covenant is written, whether outwardly circumcised or not.

But suppose Israel is now in the place where Pharaoh once was, the place of hardness of heart? Paul returns to the story of Moses' encounter with Pharaoh to reflect on God's treatment of Pharaoh:

> For the Scripture says to Pharaoh, 'I have raised you up for the very purpose of showing my power in you, so that my name may be proclaimed in all the earth.' (Rom. 9:17)

When we remember the end of the story of the exodus, how the last plague killed all of the firstborn of Egypt and how Pharaoh's army was drowned at the Red Sea, it would be easy to assume that Paul is saying that God chose Pharaoh for the very purpose of destroying him. Indeed, many readers of Romans 9:17 have assumed that Paul meant exactly that. But if we go back to an earlier point in the story, to the point at which these words were spoken, the situation looks very different. God has just sent the sixth plague (boils) upon Egypt and repeats the demand to Pharaoh: "Let my people go, that they may worship me" (Exod. 9:13). God threatens to send more plagues and adds, "By now *I could have* stretched out my hand and . . . you would have been cut off from the earth. But this is why I have let you live: to show you my power, and to make my name resound through all the earth" (Exod. 9:15–16 NRSV). In other words, God has raised up Pharaoh *not* in order to destroy him but in order to show God's power, power that leaves open the opportunity for repentance before final judgment comes. Paul is aware, of course, of the complex dynamics of the exodus story, in which two things are said: (1) that God hardens the heart of Pharaoh and (2) that Pharaoh hardens his own heart. Throughout Romans 9–11 he will refer back to this story and wonder which of the two it is with unbelieving Israel. Has God hardened their hearts so that they will not believe or have they hardened their own hearts in rejection of their own Messiah? At 9:18, Paul seems to be thinking of the first: So then God has mercy on whomever God chooses and God hardens the heart of whomever God chooses.

At this point in the argument, Paul again engages an imaginary conversation partner (interlocutor) in the style of diatribe that we have seen so often in Romans. Once more, Paul asks a rhetorical question in order to head off a faulty inference and to keep the argument on track: "You will say to me then, 'Why then does [God] still find fault? For who can resist [God's] will?'" (9:19). Following prophetic and wisdom traditions, Paul compares that question to the argument that a pot might try to make with the potter making it! The image of God as a potter was a familiar one (see Isa. 29:16; 45:9; Jer. 18:1–11; Wis. 15:7; Sir. 33:13). But then Paul develops the argument to suggest that just as a potter might wish to shape out of the same lump of clay both vessels for ordinary use and vessels for special use, so God might have God's own reasons to form different groups out of the same people. Paul takes care not to press the painful analogy to the present situation when he hints that God is God (the potter *does* have a right over the clay, 9:21) and God does have the right to create objects in order to destroy them (9:22).

Not surprisingly, where Paul *does* press the analogy is at the point of God's mercy: if some pot has been destroyed and reshaped into another pot that God has prepared ahead of time for glory (8:28–30)—again, Paul breaks off in mid-sentence (another *anacoluthon*), perhaps not wanting to think too hard about the details in the present situation. He is, after all, describing the same pattern that we saw in Romans 3:21–26, where God put forward Jesus Christ to be a sacrifice of atonement, and at Romans 5:8–9, where we have been made righteous through God's action in the blood of Jesus Christ. The major difference is that now he is forging an imaginative connection between the smashed vessel of Jesus Christ for the sake of sinners with the possible destruction of Israel, a vessel perhaps destined for destruction for the sake of the formation of the messianic people of God. That thought is terrible enough to make anyone break off in mid-sentence. . . .

When Paul lands again, he lands with considerable energy to describe a complex combination of God's merciful inclusion of the Gentiles and the preservation of at least a remnant of Israel in the messianic people of God: "including us whom [God] has called, not from the Jews only but also from the Gentiles" (9:24). Paul quotes words from the prophets Hosea and Isaiah, which in their original context spoke of the restoration of Israel after exile and the renewal of the covenant with Israel, to refer to the present situation of a messianic people in Christ composed of both Jewish and Gentile Christians. With respect to God's merciful inclusion of the Gentiles, he quotes Hosea:

> Those who were 'not my people' I will call 'my people' and her who was 'not beloved' I will call 'beloved.' (Hos. 2:23)

> And in the very place where it was said to them, 'You are not my people' there they shall be called children of the living God. (Hos. 1:10)

With respect to the preservation of a remnant of Israel, Paul's witness is ambiguous as to the size of the remnant and capable of more than one interpretation. He says he is quoting Isaiah, but he has just quoted Hosea 1:10, so if the quotation is a composite of Isaiah 10:22–23 and Hosea 1:10, then the number of the remnant may turn out to be as many as the sands of the sea (uncountable), and it would read something like this: "The number of the children of Israel will be like the sand of the sea; a remnant *will* be saved." The next verse (9:28) is obscure, but it may have the sense of Mark 13:20 that God will cut short the work of judgment for the sake of the elect, which would tend to make the number larger.

Whatever the number, Paul is clear that salvation happens only in Jesus Christ. Again he quotes Isaiah: "If the Lord of Hosts had not left us *a seed*, we would have become like Sodom and resembled Gomorrah" (Isa. 1:9). Paul has already spoken of the promise to Abraham and to his seed that he (the seed) would inherit the world (4:13), showing that he still thinks of Jesus Christ as the singular seed of Abraham (as he clearly does in Gal. 3:16). This is not incompatible with the description of Isaac as the seed in Romans 9:7, for both are singular collectives that carry forward the destiny of Israel typologically, one on the historical level, the other on the theological level.[13] Paul is also reading the chain of indictment texts in 3:10ff., "There is no one righteous, not even one," over against the story of Abraham's intervention for Sodom in Genesis 18. Therefore this text from Isaiah 1:9 may also be in the background at Romans 3:21, where "the law and the prophets" bear witness to the work of God in Christ.

To sum up the argument so far in Romans 9:6–29, then, the word of God has not fallen to the ground. Instead, God's words and actions in Scripture show that it has always been a matter of God's sovereign freedom to elect a person or a people for purposes of God's own choosing. In addition, Paul has called attention to the gracious and merciful character of God's choosing, particularly at the present time when God has chosen the Gentiles, who were not God's people, to be part of God's people along with the remnant of Israel in the people of the Messiah, Jesus Christ, the seed of Abraham. The reference back to Sodom reminds us of another way that God's election is gracious: since "no one is righteous, not even one," all humanity is in the position of the pot that has nothing to say to the Potter who could destroy it and begin again. The wonderful mercy of God is shown in God's election of God's own Son, Jesus

---

13. That Paul thinks typologically (that is, in theological patterns where one figure or story in Scripture is used by God to teach about another) has already been shown by his treatment of Abraham in Romans 4 and of Adam in Romans 5; cf. 5:14 where Adam is described specifically as a "type" (*typos*) of the One to come, Jesus Christ.

Christ, for that destruction and in God's election of humanity in Jesus Christ for salvation through the power of God's life-giving Spirit, as argued powerfully by Karl Barth.[14] Paul sees and faces the terrible possibility that the role that Israel, the people of God, may be asked to play stands in close relationship to the role that the Messiah has already played and that God may be bringing the Gentiles in at terrible cost to Israel. The argument is not over, however, as Paul's lament psalm continues. The last word in this section of the argument is the same as the first: it is the promise of the seed of Abraham, the promise of God's mercy both to Jews and Gentiles in Jesus Christ.

"WHO HAS BELIEVED OUR MESSAGE?"
(ROM. 9:30–10:21)

The next section, Romans 9:30–10:21, sees the striking return of terminology concerned with righteousness and faithfulness after its near disappearance in Romans 7, its brief reappearance at the end of Romans 8, and its virtual absence so far in Romans 9. This should not concern us and in no way implies the marginality of Romans 9–11. The issue of the righteousness of God towards Israel has been at the center of Paul's thought, even though the term "righteousness" itself does not appear until 10:3. The shift from one section of Paul's argument to the next is clearly marked, not only by the *inclusio* of "seed" (*sperma*, 9:7 and 29), which closes off the previous section, but also by a rhetorical question. Paul's question, "What are we to say then?" (9:30), marks the beginning of the new section, a pattern we have seen throughout Romans. What Paul thinks we have to say is that Gentiles, who were not striving for righteousness, have grasped it, while, paradoxically, Israel, pursuing a law of righteousness, did not attain to the law (9:30–31).

Why not? The remainder of the section attempts to explain this anomalous situation. Paul has mentioned the faith/works contrast so loved by Protestant Reformation theologians before 9:32 (at 3:27–28 and 4:4) but probably not too much emphasis should be given to that distinction here. More weight should be placed on the quotations from Isaiah in Romans 9:33, which follows. Israel has stumbled over the stumbling stone, as it stands written,

> See, I am laying in Zion a stone that will make them stumble, a rock that will make them fall, and whoever believes in it [or him], will not be put to shame. (Rom. 9:33)

---

14. Karl Barth, *Church Dogmatics* II/2, trans. G. W. Bromiley et al. (Edinburgh: T&T Clark, 1957) esp. par. 33, "The Election of Jesus Christ," and 34, "The Election of the Community," both of which involve exegetical discussion of Romans 9–11.

Once again, Paul's language about not being put to shame reminds us of his initial thesis (1:16–17) and of the fact that Romans 9–11 is structured as a lament psalm. In the first half of Romans 9:33, Paul has stitched together parts of Isaiah 28:16 and 8:14–15 in such a way that it is difficult to tell whether he means the stone of stumbling to refer to the law or to Jesus Christ. He may, of course, mean both things. Similarly, in the second half of 9:33, Paul's last line can be read either of two ways: "whoever believes in it [the rock]" or "whoever believes in him [Christ]." However, the logic of the last line, read either way, argues for a christological reading of the stone, based on an analysis of Paul's prior argument in Romans 5–8. Paul would hardly want to say that whoever trusts in the *law* will not be put to shame after all that he has said in Romans 7 about the inability of the law to oppose Sin. Moreover, there may have been a pre-Pauline Christian exegetical tradition that combined these Isaian texts and Psalm 118:22 ("the stone which the builders rejected") and read them christologically (see also Acts 4:11 and 1 Pet. 2:6–8, though these texts were both written after Romans). Finally, the fact that Paul uses the same verse (Isa. 28:16) only a few verses later, in 10:11, where it clearly refers to Jesus Christ, should resolve any remaining doubts in a christological direction.

Romans 10:1–4 is the second occasion where Paul interjects himself into the argument. (The first was 9:1–5.) Here Paul insists that his heart's desire and prayer to God for unbelieving Israel is that they may be saved. Paul can testify on their behalf that they have a zeal for God, even if their zeal is not according to knowledge. This idea may well be Paul's subsequent reflection on his own pre-Christian experience again, since he describes himself in similar terms in Philippians 3:6 ("as to zeal, a persecutor of the church"). In that case, as in Romans 7, Paul would be reasoning from his own experience—not as it felt at the time but as he reconstructed it later—and using that experience in order to analyze the situation of the rest of unbelieving Israel.

> For being ignorant of the righteousness of God, and seeking to establish their own, they have not submitted to God's righteousness. For Christ is the end of the law, so that there may be righteousness for everyone who has faith. (10:3–4)

The close parallelism between "God's righteousness," which appears twice in 10:3, and "Christ" in 10:4 leads the reader back to 3:21–26. There we saw two things. First, Paul demonstrated the close relationship between the righteousness of God and the faithfulness of Jesus Christ. Second, he told us that "the law and the prophets" have testified to the "righteousness of God" manifested apart from the law (3:21). Here in Romans 10:3–4, we are reminded of both ideas. Moreover, the connective "for" (*gar*) shows that Paul intends a logical connection between these two verses. Christ is the point of the law (its purpose and goal) from Paul's point of view, and through Christ God has done what the law could not do (8:3) by condemning Sin in the flesh.

The next section, 10:5–13, is one of the most difficult passages in Romans. In 10:3–4 Paul has just shown that a fundamental unity of purpose exists between the righteousness of God (Jesus Christ) and the law, such that God in Christ accomplished what the law was meant to do but was too weak to do. In 10:5 and 10:6, however, Paul seems to be setting up a contrast between "the righteousness from law" that is identified with Moses and Leviticus 18:5 and "the righteousness from faith" that quotes Deuteronomy 30. In Galatians 3:11–12, Paul had set up the sharpest possible antithesis between Leviticus 18:5 and Habakkuk 2:4:

> Now it is clear that no one is put right with God by the *law*, for "the one who is righteous will live by *faith*" [Hab. 2:4]. But the *law* is not based on *faith*; on the contrary, "whoever *does* them will live by them" [Lev. 18:5].

It is possible that Paul intends to make the same sharp contrast here, but it is not necessary to assume that he does. What then is the relationship between the "the righteousness from law" and "the righteousness from faith"? Or should they simply be equated with "their own righteousness" and "the righteousness of God" from 10:3 that Paul associated in 10:4 with everyone who has faith? The best solution seems to be to posit a strong contrast (though not total opposition) between these two different voices of the law that are somehow in dialectical relationship with each other.

Paul has already given us a model for this contradiction of texts three times: (1) in Romans 7:21–25 and 8:2, where two laws (the law of the Spirit of life in Christ Jesus and the law of Sin and Death) exist in opposition to each other with respect to the same person; (2) in 9:13–15, where the voice of Scripture in Malachi 1:2–3 ("Jacob I loved, but Esau I hated") is set aside in favor of the more gracious voice of Exodus 33:19 ("I will have mercy on whom I will have mercy"); and (3) in 9:27–28, where Paul lets the more generous voice of Hosea 1:10 ("Yet the people of Israel shall be like the sand of the sea, which can be neither measured nor numbered," NRSV) calculate the size of the remnant instead of the voice of Isaiah 10:22 ("Though the number of the children of Israel were like the sand of the sea, *only* a remnant will be saved"). So here in 10:5–6, two texts or two voices of the law seem to be in tension with one another, one of which is clearly privileged by Paul over the other. In this case, "the righteousness from faith" seems to articulate the position closest to Paul's own.

While Moses, writing about "the righteousness from law," is given only a restatement of the idea of Leviticus 18:5 ("Whoever does these things will live by them"), by contrast "the righteousness from faith" is allowed to give us a verse-by-verse christological interpretation of Deuteronomy 30:12–14 (with some words borrowed from Deut. 8:17 and 9:4). Paul adopts a *pesher* style (line-by-line interpretation) that is familiar to us from commentaries at Qumran but is rarely used in the New Testament. This strategy allows him to insert comments about Jesus Christ and his own preaching mission into a text that served a very different purpose in Deuteronomy 30. The words Paul adds are in parentheses:

> Do not say in your heart, "Who will ascend into heaven?"
> (that is, to bring Christ down)
> or "Who will descend into the abyss?"
> (that is, to bring Christ up from the dead),
> but what does it say? "The word is near you, on your lips and in your heart"
> (that is, the word of faithfulness that we preach).

Since Scripture says, "The word is near you, on your lips and in your heart," Paul interprets that to mean the word about what God has done in Jesus Christ, the word that Paul and his coworkers preach to the nations. The Deuteronomic writer had used these words to argue for doing what the law requires: "The word is near you . . . so that you can *do* it" (a message not unlike that of Lev. 18:5). Paul, however, has turned the implied "You can do it!" into a call to believe the gospel message about Jesus Christ. The words that follow splice phrases from Deuteronomy ("on your lips"; "in your heart") with early Christian tradition ("Jesus is Lord," cf. 1 Cor. 12:3) to form a chiastic (X-shaped) structure that would be easy to memorize. Moreover, these words may have been very close to what Paul and his coworkers actually preached:

> If you confess *with your lips* that "Jesus is Lord"
> and believe *in your heart* that "God raised him from the dead"
>   you will be saved.
> For one believes *with the heart* and is put right with God
> and one confesses *with the mouth* and is saved.
>   (Rom. 10:9–10)

The voice of "the righteousness of faith," which is also Paul's preaching voice continues:

> The Scripture [Isa. 28:16] says, 'No one who puts faith in him will be put to shame.' For there is no distinction between Jew and Greek [Rom. 3:22–23, 29–30]; the same Lord is Lord of all and is generous to all who call on him, for 'Everyone who calls on the name of the Lord will be saved'"[Joel 2:32].

Once more, Paul tells a story within the larger story of God's righteousness in Jesus Christ. This time, it is the story of his own preaching mission, which has been successful with Gentiles but not with Jews.[15] Romans 9–11 is structured as a lament psalm, which describes (in 9:1–5 and 10:1–4) Paul's anguish about Israel's continued unbelief and here (10:14–21) details Paul's complaint to God that in spite of his and his coworkers' best preaching of the gospel, Gentiles were coming into the church in great numbers while Israel's people failed to believe that Jesus Christ was the promised savior. Paul tells his story against the background of another biblical story where preachers of God's powerful good news were not effective—namely that described in Isaiah 51–55.[16]

The great theme of Isaiah 51–55 is the announcement of God's deliverance of Israel from their slavery in exile and God's call to them to return in renewal of the covenant. The call to hear God's good news is addressed to "those who pursue righteousness and seek the Lord" (Isa. 51:1), who are exhorted to look to Abraham and Sarah as examples of how God keeps covenant faithfulness: "For he was only one when I called him, but I blessed him and made him many" (Isa. 51:2). Eden, "the garden of the Lord" lost by the disobedience of Adam and Eve (Isa. 51:3), will be restored to Israel. These ideas are familiar to readers of Romans, of course: Abraham is held up as an example in Romans 4; the undoing of the disobedience of Adam in the garden of Eden is the subject matter of Romans 5–8; and Romans 9:30 set up a contrast between Gentiles "who did *not* pursue righteousness" (and found it) and Israel "who *did* pursue the righteousness from law" and did not attain the law. When this contrast is seen, Israel is directly addressed by "the righteousness from faith" who charges them with "looking for [God] in all the wrong places" when the gospel message of Paul and his coworkers is "near you, on your lips and in your heart" *so that you can do it*, so that you can believe in God's righteousness seen through the faithfulness of Jesus Christ. The irony is painful to Paul: Isaiah's message, which was intended for Israel seeking righteousness, has been heard and responded to by Gentiles, who were not even looking for righteousness, but it has not been heard and responded to by Israel!

---

15. Elizabeth E. Johnson comments, "The apparent failure of the Jewish mission is undeniably one of the factors that prompt Romans 9–11, as the immediate literary context suggests." See her "Romans 9–11: The Faithfulness and Impartiality of God," *Pauline Theology III: Romans*, ed. D. M. Hay and E. E. Johnson (Minneapolis: Fortress, 1995), 211–239 at 215.

16. J. Ross Wagner, "The Heralds of Salvation and the Mission of Paul," *Jesus and the Suffering Servant: Isaiah 53 and Christian Origins*, ed. W. H. Bellinger and W. R. Farmer (Harrisburg, Pa.: Trinity, 1998) 193–222. See also his *"Who Has Believed Our Message?": Paul and Isaiah "in Concert" in the Letter to the Romans* (Leiden: E. J. Brill, 2002). See also Richard B. Hays, "'Who Has Believed Our Message?' Paul's Reading of Isaiah" *Society of Biblical Literature Seminar Papers* (1998): 205–225.

Romans 10:14–17 consists of another stair-step argument that frames two important quotations from Isaiah. In these quotations, Paul identifies himself and his coworkers bringing the good news of Jesus Christ with the messengers in Isaiah who brought the good news of God's deliverance and call to covenant renewal. The argument takes off from Paul's quotation of Joel 2:32, "Everyone who *calls* upon the name of the Lord will be saved."

But how are they to *call* on one in whom they have not *believed*?
And how are they to *believe* in one of whom they have never *heard*?
And how are they to *hear* without someone to *preach* him?
And how are they to *preach* him unless they are *sent*?
As it stands written: "How beautiful are the feet of those who
    preach good news!"

[Isa. 52:7]

But not all have obeyed the good news, for Isaiah says, "Lord, who has
    believed our message?"

[Isa. 53:1]

So *faith* comes from *what is heard*
And *what is heard* comes through the *word about Christ.*
(Rom. 10:14–17)

The stair-step argument breaks off in the middle with the word "sent" (*apostalōsin*), from which we get the word "apostle." Paul described himself at the very beginning of Romans as "a called apostle, set apart for the gospel of God" (Rom. 1:1). As noted there, an apostle is one who is sent with a commission, "under obligation" (1:14). Paul will explain in 11:13 how his call to be "an apostle to the Gentiles" is at the same time also part of the work of proclaiming God's deliverance to Israel and calling Israel back to covenant renewal. The preaching that he and his coworkers are doing is the same work that the messengers of Isaiah did, translated into the present context. They are "those who preach good news" (Isa. 52:7) of God's salvation, salvation in Jesus Christ. Moreover, Paul and his coworkers have also experienced the same rejection described a few verses later in Isaiah 53:1. For, as Paul can testify, "Not all have *obeyed* (*hypēkousan*) the gospel, for Isaiah says, 'Who has believed our *message* (*akoē*)?'" to which the answer in Paul's case is "the Gentiles but not Israel." Notice that Paul has placed the words "obeyed" and "believed" in parallel in 10:16. His close association of the two words is evidenced by his use of the expression *eis hypakoēn pisteōs* "for the obedience of faith" in Romans 1:5 and 16:26 to form an *inclusio* for the entire letter. This same logic explains the central role of the *Shema* (Deut. 6:4–9) in Paul's argument: "Hear, O Israel" means "hearken!" or "obey!" If Paul knows some early Christian interpretation of Isaiah 52–53 as a reference to the crucified Messiah (cf. Acts 8:32–35 written some years after Romans), then he is making a three-way connection between the rejection of the messengers of Isaiah, the rejection of the message of Jesus, and the rejection of Paul and his coworkers who are preaching "the word about Christ" (10:17), the end and rhetorical climax of Paul's *sorites* in 10:14–17.

As Paul knows, the response of obedience (*hypakoē*) is evoked by "what is heard" (*akoē*), the word about Christ. Paul also knows that in order to apportion responsibility for Israel's unbelief between Israel and God, he will need to be clear about whether or not Israel has heard and understood the good news that he and his coworkers have been preaching. In a series of four rhetorical questions (10:18; 10:19; 11:1; 11:11), each one introduced by "I ask" (*legō*), Paul ponders two things. First he considers the possibility that Israel has not heard (10:18) or has not understood (10:19)—but they have heard and understood. Second, he examines the more terrible possibility that God has rejected Israel (11:1) and that their stumbling is a stumbling "so as to fall" (11:11), which means that their unbelief may be permanent. The first two questions, in 10:18 and 10:19, are easily disposed of; the last two questions, in 11:1 and 11:11, form the core of Paul's argument in Romans 11, and will be taken up in the next section.

Regarding the first possibility (10:18), can it be that Israel has not heard the good news that Paul and his coworkers have been proclaiming? That would be an attractive option, because then the problem of Israel's unbelief could be easily solved: Paul and the other apostles would just need to do more of what they had already been doing! But Paul's quotation of Psalm 19:4 aptly sums up what he will say explicitly later in the letter at 15:18–19, namely, that through Christ and the power of the Spirit he has been able "to win obedience from the Gentiles" by preaching "the gospel of Christ" in the great half-circle "from Jerusalem all the way around to Illyricum." Figuratively speaking, then, it is true of Paul and his coworkers that "their voice has gone out to all the earth, and their words to the ends of the inhabited world" (Ps. 19:4). "Israel," represented by all those Jews who did *not* respond as Paul had hoped they would to his missionary preaching, has had plenty of opportunity to hear and has in fact heard the proclamation of the word of God's righteousness manifested in Christ.

Since Israel has heard, did they not understand? Paul does not answer the question he raises in 10:19 directly, but when he listens for biblical witnesses that may clarify Israel's rejection of the gospel, it is God's voice (as reported by Moses and Isaiah) that he hears speaking about Israel. In the quotation from Deuteronomy 32:21 at Romans 10:19, God is directly in conversation with Israel:

> I myself will make you jealous of those who are not a nation; with a foolish nation I will make you angry.

In the context of Deuteronomy 32, God is portrayed as a jealous lover who responds in kind to Israel's unfaithfulnesses: just as Israel has made God jealous with "what is no god" (some stupid idol!) so God will make them jealous with "what is no people," that is, by showing favor to some other "foolish nation" in order to provoke Israel to jealousy. Paul will return to this verse (Deut. 32:21) twice more in the course of his argument, at 11:11 and at 11:14. Deuteronomy 32:21 is the key to what Paul believes God is doing with Israel and the Gentiles through his own ministry of the gospel.

In the second quotation (or, rather, pair of quotations) from Isaiah 65:1–2, Paul describes God talking about the situation with Israel. In the original context of Isaiah 65, both verses form part of God's indictment of Israel:

> I was ready to be sought out by those who did not ask, to be found by those who did not seek me. I said 'here I am, here I am' to a nation that did not call upon my name. I held out my hands all day long to a rebellious people. . . . (Isa. 65:1–2 NRSV)

But when Paul hears these verses in the context of his own missionary preaching, it is the contrast mentioned in Romans 9:30 that catches his attention. Gentiles who were not striving for righteousness—not asking, not seeking—have been the recipients of God's mercy and have responded in faith to the gospel of God's righteousness in Jesus Christ. So he redefines the first verse of Isaiah 65 to reflect his own preaching experience of God's "readiness to be sought out" in the generous inclusion of Gentiles in the covenant promises made to Israel.[17] For Paul, that contrast only serves to heighten the scandal of Israel's unbelief, because God is also saying, "Here I am, here I am" to a nation (Israel) that did not call upon *the name of the Lord* (Joel 2:32 in Rom. 10:13).[18] As in Deuteronomy 32, God is pictured as the jilted lover, spurned by indifferent and uncaring Israel: "All day long I held out my hands to a disobedient and argumentative people" (Isa. 65:2; Rom. 10:21).

---

17. Hays, *Echoes of Scripture in the Letters of Paul*, 74–75.

18. The expression "the Lord" is probably deliberately ambiguous as used by Paul here. The Septuagint (LXX) regularly uses *ho kyrios* (the Lord) to translate the holy and therefore unpronounceable name of God given to Moses in Exodus 3:14, which is also the referent in the original context of Joel 2:32. But through the power of the Spirit, those baptized into Christ now confess that "Jesus is Lord" (1 Cor. 12:3), the name that unbelieving Israel refuses to call upon in order to be saved. It is so clear to Paul that the righteousness of God has been demonstrated in the faithfulness of Jesus Christ, now exalted as the One whom every tongue should confess as the "Lord" (Phil. 2:9–11) that he cannot imagine how the rest of Israel does not see it too. For discussion of "the Name of the Lord" see C. K. Rowe, "Romans 10:13: What Is the Name of the Lord?" *Horizons in Biblical Theology* 22:2 (2000): 135–173.

While Paul has not directly answered his second rhetorical question, "Did Israel not understand?" (10:19), the textual evidence he cites strongly suggests that they *have* understood. The problem as Paul sees it, through the lens of Deuteronomy and Isaiah, is that Israel does not care. The word is very near them, the word about Christ that will put them right with God and save them. God is generous to all who call upon God's name, a generosity painfully visible in the image of God's outstretched arms all day long. The shame and vulnerability that Paul and his coworkers have experienced in Israel's rejection of the gospel is intrinsically related to the much deeper shame and vulnerability that Paul hears from God speaking through the voices of Moses and Isaiah. God has every reason to walk away and not look back. Every reason but one, that is: God's covenant love that will not give up on Israel no matter what.

THE GIFTS AND CALLING OF GOD ARE IRREVOCABLE (ROM. 11:1–36)

For the third time, here at 11:1–6 Paul interjects himself directly into the argument of Romans 9–11 (recall 9:1–5 and 10:1–4). To paraphrase Paul's question: "I ask, then, has God rejected God's people? Of course not! For I am an Israelite myself, of the seed of Abraham, of the tribe of Benjamin. God has not rejected God's people whom God foreknew." Paul, who was formerly Saul (of Tarsus, Acts 9:11) and of the tribe of Benjamin (Phil. 3:5), may be reflecting here on the story of his namesake Saul, son of Kish, also from the tribe of Benjamin (1 Sam. 9:1–2) and Israel's first king.[19] That story in 1 Samuel 9 would have particular relevance for Paul in the present context of his missionary preaching and Israel's rejection of his message about Christ because of the word spoken by God to the prophet Samuel just prior to Saul's becoming king: "They have not rejected *you*, but they have rejected *me* as their king" (1 Sam. 8:7). After God's anger is shown in the destruction of the wheat harvest, the people greatly fear both the Lord and Samuel, God's prophet, whom they ask to intercede for them. Samuel comforts them with the words "Do not be afraid," and he promises that "*the Lord will not cast away*" this people, for the sake of God's own name, "because it has pleased the Lord to make you a people" for the Lord. Samuel adds, "And, as for me, far be it from me to sin against the Lord by ceasing to pray for you" (1 Sam. 12:20–23). If Paul's words in Romans—that God has not rejected the people whom God foreknew—echo Samuel's words—that the Lord will not cast away this people—they would also

---

19. I am indebted to N. T. Wright for this intriguing suggestion.

serve to locate Paul himself *within* the continuing story of Israel's unbelief. If God has not forsaken and will not forsake Israel, then neither will Paul cease to pray for them.

The same phrase, "*God will not cast away*" God's people, appears also in Psalm 94:14 (93:14 LXX). This prayer asks God to intervene for Israel against the enemies that have harassed God's people. Written in the context of exile and return, the psalm suggests a theology of the remnant. Paul has already raised the question of the remnant at Romans 9:27–28, where he hinted that it might not be the small size threatened by Isaiah 10:22–23, but instead the huge number promised by Hosea 1:10. Here, in Romans 11:2–4, he returns to the question of the size of the remnant by telling the story of Elijah after his confrontation with the prophets of Baal on Mount Carmel. Ahab and Jezebel are seeking to kill Elijah, who is hiding out, first in the wilderness, then at a cave on Mount Horeb (Sinai). There are many parallels between the stories of Moses and Elijah at this point. In both cases the prophet stands in significant tension with the people of Israel and complains to God about them. Elijah's complaint, repeated twice (1 Kgs. 19:10, 14), frames the account of how God was not in the wind, earthquake, or fire that Elijah experienced and may or may not have been in "the sound of sheer silence" (NRSV). But on either side of that description, the word of the Lord asks Elijah what he is doing there. Elijah's response ends with the words "I alone am left, and they are seeking to take my life." In 1 Kings (19:18) God responds to the prophet with a promise: "Yet I will leave seven thousand in Israel, every knee that has not bowed to Baal, and every mouth that has not kissed him."

When Paul retells the story in Romans 11:2–5, he characterizes Elijah's complaint as a plea "against Israel" and the word of God spoken to him as a divine oracle (*chrēmatismos*). In 11:4, Paul also changes God's word to the past tense ("I *have kept* for myself seven thousand"). This retelling suggests the conclusion he reaches in the following verse: "in this way (*houtōs*) at the present time, there is a remnant, according to an election of grace" (11:5). Paul can dare to hope, in his own moments of complaining about Israel's unbelief, that God has already preserved a substantial remnant of Israel who are or are about to become believers in the gospel of Jesus Christ. It is a remnant chosen by grace, insists Paul, mindful of the sovereign freedom of God to elect some and not others that he has reviewed in 9:6–29. For if it were from works, then people could earn election and God's grace would no longer be grace.

Paul continues in 11:7, "What then? Israel failed to reach what it was pursuing" (cf. 9:31–32, where Israel's failure is also described with reference to "works"). Paul returns to that earlier point of the argument, where he had described God as laying a stone in Zion that would cause *stumbling*, a rock that would make them *fall* (9:33, quoting Isa. 28:16 and 8:14–15). He does so in order to set up his next rhetorical question, "I ask, then, have they *stumbled* so as to *fall?*" in 11:11. First, however, he reminds his readers what is at stake in election: "Israel failed to reach what it was pursuing. The elect reached it, but the rest were hardened" (11:7). If there is ambiguity in the passive "were hardened," Paul makes it clear that the hardening is God's action as he describes the terrible fate he fears for unbelieving Israel. Paul takes his words from the psalms and the prophets:

> As it stands written: 'God gave them a spirit of sluggishness, eyes that would not see and ears that would not hear up to the present day.' And David says: 'May their table become a snare and a trap, a stumbling block and a retribution to them; May their eyes be darkened so that they will not see, and keep their backs bent forever.' (Isa. 29:10; Deut. 29:4; Ps. 35:8; Ps. 69:22–23)

Having stared with horror into that abyss of the possibility of Israel's punishment at the hands of God, Paul is now ready to ask the question upon which everything turns, both for Israel and for him personally, and to answer the possibility of God's wrath with his own confidence in the certainty of God's covenant love.

> I ask, then, have they stumbled so as to fall? Absolutely not! But by means of their trespass salvation has come to the Gentiles, in order to make them [Israel] jealous. Now if their trespass means riches for the world, and if their failure means riches for Gentiles, how much more will their full inclusion (lit. fullness) mean! (11:11–12)

Here at last is the hopeful resolution for which Paul has been longing and praying these long chapters. It seems to come to him suddenly as if, like the prophets before him, he were permitted a glimpse of God's glory and a share in God's redemptive plan. Taking his clue from Deuteronomy 32:21, Paul seems to think he can see what God may be doing with Israel. God is bringing in the Gentiles not only in order to show mercy to them, as promised long ago in Israel's Scriptures, but also in order to make Israel jealous, just as God promised to do in Deuteronomy. Israel's failure to believe is a gift of opportunity (riches) for the world and the nations of the world. But if God can do this with Israel's unbelief, imagine what God can do with Israel's belief when that happens!

Once again Paul reflects on his own place in the argument that he has been making, but now for the first time in these chapters his tone is hopeful and confident about Israel. Paul's words reflect his Abraham-like trust in God, "hoping against hope" (4:18) that God will call into existence the faithful response to the gospel that does not presently exist in Israel. It is no accident that this trust in God's covenant righteousness occurs precisely at the point where, as "apostle to the Gentiles," he stands over against any Gentiles tempted to rejoice in Israel's stumbling. It would be fewer than one hundred years before Roman Christianity in the form of Marcion would attempt to define a non-Jewish Christianity for an all-Gentile church. Paul's gospel does not allow such a move, as he shows clearly in the section of the argument that begins here:

> Now I am speaking to you Gentiles. In so far, then, as I am an apostle to the Gentiles, I glorify my ministry in order to make my own flesh [Israel] jealous so that I may save some of them. For if their rejection [of the gospel] is the reconciliation of the world, what will their acceptance [of the gospel] mean but life from the dead! (11:13–15)[20]

At the time Paul wrote Romans, resurrection of the dead was an eschatological sign like the coming in of the Gentiles to worship Israel's God. Therefore, it was logical for him to associate the two ideas. He argues in hope from the lesser to the greater: since God has done one seemingly impossible thing (and one sign of the end time) by bringing in the Gentiles by means of Israel's unbelief, why should we not expect that God will do the comparable, seemingly impossible thing (another sign of the end time) by bringing about the general resurrection of the dead when Israel believes the gospel? But that it is *Israel* to whom the Gentiles come and *Israel's* Messiah whom God raised as firstfruits of the resurrection of the dead is not in doubt for Paul:

> If the part of the dough offered as firstfruits is holy, then the whole lump is holy; and if the root is holy, then so are the branches. (11:16)

Paul's point should not be missed: the word used here for "lump" of dough (*phyrama*) is the same word Paul had used in 9:21 to describe how a potter can

---

20. The text is ambiguous as to whether the rejection referred to is Israel's rejection of the gospel or God's rejection of Israel (which is often quickly assumed by interpreters). I have (perhaps prematurely) resolved the ambiguity in favor of the first option because the overwhelming logic of Paul's argument in the missionary context described here and within the strategy of making jealous assumes that it is Israel who will turn to God, who stands with outstretched arms. But the ambiguity of the hardening of heart (11:7) should probably be preserved given the Scriptures cited in 11:8–10, to reflect the possibility of the terrible typology that Paul fears: Israel related to the cross of Jesus Christ. If that is (reluctantly) preserved as an interpretive option, it must also be clearly bounded by the logic of Isaiah 54:7–8: "For a brief moment I abandoned you, but with great compassion I will gather you. In overflowing wrath for a moment I hid my face from you, but with everlasting love I will have compassion on you, says the Lord, your Redeemer." Just as the mystery of God's purpose allowed the horror of the cross before the exaltation of Christ as Lord, and God's mysterious purpose here may involve a temporary rejection of the beloved people, nevertheless God is covenantally incapable of turning away from Israel for more than the "brief moment" in which the Gentiles come in.

make vessels for different purposes out of the same "lump" of clay. If God is playing Israel and the Gentiles against one another dialectically now, it is because the same God is God of both Jews and Gentiles and, at their most fundamental level, they are one people of God.

Again Paul shifts into diatribe style to counter an imaginary Gentile interlocutor who exults in Israel's stumbling and the subsequent inheritance of Israel's privileges and prerogatives by Gentile members of the messianic people:

> But if some of the branches were broken off, and you, a wild olive shoot, were grafted in among them to share in the richness of the olive tree, do not boast over the branches, or if you do, *remember that it is not you that support the root; instead, it is the root that supports you.* (11:17–18)

Yes, grants Paul, "branches were broken off because of their lack of faith, but you stand only through faith," so "be in awe" of God (11:20).

Once more Paul refers to the story of the near sacrifice of Isaac (Gen. 22), the story still told during the Jewish "Days of Awe," by using the catchword "spare" (8:32). Like Abraham in Genesis 22, God was described in Romans 8:32 as the One "who did not spare" God's own beloved Son. When God is described here as the One "who did not spare the natural branches" (11:21) the (theo)logical implication is that the people of Israel collectively is God's beloved son, the one whose vocation and destiny it is to become the lightning rod for the world. Stand in awe of God, suggests Paul to the Gentile ready to step into Israel's place: neither will God spare you. (It is difficult to decide whether this text is to be preferred over the softer but somewhat better attested alternative text, "perhaps he will not spare you" chosen by the NRSV.) He continues his argument with another chiasm (X-shaped structure), and once more I have emphasized the terms of the chiasm for the reader:

> Observe, then, the *kindness* and the *severity* of God: *severity* towards those who have fallen, but God's *kindness* toward you (singular), provided you (singular) continue in kindness; otherwise you yourself will be cut off. (11:22)

Paul's chiastic summary was probably intended to be easy to remember, along with its punchline: the appropriate response to the experience of God's kindness is kindness practiced to others. His point is made even more effective rhetorically by his consistent use of the singular pronoun and verb form, even though he is addressing a group. This has the effect of pointing his finger at each member of the congregation and urging all of them to consider this matter carefully. God's kindness is not a license for triumphalism!

It should be said clearly that "kindness" is not the same thing as weak christology and that some forms of "inclusiveness" can be both unkind and untrue. In
particular, it is not "kindness" for Christians to downplay the centrality of Jesus
Christ in order to avoid the offense that a strong christology might cause non-
Christians in general and Jews in particular. Christians need to confess the tragically sinful history of the distortion of Christian theology that results in the idea
that Gentile Christians have *replaced* Jews as the people of God. Clearly, Paul cannot be made to say that without doing tremendous violence to his thought. (Nor
can any of the New Testament writers in fact.) But "replacement theology" does
not follow necessarily from christology, as Paul himself shows. Recently some
scholars have argued that Romans 9–11 supports the idea that there is a way of
salvation for Jews that bypasses faith in Jesus Christ entirely, as if there were one
track for Christians and another track for Jews. Whatever the merits of this
argument, and there may be some, Paul (or, more precisely, Romans 9–11) cannot possibly be cited as a witness for it, as the next few verses (11:23–24) show:

> Even those [branches broken off because of their unbelief, 11:20] *if
> they do not remain in unbelief* will be grafted in, for God has the power
> (lit. "God is powerful") to graft them in again. (11:23)

In fact, Paul fully expects that they will be grafted back into their own tree. He
argues from the greater to the lesser: since God has been able to graft branches
that did not by nature belong (Gentiles) into Israel, how much more will God
be able to regraft the natural branches back into their own tree (11:23–24)!

In the conclusion of his argument, in Romans 11:25–32, Paul continues to
address the Gentile Christians mentioned in 11:13. He warns them not to
claim to be wiser than they are (the complementary injunction to his earlier
warning to "stand in awe" of God in 11:20). Then he points to the "mystery"
of what God is doing: hardening a part of Israel "until the fullness of the Gentiles has come in" (11:25). The word "fullness" is often translated "full number," and it may be that Paul is thinking of the apocalyptic idea that God sets
times and numbers in advance. More probably, however, he means the whole-
ness or the entirety of the Gentiles, the complement of the "fullness" of Israel
in 11:12 and especially of "all Israel" in 11:26. In this way (*houtōs*), precisely by
the bringing in of the Gentiles, "all Israel will be saved."[21]

---

21. The phrase "all Israel" cannot refer to Paul's present churches composed of believing Jews and Gentiles, however, as N. T. Wright (*The Climax of the Covenant: Christ and
the Law in Pauline Theology* [Minneapolis: Fortress, 1991] 249–251), Mary Ann Getty
("Paul on the Covenants and the Future of Israel," *Biblical Theology Bulletin* 17 [1987]:
92–99; idem, "Paul and the Salvation of Israel: A Perspective on Romans 9–11," *Catholic
Biblical Quarterly* 50:3 [1988]: 456–469 at 459), and others have suggested. Instead, it
must refer to Israel as a whole. The restoration of Israel, presently scattered through-

Here and elsewhere, Paul uses the word "mystery" (*mystērion*) to refer to God's divine plan both brought about and made known in Jesus Christ (cf. 1 Cor. 2:1–7; 15:51).[22] It is therefore not surprising when, in 11:26–27, he returns to the Scriptures entrusted to Israel as oracles for the end time:

> As it stands written: 'Out of Zion will come the Deliverer; He will turn away ungodliness from Jacob. And this will be my covenant with them, when I take away their sins.'

This quotation appears to be a complexly crafted combination of several texts (at least Ps. 14:7; Isa. 59:20–21; Isa. 27:9, and perhaps others). Paul's formulation of this quotation may also be influenced by Isaiah 2:3: "Out of Zion shall go forth the law and the word of the Lord out of Jerusalem." If so, the logic of his argument reminds us of Romans 8:3: "God has done what the law . . . could not do: by sending [God's] own Son . . . to deal with Sin."

With respect to the good news that Paul and his coworkers have been proclaiming about Jesus Christ, Israel stands in a place of opposition. In that sense, the people of Israel can be described as "enemies" (of the gospel, of course, not of God, as in the NRSV). If so, they are enemies "for *your* sake." Here Paul pointedly reminds his Gentile hearers of the costliness for Israel of God's inclusion of Gentiles in Israel's covenant inheritance. He also reminds them that even as "enemies" of the gospel Paul preaches they are God's beloved, for the sake of their ancestors, "for the gifts and the calling of God are irrevocable" (11:29). Paul can only describe as a "mystery" the wonderful way that God has made use of disobedience on the part of *both* Gentiles and Jews (another pointed reminder to his Gentile hearers) to accomplish God's own purposes of showing mercy to both groups, to all of them (11:30–32).

Meditating on God's mysterious mercy and extravagant kindness leads Paul to worship. The glorious doxology, in Romans 11:33–36, that ends this section of Paul's argument is a fitting conclusion to his defense of the righteousness of God with respect to Israel; it is also a fitting conclusion to the lament psalm through which Paul has been working out his own place in God's mysterious plan. Indeed God's judgments are unsearchable and God's ways are inscrutable for humanity. No one has a claim on God, nor can anyone presume to give advice

---

out the Diaspora, was a frequent motif in Jewish apocalyptic literature. See Elizabeth E. Johnson, *The Function of Apocalyptic and Wisdom Traditions in Romans 9–11* (Atlanta: Scholars, 1989) 124–131. Paul, however, thinks his Gentile churches are part of the "all Israel" that God will restore, though it is difficult to tell exactly what he has in mind.

22. See Raymond E. Brown, *The Semitic Background of the Term "Mystery" in the New Testament* (Philadelphia: Fortress, 1968); Marcus N. A. Bockmuehl, *Revelation and Mystery in Ancient Judaism and Pauline Christianity* (Grand Rapids: Eerdmans, 1997).

to God, who shows such great mercy in sovereign freedom. Paul exclaims, "To [God] be the glory forever!" and he invites our "Amen!" (11:33–36).

Summary. Again Paul creates suspense in his telling of the narrative of God's righteousness by introducing a major complication into the plot of God's triumphant rescue mission to the lost world. The promise through Jesus Christ, the seed of Abraham, given for the Gentiles as well as for Israel, seems still to be at risk for all those Gentiles who have not yet heard the gospel. And, oddly from Paul's point of view, the promise is still at risk for Israel, too, which has not responded to the gospel of God. What about unbelieving Israel? Are the people of Israel included in God's love for "us" in Jesus Christ? Can God's rescue mission to the world be derailed by Israel's unbelief? Romans 9–11 is an account of Paul's struggle to answer that question.

Paul knows that God has always chosen some and not others and that God's choices often seem the least likely to us. As he tries to understand the mystery of Israel's unbelief, he revisits important figures (Isaac and Ishmael, Jacob and Esau, Moses and Pharaoh) and stories (the exodus from Egypt, the return from exile) that can help us to understand his argument. He also puzzles over the idea that some remnant of Israel will be saved. The question is, How big a remnant? Some days Paul feels like he is the only one, just as Elijah once did. Like the psalmist and Job, Paul questions God, but he also knows that Israel is at fault. Has Israel not heard? Or not understood? No, they have heard and understood, but not believed. Then why has God not given them the gift of faith? Has God sold Israel down the river? In an anguished cry, he asks one rhetorical question after another: Has God rejected his people? Have they stumbled so as to fall? Finally, in his struggle there seems to come a breakthrough. Paul thinks he sees what God is doing: Israel's unbelief is just the opportunity the Gentiles need to come in. Then God will use the Gentiles to make Israel jealous, and Israel will come in, too. He can end his lament psalm with a doxology or hymn of praise to God in 11:33–36.

FOR FURTHER REFLECTION

1. Paul's evaluation of his missionary preaching experience (failure with Jews, success with Gentiles) raises the question of how Christians go about assessing religious experience. What counts as failure or success for Christians? How do Christians know what God wants us to do and whether or not we are being faithful to God's will?

2. Paul was clear that faith is a gift from God: it is not something that we can achieve on our own (faith is not just one more work), so he rightly raises the

question about God's fairness to Israel. At the same time, he also holds Israel responsible for their unbelief. Can you say how these two ideas are compatible?

3. In 11:17–24, Paul tells a story (parable) of an olive tree and its branches to explain how God may be using Israel's unbelief to allow the fullness of the Gentiles to come to faith, and to warn the Gentiles not to boast at Israel's expense. Can you name some of the gifts for which Christianity will always be indebted to Judaism?

4. As a result of God's mysterious interworkings between Jews and Gentiles, Paul asserts that "all Israel will be saved" (11:26). What do you think Paul means by "salvation"? Is the salvation of Israel tied to the confession that "Jesus is Lord"? What have you heard from present-day Christian evangelists about the conversion of the Jews? Does it matter that almost two thousand years have passed since Paul wrote his letter to the Romans and that during most of that time Christians have persecuted Jews? How does the terrible holocaust of six million Jews in the twentieth century affect the question?

5. Paul's readers were invited to struggle with what were genuine questions for him: How would the story end? What was Paul's role in God's plan? Paul is convinced that God is faithful: he thinks he may even have figured out what God is doing with Jews and Gentiles, but in the end he wonders at the unsearchable ways of God that no human being can fathom. How is the "mysteriousness" of God a part of your worship, especially a part of your prayers?

6. Paul assures himself and his readers that, in spite of what looks like overwhelming evidence to the contrary at present, God's righteousness (that is, God's covenant faithfulness to Israel and God's mercy to Gentiles) is in place. How is God's righteousness known in a situation where some believe in God and some do not? Have you ever wondered whether God plays fair? What were the circumstances? How does trusting God's faithfulness make it easier for us to be faithful, or does it?

6

"Welcome . . . As the Christ Has Welcomed You"

(Rom. 12:1–15:13)

Subsequent to Berrigan's capture, Towne and I were subjected to harassment, official defamation and surveillance by the authorities, including a remarkable incident in which a government agent, once again intruding upon my work on *An Ethic*, sought to interrogate me about theology and politics. He began the interview this way: "Dr. Stringfellow, you're a theologian." (I thought his introit faintly sarcastic.) "Doesn't the Bible say you must obey the Emperor?" His query startled me, I admit, not so much for its thrust as for the evidence it gave of how minutely the ruling powers scrutinize citizens. I could not concede the simplistic premise about the Bible which his question assumed, and I rebuked him about this, taking perhaps forty-five minutes to do so.

William Stringfellow[1]

Without community there is no liberation, only the most vulnerable and temporary armistice between an individual and her oppression. But community must not mean a shedding of our differences, nor the pathetic pretense that these differences do not exist.

Audre Lorde[2]

Paul's argument shifts in Romans 12–15 as he turns his attention to the present situation of the Roman house churches. In Romans 1–4 he has described for the Roman Christians God's merciful redemption of the lost world through

---

1. William Stringfellow, *Conscience and Obedience: The Politics of Romans 13 and Revelation 13 in Light of the Second Coming* (Waco: Word, 1977) 16.
2. Audre Lorde, *Sister Outsider: Essays and Speeches* (New York: Crossing, 1984) 112.

the death of Jesus Christ, who, like Abraham before him, trusted in God's righteousness. He has shown, by contrasting Christ and Adam in Romans 5–8, how the death of Jesus Christ is related to the fallen creation and the bondage of humanity to Sin and Death. We saw in Romans 9–11 that nothing, not even Israel's unbelief and the unexpected flooding of Gentiles into Paul's churches, can separate the whole people of God (the fullness of the Gentiles and all Israel) from God's covenant love and faithfulness, even though Paul, like Abraham, must hope against hope for what he does not yet see. Now, in his concluding chapters, he must show directly and concretely the implications of his argument for the Roman Christians and their life in Christ. He must demonstrate how the story of what God has accomplished in the death and resurrection of Jesus Christ is related to his own story and to the story of his churches, including the congregation at Rome that he hopes will support his work. He does this in two distinct moves.

First, in Romans 12:1–2, Paul's argument moves from the work of God in Christ (3:21–31) and the power of baptism of believers into Christ (6:1–14) to conclude that Christians are called to the imitation of Christ. They must grow strong in faithfulness as Abraham did, for they have become part of the seed of Abraham by virtue of their baptism into Jesus Christ. This means they will exhibit his "obedience of faith" by refusing to conform to the ways of the old (Adamic) age and by "walking in newness of life" with minds transformed according to the pattern of Christ, the firstborn of the "many" who are predestined to be conformed to the image of God's Son (8:29). Paul's application of this apocalyptic ethic to the life of the Roman house churches leads him in several different directions. He begins with general exhortations about the nature of the Christ-conformed life and the discernments of God's will to which those whose minds are renewed in Christ are called (12:3–21). Then he turns his attention to specific questions about how the community ought to conduct itself toward outsiders, especially on the controversial matter of Roman taxation and its effects on the weaker members of the community. Paul's treatment of the love commandment as the fulfillment of the law is reinforced by strong eschatological language that links his appeals with the earlier language about baptism (13:1–14).

Second, Paul crafts two arguments based on the imitation of God (14:1–23) and God's Messiah, Jesus (15:1–13), as these are described in the Scriptures of Israel, in order to show his readers in what ways they are to be conformed to the image of Jesus Christ. The first argument (based on the imitation of God) has as its dual center words of liturgical or confessional tradition (14:7–9) and words of Scripture (14:10–12) that warrant the idea that judgment of the brother or sister belongs to God. Believers are urged not to let what they eat or drink destroy the work of God in Jesus Christ (14:13–23).

The second argument (15:1–13) is structured in two parts. One serves as the rhetorical conclusion to this section of the letter (15:1–6), and the other serves as the rhetorical conclusion to the argument of the letter as a whole (15:7–13). In the first place, the Roman Christians are to follow the example of Jesus, the Messiah, "who did not please himself," as Scripture attests in Psalm 69:9, but instead took on a burden not properly his own. Just as Jesus sought the good of the other, so the Roman Christians are to seek each other's good in their own house churches. They are to work together to glorify God. Paul's concluding argument in 15:7–13, based on the imitation of Christ, is that the Roman house churches should support his upcoming mission to the Gentiles in Spain. This argument is also supported by Scripture, in a series of quotations about Gentiles that climaxes in Isaiah's description of Jesus Christ (as Paul reads it) as "the one in whom the Gentiles hope" (15:12). Since the congregation at Rome results from the fulfillment of God's promise to Abraham that he would be the father of many nations (i.e., Gentiles, Gen. 17:5; Rom. 4:17), this is their opportunity to show the same grace to others that God has shown to them.

"OFFER YOUR BODIES AS A LIVING SACRIFICE"
ROM. 12:1–2

Using the rhetorical form (*parakalō*, "I appeal to you") to signal his intentions, in Romans 12:1–2 Paul first restates the theme of the letter, then applies it to the daily lives of Christian believers.[3] Paul's theme statement for the letter, in Romans 1:16–17, asserted that the gospel in which the righteousness of God is being revealed is the power of God for salvation to everyone who puts trust in God. In 3:21ff., Paul told the story of God's saving power to put things right through the faithfulness, or trusting obedience, of Jesus Christ by using three powerful metaphors of salvation from Israel's biblical tradition. The saving sig-

---

3. C. J. Bjerkelund has shown that the first *parakalō* sentence in a Pauline letter contains the essential message of the apostle (Bjerkelund, *Parakalô: Form, Funktion und Sinn der parakalô-Sätze in den paulinischen Briefen* [Oslo: Universitetsforlaget, 1967] 189). There is no reason to divide Romans between the dogmatic (theological instruction in Romans 1–8) and the paraenetic (ethical instruction in Romans 12–16). Indeed, as Margaret Mitchell has shown, the first *parakalō* sentence in 1 Corinthians (1:10) precisely identifies that letter as a whole as being paraenetic (Mitchell, *Paul and the Rhetoric of Reconciliation: An Exegetical Investigation of the Language and Composition of 1 Corinthians.* Hermeneutische Untersuchungen zur Theologie 28 [Tübingen: Mohr Siebeck, 1991]). So also throughout Romans, Paul's theology has ethical consequences and his ethics has theological foundations.

nificance of Jesus' death on the cross was described in terms of (1) *justification*, the law court model, (2) *redemption*, buying back a family member from slavery, and (3) *atonement*, the place or means by which sins are forgiven. Each of these interpretations metaphorically transformed the shameful execution of a condemned criminal into a profound theological statement about the righteousness of God. Here in 12:1–2, Paul revisits the third (atonement) metaphor.

More precisely, Paul's argument in Romans 12:1–2 combines three ideas that he has discussed before: (1) the cultic metaphor of sacrifice (3:21–26); (2) the identification of believers with the death of Christ in baptismal burial (6:1–11); and (3) the apocalyptic motifs of cosmic holy war, the two ages, and new creation (5–8). Paul combines these three ideas to show that the lordship of Christ over believers is inevitably demonstrated by their embodied actions. Because the gospel is God's powerful invasion of the world, the bodies of believers who have been conscripted into "newness of life" (6:4) are paradoxically "as good as dead" (4:19) to the powers of this world.[4] This new section of Paul's argument (12:1–2) follows the dramatic doxology at the conclusion of the extended argument for the righteousness of God towards Israel in Romans 9–11. Immediately preceding Paul's hymn of praise in 11:33–36 was his reflection upon God's mercies, both to the Gentiles and to Israel. In each case, God has managed to use the disobedience of one group to show mercy to both, imprisoning all in disobedience in order to be merciful to all (11:30–32). Paul's meditation upon God's merciful character leads him to marvel at the depth of God's riches, wisdom, and knowledge and to ascribe glory to God forever. Indeed, the mercies of God have had a prominent place throughout the entire argument of the letter. So it comes as no great surprise to the reader that when Paul makes his appeal (*parakalō*) to the Roman Christians to conform their lives to God's action in Christ, he mentions God's mercies as the basis of his exhortation. For this reason, the adverb "therefore" in his exhortation in 12:1, "I appeal to you, *therefore*, . . . by the mercies of God," represents the most important "therefore" in the epistle. Paul's request that the Roman Christians order their lives according to the pattern of Christ is based on everything that has gone before, particularly God's covenant faithfulness to Israel by means of the inclusion of the Gentiles in the covenant promises.

What Paul urges them to do reflects his assumption that they have become affiliated with Jesus Christ through baptism into his death and are no longer enslaved to Sin, which leads to Death, but now are slaves of the obedient

---

4. A fuller version of this argument can be found in Grieb, "Affiliation with Jesus Christ in His Sacrifice: Some Uses of Scripture to Define the Identity of Jesus Christ in Romans" (Ph.D. diss., Yale University, 1997) 186–227.

righteousness that leads to resurrection life in the Spirit (6:16–23; 8:4–6). He draws on the military metaphor of putting the members of one's body at the disposal of one's lord, which he had used to speak of the new life of the baptized (6:13, 16, 19). He combines that holy war language with the liturgical language of sacrifice as he begs them "to *present* your bodies as a living sacrifice, holy and acceptable to God, which is your reasonable worship" (12:1). In its new context, the word "present" means "offer" and functions as the technical term for offering a sacrifice. They are to offer their bodies (plural) as a sacrifice (singular) of the one body of Christ having many members, which Paul will discuss shortly (12:4–8). Their "bodies" by *metonymy* (a figure of speech using the name of one thing to stand for another with which it is associated) represent the entirety of their embodied existence in the world where Christians have to live and act, and thus represent the hard choices that come with the limits of finite humanity.

Paul describes the sacrifice they are to offer with three adjectives: *living*, *holy*, and *acceptable* to God. Each requires comment. Their "living" sacrifice is related both to the "newness of life" in 6:4 and to the "life lived to God" by Jesus Christ in the resurrection (6:10–11). It is also related to "living by the faithfulness of God" from Habakkuk 2:4, quoted in 1:17, and to the resurrection life of 4:17 (where it is related to new creation) and of 4:24 (where it is related to the death of Christ as sacrifice for sins). These verbal links forge the connection of baptized Christians with the righteousness of God through the faithfulness of Christ described in 3:21–26. Because they are his body, his sacrifice entails the sacrifice of their own bodies. Because they are associated with him, they are a "holy" people of God and are "pleasing" or "acceptable" to God since they no longer set their minds on the things of the flesh that is hostile to God and cannot please God (8:7–8), but focus instead on the things of the Spirit that lead to life and peace (8:6). Their life in the Spirit is at the same time their death to the power of Sin over them (6:18–23), while their slavery to God liberates them from slavery to the hostile powers (Sin and Death) that oppose God in the world. All of this means that Paul's second sentence in 12:2 restates the first:

> Do not be conformed to this age, but be transformed by the renewing of your minds, in order that you may discern what is the will of God, what is good and acceptable and perfect.

The "reasonable worship" or "spiritual service" that the community is to offer in making over their bodily existence to God in sacrifice is discerning the will of God. As the body of Christ, they are called to discover what is good, what pleases God, and what fulfills or advances God's goals in their daily lives. This is only possible for them in that they have died with Christ to the conforming powers of the world in which they still exist. The life they live they live to God, whose Spirit transforms them, creating their minds anew in conformity to the image of Jesus Christ. In this way, the total self-offering of Christians to God anticipates the resurrection of their bodies in Christ, which is a mark of the new age to which they are becoming conformed.

As Nancy Duff has shown,[5] Paul's argument leads to a redefinition of the imitation of Christ when it is understood in terms of "witness." The embodiedness of our existence functions as a demonstration of the power of the gospel in and over its messengers. What we do with our lives, our embodied existence and the materiality of daily decision making, inevitably reveals the extent of the lordship of Jesus Christ in our lives. To the degree that the living Lord has drawn us into a new sphere of power, the powers of the present age lose their ability to conform us to the world. Christians no longer "belong" to these powers because their bodies have been offered as a living sacrifice to God and belong to God as the body of Jesus Christ. Through the gracious power of God, those whose minds Christ has captured and made new are inevitably changed in such a way that their lives conform not to the world to which they have died but to the world in which they now live. The visionaries and martyrs of the civil rights movement provide an example of this new life in Christ. Like Abraham, in hope they believed against hope, fully convinced that God was able to do what God had promised (4:18, 21). They "gave glory to God" (4:20) by presenting their bodies as a living sacrifice on picket lines, at lunch counters, and in county jails. In so doing, they witnessed to the power of the gospel in and over them, a power that did not allow them to remain conformed to this age. Instead, they demonstrated by their embodied actions that they were prisoners of war in the new age of the Spirit, or as the prophet Zechariah (9:12) put it, "prisoners of hope."

"BY THE RENEWING OF YOUR MIND"
ROM. 12:3–21

Paul's appeal to the Roman Christians to demonstrate the lordship of Jesus Christ over them by the actions of their bodies in everyday existence is made somewhat more specific in 12:3–21, where he describes, in a general way at

---

5. Nancy J. Duff, "The Significance of Pauline Apocalyptic for Theological Ethics," *Apocalyptic and the New Testament: Essays in Honor of J. Louis Martyn*, ed. J. Marcus and M. L. Soards. Journal for the Study of the New Testament Supplement Series 24 (Sheffield: Sheffield Academic Press, 1989) 279–296. She draws important ethical conclusions based on the work of Ernst Käsemann, Karl Barth, and Paul Lehmann.

least, characteristics of new life in Christ. In Romans 5:1 the community was either described as being at peace with God or was exhorted to have peace with God, while in Romans 8:6 "to set the mind on the Spirit" was equated with "life and peace." We would rightly expect, therefore, that Paul's description of the community whose minds are renewed to conform to the image of Christ would at the same time largely consist of recommendations for actions and attitudes that lead to living in peace. As such, it is also the portrayal of renewed humanity—the opposite of the failure to glorify God and subsequent declension of mind in 1:18–32—and the portrayal of renewed Israel—the opposite of the venomous and bitter bloodshed of 3:9–18. In the following sections of his argument (13:1–15:13), Paul will become even more specific as he deals with particular concrete issues in the life together of the Roman house churches. Here, in 12:3–21, he provides a series of general exhortations that illustrate life in the Spirit as described in Romans 8. As we saw there, Paul is a realist with respect to the issue of Christian suffering. He expects that Christians may be asked to suffer for their faith, as he shows in his references to suffering, distress, persecution, nakedness, danger, the sword (8:35), and in his phrase "we are accounted as sheep to be slaughtered" (8:36). More than that, he knows that the activity of prayer itself opens Christians to the pain of the world around them. They share in the sufferings of the whole created world and wait with patient endurance for the redemption of their bodies, which they do not yet see in their present existence. They "see" their redemption in hope and in solidarity with the Holy Spirit, which is both assisting their prayers and sharing in their labor pains.

In the context of these admittedly trying conditions of daily existence, Paul calls upon the Christian community to be conformed to the mind of Christ and not to the mind of Adam. Just as Genesis 12, the calling of Abram, was God's antidote to the increasing immorality and violence of Genesis 1–11 (epitomized in the fall of Adam in Gen. 3), so the renewal of the mind of the Christ-conformed community is God's reversal of the characteristics of Adamic existence. If idolatry and immorality are the characteristics of fallen humanity in Romans 1:18ff., reasonable or right worship and discerning the will of God are the signs of the renewed mind of the community in Christ. Just as the opposite of Adam's grasping behavior almost certainly lies in the background of the Christ hymn and the description of the Christ-like community in Philippians 2, so also Adam is probably in Paul's mind here, as he exhorts each member of the community "not to think more highly of yourself than you ought to think" (12:3). The renewed mind does not have an exaggerated sense of its own importance, but instead assesses itself and its apparent needs in proportion to the faith or faithfulness that God has assigned. The meaning of both "measure of faith" in 12:3 and "analogy of faith" in 12:6 are disputed, but they are probably related and describe the ability to see ourselves as God sees us and not as we idealize ourselves in Adamic existence, which has been deceived by Sin.

The renewed mind also sees itself not as an isolated individual around which the world revolves (the star of our own show) but as part of a larger community with legitimately competing needs and interests that have to be taken into account if the community is to live in peace. Paul expresses this dialectic with the same metaphor he uses in 1 Corinthians 12:12–30, the one body with many members, but here he applies the analogy to stress the functions of the body in terms of the tasks that the community needs to have done (12:4–8). When all the members of the body perform their functions appropriately, the benefits of the differing gifts of the various members accrue to all as members of one another. Verses 9–13 press the theme of doing whatever it is that you do well. Paul describes a healthy competition that strives to excel in building up the body. What looks at first like a laundry list of general exhortations (e.g., "rejoice in hope, be patient in distress, remain constant in prayer" 12:12) is shown to be more carefully crafted by the pun that Paul employs as a transition between verses 13–14: "pursue (*diōkontes*, practice) hospitality to strangers" and "bless those who pursue (*diōkontas*, persecute) you, bless and do not curse them," both of which may be a reference to the tradition about Jesus' teaching (see Luke 6:28).

This transition focuses the discussion specifically on living in peaceful coexistence with others, especially with enemies. Recommendations to live imaginatively into the situation of the other ("rejoice with those who rejoice; weep with those who weep," 12:15) and to live in harmony are paired with injunctions to avoid community-disrupting behaviors: "Do not be proud"; "Do not pretend to be wiser than you are"; and especially "Do not repay anyone evil for evil, but consider what is noble in the sight of all" (12:16–17). Verses 17–21 (marked by an *inclusio* on the subject of dealing with evil) deal specifically with the active peacemaking behavior that is expected of the community conformed to the mind of Christ. "If it is possible, so far as it concerns you, live peacefully with all" (12:18). One of Paul's strongest imperatives follows:

> Beloved, *never* avenge yourselves, but allow the wrath [of God] to take its course, for it stands written: 'Vengeance is mine, I will repay, says the Lord.' (12:19, quoting Deut. 32:35)

Right behind it is another biblical warrant for not seeking revenge upon enemies, based on Proverbs 25:21–22. Instead,

> If your enemy hungers, feed him; if he thirsts, give him something to drink; for by doing so you will heap burning coals on his head. (12:20)

These two quotations, when taken in conjunction, have often been read to mean that the Christian who does not seek revenge will have the pleasure of knowing that God will torment the enemy in hell. But, given the context, it is far more likely that the reference to "heaping burning coals on the head" of the enemy is metaphorical language that refers to shaming or embarassing the enemy (making the face red) through the discipline of nonretaliation and through acts of kindness in place of vengeance.

Once more, Paul's argument is clarified by means of a story, this time one found in 2 Kings 6:8–23. That story is so well summarized by Proverbs 25:21–22, read the way I have suggested, that it is tempting to think it may have been in Paul's mind; there is no way to be certain, since he doesn't reference it specifically. Once when the Arameans attacked Israel, the prophet Elisha, who had been providing military intelligence to the king of Israel, was surrounded by the Aramean armies. Elisha prayed to the Lord, and they were stricken with blindness. He then led them into Samaria and reopened their eyes. They saw that they were in the hands of the king of Israel, who gleefully said to Elisha, "Shall I strike them down? Shall I kill them?" But the prophet replied, "No, did you capture with your sword and your bow those whom you want to strike down? Rather, set food and drink before them so that they may eat and drink, before they return to their master." So the king of Israel prepared a great feast for his enemies and sent them on their way home. The last line of the story reads, "And the Arameans ceased raiding operations in the land of Israel!" Elisha's point was that it was not the king of Israel but *God* who had captured the enemy and had the right to take vengeance. Then he taught another way to overcome the enemy. So, advises Paul, "Do not let yourselves be conquered by evil, but conquer evil with good" (12:21).

BE SUBJECT FOR THE SAKE OF THE NEIGHBOR
ROM. 13:1–14

When Romans is read primarily as a compendium of Christian doctrine, particularly when that reading is accompanied by an ethical doctrine of the two kingdoms or a theology that stresses the orders of creation, then Romans 13:1–7 is where one goes to find Paul's teaching on church and state. Sometimes, as in Oscar Cullmann's typology,[6] it is held in tension with Revelation 13:1–18, and sometimes Acts 5:27–29 is brought into the discussion, but these

---

6. Oscar Cullmann, *The State in the New Testament* (New York: Charles Scribner's Sons, 1956).

texts usually serve only to qualify what is said categorically in Romans 13 about being subject to governing authorities. This hermeneutical strategy does not work well, however, because each of the texts is rooted in such a distinctive historical context that they can hardly be placed in conversation with each other. Another interpretive strategy isolates Romans 13:1–7—and in that way attempts to control the damage done by reading it as the definitive doctrine of church and state—by treating it as the interpolation of a later writer into Paul's letter. There is, however, no textual support for this view. It is wiser to read the passage in its historical context than to read it as if it were a timeless source for a Christian doctrine of church and state.

Paying attention to the historical context of Romans 13:1–7 does not obligate us to envision Paul as actually recommending the emperor Nero in particular, even if it is true, as some historians have suggested, that the early years of Nero's reign looked promising for religious toleration. Shortly before Paul wrote, the emperor Claudius had been murdered (he was promptly deified by the Roman Senate), an act that brought Nero to the throne. Roughly contemporary with Romans are two fragmentary eclogues (poetic selections) of the Einsiedeln Papyrus that laud the accession of young Nero as the beginning of the golden age. But it is extremely unlikely that Paul shared that optimistic view. Elsewhere in his letters he refers to "the present evil age" (Gal. 1:4), assumes that "the external form of this world is passing into nothing" (1 Cor. 7:31), and states that "the rulers of this age, who are being destroyed" did not understand God's wisdom "for if they had, they would not have crucified the Lord of glory" (1 Cor. 2:6–8)—the latter, a clear reference to the Roman empire. Then why does Paul use such unqualified language about the need for the Roman Christians to be subject to the governing authorities, describing them as having been instituted by God and functioning as servants of God?[7] Moreover, why is this passage found where it is—preceded by recommendations for living peacefully insofar as it is possible and followed by the description of the commandment to love the neighbor as oneself as fulfilling the whole law—all of it set in the context of the coming parousia?

7. Luise Schottroff comments, "The radicality and singularity of Rom. 13:1–7 becomes clear if one compares this text with a philosophical explanation from antiquity about the power of the state, about different constitutional forms and their quality. A philosopher who is a loyal supporter of the government will naturally differentiate between good and bad constitutions" ("'Give to Caesar What Belongs to Caesar and to God What Belongs to God': A Theological Response of the Early Christian Church to Its Social and Political Environment," *Love of Enemy and Nonretaliation in the New Testament*, ed. Willard M. Swartley [Louisville, Ky.: Westminster/John Knox, 1992] 223–257 at 238).

Neil Elliott[8] has proposed a historical reconstruction that makes sense of most of the puzzling features of Romans 13:1–7. Following Ernst Käsemann,[9] he argues that while Paul's language is framed as if it spoke of universally valid realities, in actuality it reflects commonplace assumptions within Diaspora Jewish thought about how to get along with the various secular authorities to which the Jews were subject. Given the extremely precarious situation of Jewish communities throughout the empire, and especially the Jews in Rome who had already been expelled under emperors Tiberius (19 C.E.) and Claudius (49 C.E.), Jews (including Jewish Christians) were advised to avoid the hostility of local populations and to keep a low profile with respect to the Roman government. This was already difficult because, in the context of an aggressive imperial taxation system, the special, negotiated arrangements by which Jews paid a temple tax seemed to many Gentiles a form of tax evasion, and this perception resulted in increased antagonism towards Jews. In that context, Paul's admonition to be subject to authorities, especially on the matter of paying taxes and revenues, would have functioned practically to advocate for the safety of Jews and Jewish Christians in Rome. These weaker members of the community were particularly vulnerable to the social hostilities of the surrounding Gentile population.

Elliott's reading accounts for a number of distinctive features in the text of Romans 13:1–7. Paul's argument moves from the conventional language of "political realism," typical of Philo and other Diaspora Jewish writers of his time (about getting along under foreign rule), to focus specifically on the issue of taxation. The argument is structured to highlight its conclusion:

> Pay to all what is owed them—taxes to whom taxes are due, revenue to whom revenue is due, respect to whom respect is due, honor to whom honor is due." (13:7)

That sentence is rhetorically crafted to be memorable, for it uses the devices of alliteration and *anaphora* (repetition of a word or phrase for emphasis), which are even more pronounced in the Greek. In the course of the argument, Paul hints that the authorities command a respect that is closer to "fear" or "terror" (13:3). In contrast to the idealized portraits of *Pax Romana* and imperial propaganda that portrayed Nero as the emperor with the "idle sword," Paul cautions the community that the authority "does not wear the sword in vain" (13:4). For those with ears to hear, Paul's apparently conventional advice

---

8. Neil Elliott, "Romans 13:1–7 in the Context of Imperial Propaganda," *Paul and Empire: Religion and Power in Roman Imperial Society*, ed. Richard A. Horsley (Harrisburg, Pa.: Trinity Press International, 1997) 184–204.

9. Ernst Käsemann, "Principles of the Interpretation of Romans 13," *New Testament Questions of Today*, trans. W. J. Montague (Philadelphia: Fortress, 1969) 212–213.

to "be subject" and his flattering description of the empire serve as subtle reminders that the imperial sword is *not* idle: it continues to threaten destruction of the most vulnerable population, namely, the Jews around and among the Roman Christians. Disruptive actions on the part of the Roman Gentile Christians would place the lives of their Jewish and Jewish Christian neighbors in danger.

Paul's use of the catchword "owe" to bridge 13:7 ("Pay to all what is owed them") and 13:8 ("Owe nothing to anyone") suggests that it is these Jewish Christian neighbors who are particularly in view. In 13:8, Paul relates "not owing any debts," that is, having paid taxes and revenues as necessary, to "owing the debt" of love to the neighbor and thereby fulfilling the law. He lists four representative commandments from the Torah—no adultery, no killing, no stealing, no coveting—that are undeniably critical for life in community, and he insists that all the commandments are summed up by one commandment from Leviticus 19:18: "You shall love your neighbor as yourself." He counsels the Roman Christians that "love does no harm to a neighbor; therefore love is the fulfillment of the law" (13:10). It is striking that in the context of Leviticus 19, from which the love commandment is taken, the other half of the verse immediately preceding it speaks of avoiding vengeance: "You shall not take vengeance or bear a grudge against any (lit. the sons) of your people, but you shall love your neighbor as yourself: I am the Lord" (Lev. 19:18). This suggests that John Howard Yoder[10] was right to insist that Romans 12 and 13 ought to be read together and that the people of God—who are enjoined not to take vengeance—are being contrasted with the administration of empire, which does not bear the sword in vain but is the servant of God to execute wrath on the wrongdoer. The solemn eschatological warning that concludes chapter 13 serves, among other things, to destabilize the apparent facticity of the reigning Roman empire and to describe the alternative community that wears "weapons of light" (13:12) because it belongs to the coming Day of the Lord and not to the present time of darkness (13:12–13).

Finally, the irony of the history of interpretation of this passage should be noted. Paul himself was almost certainly a prisoner when he finally arrived in Rome, the city where he would be tried and executed during Nero's reign, according to the traditions of the early church in Acts 28:16 and 1 Clement 5. The political realism that lies behind what looks like the double message of Romans 13:1–7 reminds us of Paul's earlier listing of rulers and powers along with persecution, danger, and sword in Romans 8 as among the things that

---

10. John Howard Yoder, *The Politics of Jesus: Vicit Agnus Noster*, 2d ed. (Grand Rapids: Eerdmans, 1993) and idem, *The Christian Witness to the State* (Newton, Kans.: Faith and Life Press, 1964).

could not separate us from the love of God in Christ. If Paul himself was taken as a "sheep to be slaughtered" at the hands of the Roman empire, it is indeed ironic that his warning that the authority "does not wear the sword in vain" should have functioned for so many centuries as the warrant for unquestioning obedience of Christians to the state.

"WELCOME THE WEAK . . .
GOD HAS WELCOMED THEM"
ROM. 14:1–23

Paul continues to address particular issues in the life of the Roman house churches in Romans 14:1–23, the next section of his argument. Here he returns to the diatribe style of addressing rhetorical questions or exhortations to imagined dialogue partners who represent specific groups or advocates of theoretical positions within the community. This rhetorical strategy allows Paul to address controversial issues that are threatening to divide the community in such a way that the issues themselves are relativized and attention is shifted to the neighbors that the community has just been exhorted to love as themselves (13:9). It enables him to repeat and challenge slogans, such as "everything is clean" in 14:20, that may be true but are being used in a way that is destructive of community. Paul's rhetorical style also allows the Roman Christians to listen nondefensively (since positions are described anonymously). At the same time it invites them to abandon their own tendencies to judge or despise one another by reflecting on their common destination: the judgment seat of God.

Paul's argument in this section is strongly theocentric, as in Romans 9–11. This suggests that some of the same tensions that have arisen because of Jewish priority and Gentile numerical superiority may be at work here. It is significant that Paul never actually identifies the "strong" or the "weak," except to say in 14:2 that the "weak" person eats only vegetables. He may have picked these terms up from whatever he has heard about the situation in the Roman house churches, terms that one group (presumably the "strong") has adopted to describe the situation. If that is the case, Paul identifies himself with that group's position on matters of food and observance of days in 15:1 when he says "*we* who are 'strong',", but not with their stance towards those whom they consider "weak." Perhaps Paul shares the assumption of many of his later readers that the "strong" are Gentile Christians and Jewish Christians, such as Prisca, Aquila, and Paul himself, who no longer observe dietary laws or keep the sabbath. In this view, the "weak" are Jewish Christians who still consider themselves bound to keep these regulations, as well as Gentiles like those in Galatia who thought they needed to take on the observance of particular days

(Gal. 4:10). If this hypothesis is correct, Paul's refusal to name these groups specifically is probably a deliberate tactic to avoid strengthening the very divisions he wishes to question. But it is also possible that the behaviors and attitudes that divide the community do not correlate neatly with ethnic divisions, since there were also Gentiles who ate only vegetables and the observance or nonobservance of particular days could refer equally to Jews or to Gentiles.

What is immediately apparent in this argument is that Paul does not focus on the sources or causes of differing perspectives, such as ethnic divisions, or on the differing perspectives themselves, such as eating anything or eating only vegetables, and treating all days alike or treating some days as distinctive. He focuses, instead, on the *attitudes* towards others who have made different decisions about these issues.

> Those who eat must not despise those who refrain, and those who refrain must not judge those who eat; for God has welcomed them."
> (14:3)

Paul's rhetorical question in 14:4—"Who are you to judge the household servant of another?"—builds on his earlier argument at 12:1–2 that in baptism believers have become the possession of their Lord and demonstrate that lordship in their embodied actions.

In the following verses, Paul builds on another earlier argument: that because God is One, and the same God is God of both Jews and Gentiles, the community of Jewish Christians and Gentile Christians is also one (3:27–31). Therefore, those who observe a given day, keep it in honor of the Lord. Similarly, those who eat, eat in honor of the Lord and give thanks to God, while those who refrain, refrain in honor of the Lord and also give thanks to God (14:6). Paul invites those who have made different decisions about how to honor the Lord to recognize that it is the same Lord they are honoring with their different behaviors about food and observation of days.

The next step in Paul's argument is to relativize the importance of these particular decisions about admittedly central aspects of Christian life by insisting that all of Christian life is lived *coram Deo*, in the presence of God, and that everything Christians do is done *sub specie aeternitate*, under the aspect of eternity. Paul may be drawing on traditional hymnic or creedal material familiar to the Romans to underline his point:

> We do not live for ourselves, nor do we die for ourselves.
> If we live, we live for the Lord, and if we die, we die for the Lord;
> Therefore, whether we live or die, we are the Lord's.
> For to this purpose Christ died and lived again:
> That he might be Lord over both the dead and the living.
> (Rom. 14:7–9)

Moreover, Paul argues that Christians are just as accountable to God for their *attitudes* towards their brothers and sisters with whom they disagree as they are accountable for the *decisions* they have made that divide them from one another. Paul's pointed rhetorical questions ("Why do you judge your brother [or sister]? Or you, why do you despise your brother [or sister]?") form an *inclusio* with the earlier question in 14:4 and bring the first half of this section of the argument to a close. They are combined with the vivid image of the entire community standing before the judgment seat of God and with the powerful word of the Judge spoken to the community through the words of Scripture:

> As I live, says the Lord, every knee shall bow to me, and every tongue
> shall confess God. (14:11)

Paul has enhanced an already potent word from Isaiah 45:23 with a solemn oath formula ("as I live," perhaps from Isa. 49:18) for the strongest possible effect: the community is dramatically called to account for their present judging and despising behavior by the very Lord in whose honor they are doing the activities that divide them! Paul has only to underline the point: "So then, each of us will have to render an account to God" (14:12).

Paul has employed a combination of moving liturgical cadences, vivid judgment imagery, and powerful biblical language to question the divisive attitudes that accompany decisions about religious behavior within the Roman house churches. In the second half of this section of his argument, he turns his attention to the debated matters themselves, or at least those dealing with food and drink. The word "therefore" in 14:13 signals that Paul is building on the argument just completed as he exhorts the community to let go of one attitude and adopt another. "Let us *therefore* no longer judge one another, but rather decide (lit. judge) never to put an obstacle or stumbling block in the way of another (lit. a brother)" (14:13). Not until then does Paul state his own position: "I know and am convinced in the Lord Jesus that nothing is unclean in itself; instead, it is unclean for the person who considers it unclean" (14:14). Once again, Paul may be alluding to early Christian tradition about Jesus' teaching (see Mark 7:15, 19) as also in 12:17 and 13:9, particularly since his solemn declaration includes the emphatic words "in the Lord Jesus," but these may also be a shorthand reference to the authority of the risen Lord who commissioned Paul as an apostle with a law-free mission to the Gentiles. Either way, Paul is less interested in the teaching of Jesus than in his saving death, which he also describes as "the work of God" (14:20). Paul's injunctions ("Stop destroying the one for whom Christ died by what you eat," 14:15, and "Do not, for the sake of food, destroy the work of God," 14:20; cf. 1 Cor. 8:8–13) once more function to relativize the importance of the religious behaviors that are dividing the community by contrasting them with the work of God in Christ.

Paul rarely speaks of the kingdom of God. When he does, it is sometimes in connection with a list of vices to make the point that those who do such things will not enter the kingdom of God (1 Cor. 6:9–10; Gal. 5:21). It is significant, therefore, that he mentions the kingdom here with the opposite effect: the kingdom of God is *not* about food and drink; it consists of righteousness, peace, and joy in the Holy Spirit (14:17). In the interests of peace and mutual upbuilding of the community, Paul will not allow the "strong" their slogan "everything is clean!" (14:20)—even though he agrees with them—if by eating meat or drinking wine or doing anything else they cause another member of the community to stumble and fall. With respect to observing days or not, Paul had said earlier, "Let each be fully convinced in his [or her] own mind" (14:5). The same thing applies to food: those who are clear about their convictions about what God wants and follow them are blessed, since they have no reason to condemn themselves for their actions. But those who are unsure and eat or drink what they think may be wrong to eat or drink are condemned because their actions do not stem from faithful obedience to God but from sin (14:23).

You may have noticed that I have not talked about the "strong in faith" or the "weak in faith" at all in this passage, even though most commentators adopt this terminology. They do so presumably because they read 14:1 to speak of welcoming the "weak in faith" and then extend that reading through the rest of chapter 14. But Paul never actually uses the word "strong" in chapter 14 and only uses the word "weak" in verses 1–2. (Where both words appear in 15:1, the apparent qualifier "in faith" is strikingly absent.) Moreover, the phrase "in faith" or "in faithfulness" in 14:1 may just as easily modify the verb "welcome" as the adjective "weak." In that case, Paul would be opening and closing this section of his argument (Romans 14) with language exhorting Christians to welcome in faithfulness the "weaker" others—not disputing about opinions, but confident of God's blessing upon their own faithful obedience. Paul urges the "strong" Christians to protect the less-confident brothers and sisters for whom Christ died so that the others might enjoy that same blessing and escape the condemnation that comes from doublemindedness.

"WELCOME . . . AS THE MESSIAH HAS WELCOMED YOU" ROM. 15:1–13

Romans 15:1–13, the climactic summary of Paul's argument, shows how important particular passages of Scripture were in shaping Paul's exhortation to the Roman house churches. These "oracles of God" (3:2) for the end time were written for the instruction of the messianic community of Jewish and Gentile Christians living in the eschatological age of the Spirit. In carefully paired twin arguments (15:1–6 and 15:7–13), Paul reads Scripture christolog- ically to describe Jesus, the Messiah, as normative both for the community's life together (like the Christ, they are not to please themselves but to build up their neighbors) and for their apostolic vocation (like the Christ, they are to serve the circumcision and to bring hope to the Gentiles). In the first argu- ment (15:1–6), Paul makes the imitation of Christ appeal explicitly in the text of Romans. The second argument (15:7–13), however, depends on the more subtle suggestions that scriptural quotations identifying Jesus as servant to both Jews and Gentiles (1) foreshadow the success of the gospel among Gen- tiles, (2) mandate Paul's own apostleship to the Gentiles, and (3) compel the support of that mission by the Roman Christians in imitation of Christ.[11]

That Romans 15:1–13 should be treated as a unit is apparent from the close parallelism between the structures of 15:1–6 and 15:7–13. In each case, there is a four-part argument, consisting of (1) an appeal to the community to act in a particular way; (2) the identification of the Messiah as the pattern for the rec- ommended behavior; (3) exegetical warrants introduced by standard formulas for citing Scripture; and (4) a prayer that God will empower the community to enact the christological pattern just described. Romans 15:1–6 is directed to the internal life together of the community at Rome. Romans 15:7–13 refers to the larger mission to the Gentiles and leads naturally to Paul's request for support for the upcoming mission to Gentiles in Spain.

Romans 15:1–6 summarizes the discussion in Romans 14 of the primary responsibility of the powerful to accept the weaknesses of the powerless as their burden, this time in a christological framework. As James Dunn[12] suggests, the logic of Romans 15:1–3 runs parallel to that of Galatians 6:2, where bearing one another's burdens is equated with fulfilling the law of Christ. The appeal to the death of Christ on behalf of the same powerless ones (14:15) is dramat- ically recalled by the quotation of Psalm 69:9 (68:10 LXX) in Romans 15:3. The exegetical warrant for Paul's assertion that "the Messiah did not please him- self" (note the titular use of *ho Christos* in both 15:3 and 15:7) is remarkable: Paul not only reads the psalm quotation christologically but also directly attrib- utes the words of the psalm to Christ himself in a striking parallel to 14:11, where Paul has God as Judge address the community directly in the words of Isaiah. By allowing the Roman Christians, particularly the "strong" (15:1), to

---

11. A fuller version of the following argument can be found in Grieb, "Affiliation with Jesus Christ in His Sacrifice," 229–262.

12. James D. G. Dunn, *Romans*, 2 vols., Word Bible Commentary 38 (Dallas: Word, 1988) II:836.

overhear, as it were, the expressed willingness of the Messiah to take on the additional burden of reproaches not properly his own, Paul gives them a model for their own attitudes towards those with whom they disagree.

Paul is claiming not only that the death of Jesus the Messiah on the cross fulfills Scripture (cf. 1 Cor. 15:3ff.) but also that the Jesus who died for others is a paradigm for Christian obedience. Hence his "aside" to the reader in 15:4, where he explains that "these things were pre-written" (e.g., Ps. 68:10 LXX) "for our instruction." The nature of that instruction is the enkindling of hope, which points forward to the eschatological uniting of the church of Jews and Gentiles. God's integrity (the basis for our hope) is thus also the grounds for Christian ethics, since the correspondences between the Jesus narrative and the Scriptures of Israel reveal God's trustworthiness and truthfulness. It is this God of steadfastness and encouragement who speaks of hope through the steadfastness and encouragement of the Scriptures. Paul closes this section of his conclusion with a prayer—that the God of hope will unite the community of Christians at Rome, powerful and powerless together, in conformity to the pattern of the Messiah and therefore as a sign of the coming eschatologically united community of Jews and Gentiles.

In Romans 15:1–6, Paul used the christological convention of Christ speaking in Psalm 68:10 LXX—singling out a single poignant moment in the life of Jesus—to exhort the community at Rome to please one another in order to build up the community, the stance toward temporary opponents that is appropriate to those who look ahead in hope. Now, in Romans 15:7–13, the thrust of Paul's argument is outward: the united community at Rome, glorifying God and bearing witness to their unity in Christ, are called to envision an even more comprehensive unity—based once more on the story of Jesus. Paul tells the story of Jesus in a tightly compressed summary (15:8–9) that both justifies the Gentile mission and mandates Paul's own apostleship to the Gentiles. Then, in a series of biblical quotations (15:9–12), he shows how this story of Jesus found in the Scriptures of Israel speaks directly to the present situation of Paul and his churches.

The extremely compact summary of the work of God in Christ in 15:8–9 is striking both for its brevity and its comprehensiveness. As Wayne Meeks has shown,[13] the strange indirection of this claim—Christ has welcomed *Gentile* Christians by being a servant of the *Jews*, in order to fulfill promises made to *Jewish* patriarchs about *Gentiles*—is all the more remarkable when it is seen that it summarizes the themes, not only of Romans 9–11 but of the entire letter, leading up to Paul's restatement of his own mission that follows it. The

---

13. Wayne A. Meeks, "Judgment and the Brother: Romans 14:1–15:13," *Tradition and Interpretation in the New Testament: Essays in Honor of E. Earle Ellis*, ed. G. F. Hawthorne and O. Betz (Grand Rapids: Eerdmans, 1987) 291–292.

"truthfulness of God" is the aspect of God's righteousness that is singled out for attention (as in 3:7) because of the close relationship between the *words* of God in the Scriptures of Israel and the *work* of God in the death and resurrection of the Messiah, the event that has inaugurated the end time in which Paul and his churches are living. For this reason, Paul drives home the point that God had always intended the union of Jews and Gentiles with a string of scriptural quotations that speak of Gentiles praising God, rejoicing with the people of Israel, and, finally, hoping in the root of Jesse who rises to rule the Gentiles.

Once again Paul reads Scripture christologically, and in at least two of the quotations the christological pattern has ethical implications. When Paul reads Isaiah 11:10 LXX—"the root of Jesse will appear, the one who rises to rule the Gentiles" (Rom. 15:12)—he hears the prophet describe the coming one who will be the hope of the Gentiles, recognizes Jesus the Messiah as the one so described, and assumes that the text is prophesying the success of the Christian mission to the Gentiles that Paul is already experiencing. When Paul reads Psalm 17:50 LXX—"Therefore, I will confess you among the Gentiles and *psalm* your name" (Rom. 15:9)—he hears the voice of Christ praying the psalm in the midst of a congregation of Gentiles and concludes that followers of the Messiah will be there as well. Thus both of these texts mandate Paul's own apostleship to the Gentiles in imitation of Christ and warrant his request for support for the Gentile mission. With Isaiah's words "in him shall the Gentiles hope" (Isa. 11:10 in Rom. 15:12) still ringing in their ears, Paul concludes his argument to the Roman Christians with the prayer that "the God of hope" will fill them with all joy and peace in believing through the power of the Holy Spirit, in order that they may abound in hope (15:13). Rhetorically, this serves as an open invitation to join in the work God is doing through Paul's upcoming mission in Spain. At the same time, it underlines the unity of the Roman Christians in their worship of the truthful and trustworthy God.

Summary. As Paul turns his attention to the situation of the Roman house churches, his argument becomes increasingly concrete and specific. First, he describes how all baptized Christians participate in the death of Christ by offering themselves as a living sacrifice to God. They are no longer to be conformed to Adamic existence but to be transformed by the renewing of their minds into those who discern what is the will of God. This transformation will cause them to take up behaviors that lead to peaceful coexistence with neighbors and to the building up of community. Specifically, they will act towards the governing authorities in ways that protect the most vulnerable around and among them, the Jews and Jewish Christians whose rights in the empire were imperiled. Loving the neighbor as oneself in this context means being subject and paying taxes, until the Day of the Lord comes.

Loving the neighbor also has implications for the Roman Christians in their life together. They ought to welcome one another because God and Christ have already welcomed the other. Paul uses the language of relation to redescribe the neighbor as "the work of God" and as "the brother or sister for whom Christ died" in such a way that gratitude to God and Christ for the work of redemption accomplished on the cross is naturally expressed in the serving of the neighbor who is likewise the recipient of the same gracious mercy. Finally, loving the neighbor means imitating the Messiah in whom the Gentiles hope by following him in mission to the Gentiles. Paul reads Israel's Scriptures as a mandate for his own apostleship to the Gentiles and as the warrant for his request that the Roman house churches support the upcoming mission to the Gentiles in Spain.

FOR FURTHER REFLECTION

1. On April 3, 1968, the evening before his assassination, Martin Luther King Jr. gave a speech in Birmingham, Alabama, in which he said, "Like anybody I would like to live, but that doesn't matter to me now, because I have seen the promised land. . . ." In what ways does this language reflect Paul's appeal to the Roman Christians in Romans 12:1–2 to offer their bodies as a living sacrifice and no longer to be conformed to this age?

2. While in 1 Corinthians 13, Paul speaks of Christian love in terms of general attitudes and habitual practices, in Romans 12:9–21 the focus of his comments is specifically the peacemaking praxis of the church. What does it mean, practically speaking, for the church to be the place where the forgiveness of sins is practiced? How does the church imitate Christ in its nonretaliation for wrongs done, in its overcoming evil with good?

3. Ernst Käsemann comments about Romans 13:1–7, in ironic understatement, that this passage "has given rise to particularly lively debate during the past generation in the German-speaking areas." Käsemann himself was imprisoned by the Nazis as a young man. Karl Barth, as a member of the Confessing Church, had to work through this passage several times in the course of his career. Romans 13:1–7 also played an important role in the movement to end apartheid in South Africa and in the civil rights movement in the United States. What is at stake for the life of the church if this passage is read as a timeless discussion of Paul's doctrine of church and state rather than as Paul's assessment of how the Roman churches ought to live out the command to love their neighbors—specifically in the context of payment of taxes to the Empire?

4. Augustine describes with great power in his *Confessions* (Book VIII, 29) the role that Romans 13:13–14 played in his conversion. As he sat weeping

over his inability to reform his dissolute life, he heard a child's voice saying again and again, "Pick up and read, pick up and read," which he heard as a divine command to open the Bible. He seized the book and his eyes fell upon the words, "Let us walk in a well-formed way, as in the day; not in orgies and drinking bouts, not in sexual immorality and licentiousness, not in strife and jealousy, but put on the Lord Jesus Christ and do not provide for the flesh, to gratify its lustful desires" (Rom. 13:13–14). Augustine reports that he needed nothing else; all his anxieties were at once relieved, and all his doubts were dispelled. When Paul says, "What was written in advance was written for our instruction" (Rom. 15:4), what is he saying about the power of Scripture to shape Christian lives and Christian communities today? Do you think Augustine and Paul are saying the same thing, or are they reading Scripture in different ways?

5. How is the imitation of Christ to be lived out in Christian community? Readers of Paul's last few chapters of Romans will find themselves challenged by his strong theocentric, christocentric, and ecclesiocentric ethics. This is where Paul the evangelist invites his readers to "close with Christ" on a deeper level. He is in effect asking us, What difference does it make to you personally that Jesus Christ was crucified? What difference does it make to your community of faith? How would it change your concept of your neighbor to think of Christ's death on behalf of him or her? Can we also imagine the neighbors that we have never seen as brothers and sisters for whom Christ died?

7

"I Hope to See You . . . As I Go to Spain"

(Rom. 15:14–16:27)

Prayer is *not* personal in the sense of a private transaction occurring in a void, disconnected with everyone and everything else, but it is *so* personal that it reveals (I have chosen this verb conscientiously) every connection with everyone and everything else in the whole of Creation throughout time. . . . Prayer, in quintessence, therefore, is a political action—an audacious one, at that—bridging the gap between immediate realities and ultimate hope, between ethics and eschatology, between the world as it is and the Kingdom which is vouchsafed.

William Stringfellow[1]

The conclusion of Paul's letter summarizes the story so far and hints at the next chapter of the story of Romans: Paul's mission to the Gentiles in Spain. The story is left open-ended, and the conclusion, to some extent at least, is in the hands of its readers. Since, as Paul seems to assume, God does not coerce the Roman Christians to become part of the plot but rather welcomes them into the narrative and invites their response, this section of the letter was probably the most demanding for Paul himself. It would require the utmost tact and diplomacy to move from his theological vision of God's salvation-creating righteousness, working itself out dialectically in the interaction of Jews and Gentiles, to his own current plans and his hopes for the future. Here his rhetoric creates an opportunity for concrete response on the part of the Roman house churches.

---

1. William Stringfellow, *A Simplicity of Faith: My Experience in Mourning* (Nashville: Abingdon, 1982) 67–68.

Specifically, he requests their support for Phoebe; he asks that they keep him in prayer as he undertakes the dangerous and challenging journey to Jerusalem, and he suggests that they will want to prepare for his own upcoming visit to Rome by gathering resources with which to support his work in Spain. Paul makes a point of sending his personal greetings to a number of people in the congregation, both Jewish Christians and Gentile Christians, underlining at the end that the same God is God of all the Roman Christians as well as of Paul himself. He also warns them about false teachers who could threaten the vision of unity he has worked so hard to describe in this letter. Then, after sending greetings from his coworkers, he closes the letter with another doxological hymn that summarizes one more time the main themes of the letter and forms a rhetorically pleasing *inclusio* with its opening sentences.

"I HAVE WRITTEN TO YOU RATHER BOLDLY"
ROM. 15:14–21

Paul begins his concluding comments with a compliment to his hearers: he expresses his confidence that the Roman Christians are full of goodness and knowledge and able to instruct one another (15:14). The implied corollary is that they do not need anyone from outside their community to provide them with theological insight or to direct their ethical behavior. Once again, Paul is at his diplomatic best, showing the same care that he exercised before, in Romans 1:12, not to assert his authority over the community. Then, in another diplomatic move, common in Hellenistic letter writing, he acknowledges his "boldness" at some points in the letter to remind them of these things they already know, because of his distinctive calling from God or "the grace given me by God" (15:15).

Paul had appealed to this "grace" at the very beginning of his letter in his self-description:

> Paul, a slave of Jesus Christ, called to be an apostle, set apart for the gospel of God, . . . Jesus Christ our Lord, through whom we have received grace and apostleship to bring about the obedience of the Gentiles. (1:1–5)

He had returned to the same "grace" earlier, at the beginning of the last major section of his letter ("by the grace given to me," 12:3) where he had used specifically cultic language: "I appeal (*parakalō*) to you therefore . . . to present your bodies as a living sacrifice, holy and acceptable to God which is your reasonable worship" (12:1). Here he gives a much fuller account of the grace of God given to him and its purpose as he sees it:

> to be a minister of Christ Jesus to the Gentiles, serving the gospel of
> God as a priest, so that the offering of the Gentiles may be acceptable,
> having been sanctified by the Holy Spirit. (15:16)

The cultic language of offering and sacrifice reappears here, although the attribution of sanctification specifically to the Holy Spirit is new in Romans (see 1 Cor. 3:16; 6:19).[2]

This language may be part of the way that Paul conceives of the unity of the Gentiles with Israel, since he had used similar language about Israel in 11:16, where he argued, "If the firstfruit is holy, then also the lump; if the root is holy, then also the branches." Gentiles who have been grafted into Israel partake of the "richness of the root" of Israel's holiness.[3] This cultic language also reflects the unity between "the apostle to the Gentiles" and the "offering, which is the Gentiles" (reading the genitive of 15:16 epexegetically, that is, as explanatory), since elsewhere Paul refers to himself as "being poured out as a libation over the sacrifice and the offering of your faith" (Phil. 2:17). The credibility of Paul's own apostleship and the success of the Gentile mission are tied together symbolically in the collection of money for Jerusalem, which was the one thing (Gal. 2:10) that the authorities in Jerusalem had requested of Paul as, "recognizing the grace given" to him, they had extended "the right hand of partnership" to Paul and Barnabas to carry out the Gentile mission. It is not surprising that Paul will request the prayers of the Roman house churches that "his ministry," the delivery of this highly symbolic collection from the Gentile churches, may be "acceptable to the saints" in Jerusalem (15:31).

As Paul reflects on his apostolic endeavors, he returns in 15:17–18 to the theme of "boasting" or "rejoicing" (*kauchēsis*) that has played a major role in his argument in Romans:

> In Christ Jesus, then, I have cause to boast in my work for God. For I
> will not dare to speak of something other than what Christ has accom-
> plished through me to win obedience from the Gentiles, in word and
> in deed."

---

2. Luke Timothy Johnson, *Reading Romans: A Literary and Theological Commentary* (New York: Crossroad, 1997) 209.

3. Paula Fredriksen has shown that Paul did not see the particular form of his apostleship to the Gentiles as constituting a break with Judaism. Instead, he exchanged one understanding of Judaism for another (messianic) understanding. Paul's own commission as a missionary was to bring the Gentiles "to Zion" (Jerusalem), even though the symbolic way in which this was to occur (through the collection) would be somewhat different from the traditional expectation of the way the Gentiles would come to Zion ("Judaism, the Circumcision of Gentiles, and Apocalyptic Hope: Another Look at Galatians 1 and 2," *Journal of Theological Studies* 42 (1991): 532–564).

Paul will only speak of what Christ has done through him in his work for God concerning the Gentiles. Boasting in one's own efforts apart from God's grace has been excluded by Paul (in 3:27; 4:2), but boasting in the things of God is appropriate in his view. So, recalling Romans 5:1–11, those whom God has made righteous through the faithfulness of Christ boast (or rejoice) in their hope of sharing the glory of God (5:2), in the sufferings that are building their character and leading them to hope in God (5:3), and even in God (5:11) through Jesus Christ through whom they have now received reconciliation. Here Paul boasts of God's power ("by the power of signs and wonders, by the power of the Spirit of God," 15:19) working in him "in word and in deed" (15:18). It is not clear grammatically if (1) this last phrase best describes the genuineness of the "obedience from the Gentiles"—they are obedient in speech and in action—or (2) it serves as the first of three parallel phrases describing what Christ has accomplished in Paul—by word and deed, by signs and wonders, by the Spirit. Either way, the saving power of the gospel of God is attested to by the success of Paul's apostleship to the Gentiles. The phrase "signs and wonders" sets the miraculous demonstrations of the power of the Spirit in the preaching of the gospel and the founding of Christian communities in the context of the exodus tradition (for example, Exod. 7:3 as in 2 Cor. 12:11–12).

Paul's success has been remarkable by any measure, even allowing for some hyperbole (rhetorical exaggeration) in his description of the scope of his apostolic labors: for example, his comment in 15:19, "So that from Jerusalem and as far around as Illyricum I have fully proclaimed the gospel of Christ." Paul describes his missionary activity in terms of a great circle (*kyklō*) or arc from Jerusalem to the Roman province of Illyricum on the eastern shore of the Adriatic Sea (present-day Albania, Croatia, Bosnia, Serbia). It is both theologically and politically significant that he characterizes his mission as starting "from Jerusalem."[4] Jerusalem is associated not only with the gospel Paul proclaims and with his immediate travel plans concerning the collection of funds from the Gentile churches, but also with the group of Jewish Christians that served as an important accountability structure for his ministry, whether seen through the polemical lens of Galatians 2 or the more benign picture of Acts 15. Throughout Romans Paul has used the framing device of "the Jew first and also the Greek" to describe God's salvation-creating righteousness, and in 11:13–14 he describes his own vocation as a part of God's own plan expressed in Deuteronomy 32:21 LXX—to make Israel jealous—for the ultimate reconciliation of Jew and Gentile (10:19). His past-tense description of his apostolic labors in 15:19 provides geographical confirmation that Paul has been living his theological vision.

---

4. Johnson, *Reading Romans*, 212.

What motivates Paul to make such extraordinary efforts and expenditure of self in the service of the gospel of God is his drive to push beyond the boundaries of the familiar and the established ministries of others to the edges of the Lord's territory, the frontiers of the Spirit: "Thus I make it my ambition to preach the gospel, not where Christ has already been named, so that I do not build on someone else's foundation" (15:20; see 1 Cor. 3:10–15 for another use of the same "building on a foundation" metaphor with respect to his ministry). Paul's missionary zeal probably reflects both the urgency of the gospel of reconciliation itself for its ambassadors (see 2 Cor. 5:20–6:2) and the eschatological pressure present in Romans 13:11–12a ("For now salvation is nearer to us than when we first came to believe; the night has advanced; the day has drawn near"). His description of himself here in terms of drive or ambition need not conflict with his earlier self-presentation as a man "under obligation" (1:14; see also 1 Cor. 9:16) or a "slave" of Jesus Christ (1:1). Paul seems to have loved his work and to have been powerfully moved by the revelation (apocalypse) of Jesus Christ that determined his future direction. This is evident in the biblical warrant he gives for his ministry in 15:21. Paul reads Isaiah 52:15 christologically: "Those to whom nothing about him has been told shall see, and those who have never heard [of him] shall understand." This text, which immediately precedes the complaint "Lord, who has believed our message" (Isa. 53:1, quoted in Rom. 10:16), is taken from that section of Isaiah in which Paul identifies the experience of the earlier prophet with that of himself and his coworkers. In both cases, the rejection that the heralds of the gospel of God experience only seems to fuel their determination to get it across.

"BUT NOW I AM GOING TO JERUSALEM"
ROM. 15:22–29

It may be Paul's ongoing experience of rejection as much as his sense of successful completion of a certain phase of the work that accounts for Paul's next statement. After explaining that his efforts in the eastern regions surrounding the Mediterranean Sea have so occupied his time and energy that he has "so many times been hindered from coming to you," he adds, "but now, since I have no further place in these regions, I desire, as I have for many years, to come to you when I go to Spain" (15:22–24a). Paul's words here remind me of some of the pastors who come through the seminary's continuing education program. After years of engagement with a parish or a diocese, they sense that it is time to do something else and are not quite sure whether to characterize their past ministry as a trial that has gone on long enough or as a pattern that has become too much of a good thing. Either way, Paul is getting closure on the past and turning his attention to the future.

Paul now wants to work in Spain, and he therefore writes to the Roman Christians that he hopes to "be sent on his way" by them, once he has enjoyed their company for a while (15:24). The Greek word for "speed on a journey" (*propempein*) is used technically to mean providing the necessary staff and supplies for an expedition. In another few verses (15:32) Paul will mention his hope to be "refreshed" (*synanapauesthai*) by them, another word that strongly suggests monetary support.[5] In other words, Paul is alerting them that he intends to ask for their financial backing for his proposed mission to Spain. He may have been hinting at this desire for support in the opening of the letter when he mentions that he had desired to "reap some harvest" among the Roman Christians as among the other Gentile churches (1:13), especially if it had been Paul's hope at one time to include an offering from the Roman house churches in the Jerusalem collection project. That had not been possible for whatever reasons, but now Paul is offering them the opportunity to be his base of operations for the western mission. It was Paul's pattern, as he describes it in other letters, to "preach the gospel free of charge" (2 Cor. 11:7) so as not to burden the community receiving it. Paul seems to have accomplished this in a combination of two ways: by "working with his own hands" (1 Cor. 4:12) in self-support (1 Thess. 2:9) and by allowing certain churches with whom he had a special relationship to be in financial friendship or partnership (*koinōnia*) with him (Phil. 4:15–16). It is probable that one of the reasons Paul has stressed the unity of the Roman Christians (e.g., 15:6) is that a divided community is less likely to fund his vision for the Spanish mission.

Before Paul can turn his attention to these long-range plans, however, he needs to complete the project that has preoccupied him during much of his previous ministry: "At the moment, however, I am going to Jerusalem as a minister to the saints" (15:25). Paul intends to deliver to the church in Jerusalem the funds that he had been collecting for many years in order to fulfill his promise to the "pillars" at Jerusalem "to remember the poor, the very thing I had already been eager to do" (Gal. 2:10). Acts 11:27–30 suggests that the Jerusalem Christians were chronically poor and seriously in need of financial support. As noted above, the collection of funds for the Jerusalem church also had great value—probably both to Paul and to the church leadership at Jerusalem—as a symbol of the way Paul's law-free Gentile churches and the Torah-observant Jewish Christian community at Jerusalem were nevertheless one in Christ. Paul had devoted himself to the effort and must have been anticipating the relief of bringing the project to its long-awaited conclusion. We

---

5. Ibid., 216.

hear some of his theological reflection about it, which may also be a summary of his fund-raising appeal (see 2 Cor. 8–9), in the next few verses:

> For Macedonia and Achaia were pleased to form a partnership with the poor among the saints at Jerusalem. For not only were they pleased to do this, but indeed they are under obligation to them; for if the Gentiles have participated in their spiritual blessings, they also ought to minister to them in material (lit. fleshly) goods. (Rom. 15:26–27)

For Paul, as for others in the Greco-Roman world, serious friendship implied financial partnership (friends hold all things in common) and was only possible between "equals." In 2 Corinthians 8:13–15, for instance, Paul speaks of "equality" (*isotēs*) between givers and receivers. Here in Romans, Paul uses language that formally balances the gifts being exchanged—"spiritual things" and "fleshly things"—which is a nod to the "equality" tradition of friendship. But in the context of his argument, the scales are not truly in balance: the Gentiles "owe" the Jerusalem church. Paul is not appealing for their charity but for justice (another term for "the righteousness of God") in the specific context of the Gentile mission. There may be just a hint of the olive tree metaphor that Paul had used in 11:17–18 to talk about unbelieving Jews and Gentile Christians. The "rich root" or "richness" of Israel is what supports the later Gentile branches. Here, the Gentile Christian churches are shown to be in debt (under obligation) to the Jewish Christian church in Jerusalem, the city from which God's saving act in the Messiah came. Whatever Paul means by the expression "when I have sealed to them this fruit" (15:28), it is clear that he is thinking organically about the relationship of the root church and its fruit-bearing branches. Hopeful that the completion of the collection will soon be behind him, Paul concludes the paragraph with another reference to his next project: "I will go on, by way of you, to Spain; and I know that in coming to you, I will come with the fullness of the blessing of Christ" (15:28–9).

"STRIVE TOGETHER WITH ME IN PRAYER TO GOD" ROM. 15:30–33

Ernst Käsemann, who sees Romans 15:30–33 as "the true ending of the epistle,"[6] comments that it is not unusual for an apostle writing to an unknown congregation to conclude with a blessing, with or without greetings:

---

6. Ernst Käsemann, *Commentary on Romans*, trans. G. W. Bromiley (Grand Rapids: Eerdmans, 1980) 406.

What is unusual is that the conclusion should consist of an urgent request for prayer, which is based on very strong fears. Paul obviously expects—and Acts bears him out—that he will run into serious complications in Jerusalem, and he does not even rule out danger to his life."[7]

That Paul had a keen sense of the danger that he faced from "the unbelievers in Judea" is shown by the solemn formula with which he begs the Roman Christians to pray for and with him. The "I beseech you" (*parakalō*) formula that Paul used at 12:1–2, also in a cultic or liturgical context, reappears here toward the end of his letter. Evidence from Paul's other letters (1 Thess. 2:14–16; 2 Cor. 11:32–33) and from Acts (9:23–25, 29) describes how, from the time of his conversion, Paul experienced harassment from "his flesh." It is not difficult to see how someone who preached a law-free gospel about a crucified messiah to uncircumcised Gentiles would attract the hostility of Jewish religious leaders. An account of Paul's later arrest in Jerusalem and plots against his life is also found in Acts (21:27–36; 23:12–15; and 25:2–3), showing that his fears were well grounded.

Paul asks the Roman Christians to join in a prayerful struggle with him in his prayers to God (15:30). He asks them to pray for two things: that he might be delivered from the unbelievers in Judea and that his ministry for Jerusalem might be acceptable to the saints (15:31). Paul is confident that if these two requests are granted, the rest of his plans will fall in place, and he will be able to come to the Roman Christians with joy and be refreshed in their company. Having asked for their prayers, Paul reciprocates by praying for them: "The God of peace be with all of you. Amen."

That Paul includes here near the end of his letter "an urgent request for prayer, which is based on very strong fears" should not particularly surprise us. Romans contains more prayers than any of the rest of Paul's letters and perhaps more than all of them combined.[8] The prayers of Romans are important in the letter at both the rhetorical and the theological levels.

Rhetorically, prayer is part of the apostle's self-presentation to the community at Rome, which he did not found. He offers the usual prayer of thanks-

---

7. Ibid., 406.

8. John Koenig, *Rediscovering New Testament Prayer: Boldness and Blessing in the Name of Jesus* (San Francisco: Harper, 1992); Gordon P. Wiles, *Paul's Intercessory Prayers: The Significance of the Intercessory Prayer Passages in the Letters of St. Paul* (Cambridge: Cambridge University Press, 1974); Carolyn Osiek, "Paul's Prayer: Relationship with Christ?" in *Scripture and Prayer: A Celebration for Carroll Stuhlmueller*, ed. C. Osiek and D. Senior (Wilmington, Del.: Michael Glazier, 1988), 145–157; David G. Peterson, "Prayer in Paul's Writings" in *Teach Us to Pray*, ed. D. A. Carson (Exeter: World Evangelical Fellowship, 1990) 84–101.

giving for them (1:8–15), and within that paragraph he identifies himself as a person of prayer (1:9). Paul's Jewish identity is underlined, for the *Shema* (Deut. 6:4ff.), Israel's great prayer of praise, plays a prominent role in his argument at 3:30; he speaks of circumcision of the heart at 2:29; and the charge that Israel has blasphemed God's name provides a damaging rhetorical blow at 2:24. The power of baptismal adoption is recalled in the "Abba, Father" prayer at 8:15 and probably also the references to "putting on" (weapons of light and the Lord Jesus Christ) in 13:12 and 13:14. In a prayer-like moment, the entire community at Rome hears the direct address of God as Judge, reminding them that they will all appear before the judgment seat of God (14:11; see also 12:19). Benedictions, thanksgivings, and doxologies often form the concluding phrase or sentence of a section of his argument (1:7; 7:25; 8:39; 9:5; 11:33–36; 15:5–6, 13, 33; 16:20, 25–27) or tag an important point in the argument (1:25; 14:22). The concluding refrain "in" or "through Jesus Christ our Lord" marks subsections of the argument, especially in Romans 5–8 (5:11, 17, 21; 6:11, 23; 7:25; 8:39). Finally, in prayer, Paul identifies with the Roman Christians at the conclusion of his argument (15:3–6, 13). He implies by his request that he and the Christians in Rome stand in the same place with respect to God.

Theologically, it is significant that at several points in the letter, as here, prayer is portrayed in terms of a struggle or contest (*agōn*) (1:9–10; 3:19–20; 7:24; 8:18–27, 31–39; 9:3; 10:1) and in connection with the unfathomable mystery of God's mercy (11:33–36; 16:25–27). Paul's strikingly dense use of Scripture in Romans draws heavily on the Psalms, the prayer book of Israel, including a *catena* composed mostly of psalms that confess sin (3:10–18). Moreover, Paul employs quotations, allusions, or echoes from Israel's prophets. In the course of Paul's argument, the prophets Elijah (11:3), Moses (9:3, 15), Isaiah (9:20, 27; 10:16), Jeremiah (8:36), and Hosea (9:25) have appeared, together with other figures, like David (3:4; 4:6–8), Pharaoh (9:17), and Job (11:34–35), all speaking words to God or from God. In addition, the assurance that the word of God has not fallen (9:6), the "nearness" of the word of God (10:6–8), the promise from Habakkuk (1:17), the assurance of Joel in 10:13 that "everyone who calls on the name of the Lord will be saved," and Paul's tendency to personify Scripture (1:2–3; 3:2, 19, 21; 4:3, 23; 7:7; 8:2; 9:17; 10:11; 11:2, 4; 15:10; 16:26) and even to create a character called "the Righteousness from Faithfulness" (10:6), all strengthen the relationship between the study of the Scriptures and the discipline of prayer. A description of Abraham's prayer life appears at 4:17–22, followed by an account of the access Christians have to God in 5:1–11.

The last two points of theological significance are actually the most important: first, the entirety of Romans 9–11 can be described as a record of Paul's own prayerful struggle with God. Second, and finally, the prayers of Israel's own Messiah, Jesus, appear at the rhetorical climax of Paul's theological argument (15:3, 9).

PERSONAL GREETINGS AND FINAL INSTRUCTIONS
ROM. 16:1–27

Romans 16:1–2 serves as a letter of recommendation for Phoebe, described as a deacon (*diakonos*) at Cenchreae, a port to the east of Corinth and a supporter (*prostatis*) of Paul and of many others as well. It is quite possible that Phoebe is the bearer of Paul's letter and that she will read and interpret it at Rome. She may also be Paul's financial representative, who will assist him in gathering material resources for the mission to Spain, especially since, as Johnson notes,[9] Paul consistently uses "*diakonia*" to describe his collection (Rom. 15:31; 2 Cor. 8:4; 9:1, 12, 13). Paul urges the community to "welcome her in the Lord in a way that is worthy of the saints" and to "stand ready to assist her in whatever she may need from you" (16:2). Paul calls her "our sister Phoebe," which is typical of the social kinship language used by the early Christians to express solidarity.[10]

The list of greetings to friends in Rome (16:3–16) and from coworkers (16:21–23) also functions as a recommendation for Paul himself, presumably showing him to be both well-informed and well-connected. A great deal of information can be derived from the names listed in this chapter, especially since a few of them are known to us from other letters and from Acts. It is clear, for example, that Paul counted many women as coworkers or as leading members of this church. Nothing in Romans suggests that Paul had any difficulty with women exercising leadership functions or any reason to doubt their reliability as teachers and preachers. Phoebe is the first of many such examples in Romans 16. Paul also names Prisca, together with her husband, Aquila, as "coworkers in the Lord who risked their necks for my life" (16:4–5; see Acts 18 and 1 Cor. 16:19, where Prisca is also listed first). Paul mentions by name Mary, "who has worked hard among you" (16:6); Tryphaena and Tryphosa (perhaps sisters), "workers in the Lord" (16:12); Persis, "who has worked hard in the Lord" (16:12); Rufus's mother, "a mother to me also" (16:13); Julia; and the sister of Nereus (16:15). More controversial is Junia in 16:7, who, with Andronicus, is described as having been "from the same nation," "in prison" with Paul, "prominent among the apostles," and "in Christ" before Paul. If, as

---

9. Johnson, *Reading Romans*, 217.

10. Wayne A. Meeks, *The First Urban Christians: The Social World of the Apostle Paul* (New Haven, Conn.: Yale University Press, 1983) 85–89.

seems highly probable, Junia is a woman, then she and Andronicus are probably another missionary couple like Prisca and Aquila, who shared in Paul's apostolic labors.[11]

The list of people Paul greets clearly contains both Gentile Christians and Jewish Christians, some of whom Paul points out specifically, like Andronicus and Junia (16:7) and Herodion (16:11). In addition, Paul identifies four separate communities, at least two of which are house churches, in connection with Prisca and Aquila (16:3–5); Aristobulos (16:10); Narcissus (16:11); and the combination of Philologus, Julia, Nereus, his sister, and Olympas (16:15). The Roman church was probably made up of a mixture of people from around the world, from different ethnic backgrounds, some of whom had worked with Paul in other places and ended up in Rome. We get more information about the social composition of the early Christian communities from the names of people sending greetings to Rome. Tertius (16:22) and Quartus (16:23) may have been slaves (their names mean "third" and "fourth" respectively), but Tertius serves as the *amanuensis*, or scribe, for Paul's letter, and Quartus is referred to as "our brother" by Paul. "Gaius, who is host to me and to the whole church" and "Erastus, the city treasurer" (16:23) are probably well off, whether or not they are related to others with the same or similar names mentioned elsewhere in the New Testament. Timothy is described as Paul's coworker (16:21) while Lucius, Jason, and Sosipater are described as "from the same tribe" (16:21).

Between the list of people to whom Paul sends greetings at Rome and the list of those who, with Paul, are sending their greetings to Rome, appears a paragraph of warning about "those who cause dissensions and difficulties (lit. stumbling blocks) in opposition to the teaching that you learned" (16:17). They are to be avoided! Their behavior is described in general terms using stock phrases to caricature opponents, as elsewhere in Paul's letters (see Phil. 3:18 and 1 Thess. 2:5). Then the community is enjoined to be discerning about good and evil (16:19) and to trust that "the God of peace" will crush Satan under their feet (16:20).[12] The paragraph concludes with a standard grace wish

---

11. This is assumed by J. Louis Martyn: "Another missionary couple, Andronicus and Junia, is said by Paul to be Jewish, but he adds that they were 'in Christ before me' (Rom 16:7; cf. 16:11)" (*Galatians: A New Translation with Introduction and Commentary*, Anchor Bible 33A [New York: Doubleday, 1997] 215).

12. James Dunn notes that the influence of Genesis 3:15 ("He will strike your head" spoken to the serpent) is probable but almost certainly indirect (through many other Jewish eschatological writings that speak of the final defeat of angelic powers hostile to God) since Genesis 3:15 LXX uses different language (J. D. G. Dunn, *Romans*, 2 vols. Word Biblical Commentary 38 (Dallas: Word, 1988) II:905). If so, this is one last allusion to the story of Adam's fall, an important part of the narrative substructure of Paul's argument throughout Romans.

(16:20b). While the placement of the paragraph seems unusual and some of its contents seem out of place in Romans (for example, this is the only reference to Satan in the letter), it does not need to be a later interpolation, as some scholars have argued. Polemical afterthoughts at the end of the letter are not that unusual in Paul (see Gal. 6:11–17), and polemical asides interjected into an argument are even less unusual (1 Thess. 2:14–16; Gal. 3:1; 4:17; 5:7–12; Phil. 3:2, 18–19; 1 Cor. 4:18–21; 11:16; 14:38; 16:22; 2 Cor. 3:1; 6:14–16a; 10:10–11; 11:4, 13–15; 12:11–13; 13:2).

Neither should the concluding doxology be dismissed as a later interpolation, in spite of its absence in some manuscripts and its appearance after 14:23 or 15:33 in others. These text-critical issues probably reflect the problem of the particularity of Paul's letters for the early church as a whole.[13] Romans 16, with its long list of the names of people whom nobody knew anymore, would be particularly offensive in that regard. If we assume that the paragraph is authentic, the letter ends perfectly. The doxological prayer consists of a single long sentence that provides a rhetorically compelling and theologically precise summary of the argument of Romans as a whole. It also provides a graceful *inclusio* with the opening long sentence, which also speaks of the gospel of God, of the prophetic character of Israel's sacred writings concerning Jesus Christ, and of "the obedience of faith" that Paul has been commissioned to win from the Gentiles according to the plan of God. The language of "mystery" (16:25) recalls the description of God's gracious mercy shown to Jews and Gentiles in 11:25, and the closing words appropriately give God the glory, as faithful Abraham did (4:20), as faithless idolators refused to do (1:21), as Paul urged the Roman Christians to do "with one voice" (15:6), and as the Messiah came so that Gentiles would do (15:9). It would be difficult to write a better conclusion to this letter than the powerful words that actually appear at its end.

CONCLUSION: THE REST OF THE STORY

Romans, the story of God's righteousness as it comes to us in Paul's "final account"[14] of his theological vision, is unfinished. Its rhetorical conclusion is

---

13. Nils Alstrup Dahl, "The Particularity of the Pauline Epistles as a Problem in the Ancient Church," *Neotestamentica et Patristica. Eine Freundesgabe, Herrn Professor Dr. Oscar Cullmann zu seinem 60. Geburtstag überreicht*, Supplements to Novum Testamentum, vol. 6, ed. A. N. Wilder et al. (Leiden: E. J. Brill, 1962) 261–271.

14. Krister Stendahl, "Romans is Paul's final account of his theology of mission. . . . Although not intended by Paul to be 'final,' this account of his mission became so." (*Final Account: Paul's Letter to the Romans* [Minneapolis: Fortress, 1995] ix).

deliberately left open-ended: Will the members of the Roman house churches welcome one another (their brothers and sisters who are the work of God and for whom Christ died) in imitation of God and of the Messiah? Will they refrain from simply pleasing themselves in order to please their neighbors and so build up the community, in imitation of Jesus Christ's death on the cross? Will they join with Paul in support of his mission to the Gentiles in Spain, in fulfillment of God's purposes as foretold by God's prophets in the holy Scriptures concerning God's Son and in imitation of the root of Jesse in whom the Gentiles hope? He writes to them, as he says, "rather boldly" because he is a prisoner of hope and of the God of hope.

As for "the rest of the story" as it is reconstructed historically apart from Paul's letter to the Romans, Paul probably never made it to Spain. Our best information indicates that he was right to be worried about his safety during the upcoming trip to Jerusalem with the collection for the saints. According to Acts 28:16, when he finally did arrive at Rome, he was a prisoner under house arrest. It is one of the ironies of history that Paul was probably killed by the empire he described so flatteringly as "God's agent for good" for Christians who wanted to live peacefully. Tradition has it that both Paul and Peter perished at the hands of the emperor Nero, who needed scapegoats for the terrible fire that swept through the crowded city of Rome in the mid-60s, though some scholars think the two events are unrelated. If Paul did indeed die by the sword in the coliseum at Rome, there is special poignancy to his words about being "accounted as sheep for slaughter" and his ringing conviction that nothing—not "nakedness, danger, or the sword," or anything else in all creation—can separate us from the love of God in Christ Jesus.

There remains the narrative defense of God's righteousness that is Romans in its canonical placement, at the head of Paul's own letters and other letters written in the name of Paul, in the New Testament of the Christian Bible. As is well known, the historical process by which the letters of Paul were redacted and circulated in differently ordered collections prior to their placement in the New Testament canon is complex and controversial. However, with the possible exception of the Pastoral Epistles, chronological concerns do not seem to have guided the canonical ordering of the collection of letters that presently appears in the New Testament under the name of Paul. Instead, the letters seem to be ordered primarily by length (except 2 Thessalonians), with some attention given to the corporate or individual nature of the addressees. That the Pastorals are treated as a unit and that Hebrews is placed separately show that theological and rhetorical judgments (perhaps as to authorship) also mattered.

What then shall we say? In spite of the complexities of circulation and canonical ordering, the final canonical placement of Romans is both fitting and appropriate to the theological and pastoral weight of the book for the church.[15] Romans easily deserves its place at the beginning of Paul's letters and, arguably, as the work of the mature apostle, ought to function as a standard by which to measure Paul's other, earlier letters as well as the letters written in his name by later writers. This is particularly true for the issues of the relations between Jews and Gentiles, the role of women in apostolic leadership, and the peacemaking function of the community conformed to Christ. In addition, Romans seems to have been "written for our instruction" (15:4) on a variety of other important topics, such as the appropriate way to live with those who hold different views about how or when to worship God; the implications of baptism for the ethical life of Christians; our solidarity with unredeemed creation and with other creatures; and our confident assurance that since God is for us, it does not matter who might be against us, because—whether we live or die, we belong to the Lord.

Summary. The conclusion of Paul's letter to the Roman Christians returns to many of the themes of its introductory section (1:1–17). Paul is at his most diplomatic as he prepares the members of the several house churches at Rome for his upcoming visit. He gives the fullest statement yet of his purpose and vision before hinting that he has money on his mind. Paul intends to ask for their support for the mission to Spain, but first he is on his way to Jerusalem to pay an important debt that represents both his own apostleship and the resulting Gentile churches among whom he has labored for many years. Paul describes a turning point in his career: the closing of one chapter in the eastern regions of the Mediterranean and the opening of another new chapter in the west, for which he hopes Rome will be his base of operations. The relief Paul expects to feel after delivering the collection to Jerusalem is overshadowed by the fears he presently feels, not only for his own safety but also for the successful resolution of the project that has occupied his attentions from the beginning of his ministry and has become symbolic of it. He begs for the prayers of the Roman Christians as he offers a prayer that the "God of peace" will be with them. Finally, Paul endorses Phoebe; greets by name many members of the Roman church, listing the various house churches he knows; warns against those who would threaten the unity of the church; sends greetings from his coworkers; and closes with a doxological prayer summarizing the themes of the letter with language that imitates its opening verses.

---

15. Beverly Roberts Gaventa, "Romans," *Women's Bible Commentary*, exp. ed. with Apocrypha, ed. Carol A. Newsom and Sharon H. Ringe (Louisville, Ky.: Westminster John Knox, 1998) 405.

FOR FURTHER REFLECTION

1. What do you make of Paul's impassioned request for the community to join him in his prayer/struggle with God in Romans 15:30–33? Where else does prayer play an important role in the letter to the Romans?

2. One way to assess the effectiveness of an argument is to enter imaginatively into the historical situation of those who first heard and read it. If you had been part of one of the house churches in Rome, do you think you would have been persuaded by Paul's letter? Why or why not?

3. Paul's letter to the Romans has now become part of "the oracles of God" or "the Holy Scriptures concerning his Son" that Paul believed were "written for our instruction." It comes to us, as it came to the Roman Christians, as a word from a trustworthy apostle who challenges us to become part of "God's plot" for the redemption of the world. Where do you see God calling you to redefine the boundaries of neighborhood and neighbor?

4. To read Romans rightly is, therefore, inevitably to enter into a process of vocational discernment about contemporary opportunities to preach "the gospel of God" as apostles of Jesus Christ. If Paul were writing a letter telling the story of God's righteousness to your Bible study group today, for what specific projects do you suppose he would be trying to recruit you?

5. Paul spent much of his career working for church unity and raising funds for the poor. What is your community of faith doing on these fronts?

6. How is your community of faith engaged in the ongoing conversation with Jewish brothers and sisters, who do not confess that Jesus is the Messiah? What do they have to teach us about the Scriptures of Israel so beloved by Jesus and Paul, about the mysteries of election and suffering, and about the eschatological reservation by which we confess how much we still do not know about the righteousness of God?

Selected Bibliography

Adams, J.P. *Peacework: Oral Histories of Women Peace Activists*. Boston: Twayne, 1991.

Ancient Christian Commentary on Scripture: New Testament VI: Romans, edited by G. Bray. Downers Grove, Ill.: InterVarsity, 1988.

Ambrose. *On the Death of His Brother Satyrus*. In *Fathers of the Church: A New Translation*, edited by R. J. Deferrari. Washington, D.C.: Catholic University of America Press, 1947.

Auerbach, E. *Mimesis: The Representation of Reality in Western Literature*, translated by W. Trask. Princeton, N.J.: Princeton University Press, 1953.

Augustine. *Confessiones* (*The Confessions of Saint Augustine: A New Translation with Introduction*). Edited by E. M. Blaiklock. Nashville: Thomas Nelson, 1983.

Barrett, C. K. *From First Adam to Last: A Study in Pauline Theology*. New York: Charles Scribner's Sons, 1962.

Barth, K. *Against the Stream: Shorter Post-War Writings 1946–52*. New York: Philosophical Society, 1954.

———. *Christ and Adam: Man and Humanity in Romans 5*, translated by T. A. Smail. New York: Collier, 1962.

———. *Church Dogmatics*, II/2, translated by G. W. Bromiley et al. Edinburgh: T&T Clark, 1957.

———. *Deliverance to the Captives*, translated by M. Wieser. New York: Harper & Row, 1978.

———. *The Epistle to the Romans*, 6th ed., translated by E. C. Hoskyns. London: Oxford University Press, 1933, 1950.

Bartlett, D.L. *Romans*. Louisville, Ky.: Westminster John Knox, 1995.

Bassler, J.M. *Divine Impartiality: Paul and a Theological Axiom*, Society for Biblical Literature Dissertation Series 59. Chico, Calif.: Scholars, 1982.

———. "Paul's Theology: Whence and Whither?" in *Pauline Theology II: 1 and 2 Corinthians*, edited by D. M. Hay, 3–17. Minneapolis: Fortress, 1993.

Bjerkelund, C.J. Parakalô: *Form, Funktion und Sinn der* parakalô-*Sätze in den paulinischen Briefen*. Oslo: Universitetsforlaget, 1967.

Bockmuehl, M. *Revelation and Mystery in Ancient Judaism and Pauline Christianity*. Grand Rapids: Eerdmans, 1997.

Boyarin, D. *A Radical Jew: Paul and the Politics of Identity*. Berkeley, Calif.: University of California Press, 1994.

Brauch, M. T. "The Righteousness of God in Recent German Scholarship." In *Paul and Palestinian Judaism*, by E. P. Sanders, 523–542. Philadelphia: Fortress, 1977.

Brooten, B. J. *Love Between Women: Early Christian Responses to Female Homoeroticism*, Chicago: University of Chicago Press, 1996.

Brown, A. R. *The Cross and Human Transformation*. Minneapolis: Fortress, 1995.

Brown, R. E. *The Semitic Background of the Term "Mystery" in the New Testament*. Philadelphia: Fortress, 1968.

Brueggemann, W. *Biblical Perspectives on Evangelism: Living in a Three-Storied Universe*. Nashville: Abingdon, 1993.

———. *Texts Under Negotiation: The Bible and Postmodern Imagination*. Minneapolis: Fortress, 1993.

Bultmann, R. "Adam and Christ in Romans 5." In *Current Issues in New Testament Interpretation*, edited by W. Klassen and G. F. Snyder, 43–165. London: SCM Press, 1959.

———. "Romans 7 and the Anthropology of Paul." In *Existence and Faith*, 173–185. 1932, reprint, London: Hodder & Stoughton, 1960.

———. "The Significance of the Old Testament for Christian Faith." In *The Old Testament and Christian Faith*, edited by B. W. Anderson, 8–55. New York: Harper & Row, 1963.

Callaway, M. C. "A Hammer That Breaks Rock in Pieces: Prophetic Critique in the Hebrew Bible." In *Anti-Semitism and Early Christianity: Issues of Polemic and Faith*, edited by Craig A. Evans and Donald A. Hagner, 21–38. Minneapolis: Fortress, 1993.

Calvin, J. *Calvin's New Testament Commentaries: The Epistles of Paul the Apostle to the Romans and Thessalonians*, translated by R. MacKenzie; edited by D. W. Torrance and T. F. Torrance. Grand Rapids: Eerdmans, 1960.

Coles, R. *The Call of Stories: Teaching and the Moral Imagination*. Boston: Houghton Mifflin, 1993.

Cousar, C. B. *The Letters of Paul*. Nashville: Abingdon, 1996.

———. *A Theology of the Cross: The Death of Jesus in the Pauline Letters*. Minneapolis: Fortress, 1990.

Cranfield, C. E. B. *A Critical and Exegetical Commentary on the Epistle to the Romans*, ICC, 2 vols. Edinburgh: T&T Clark, 1975, 1979.

Cullmann, O. *The State in the New Testament*. New York: Charles Scribner's Sons, 1956.

Dahl, N. A. "The Atonement—An Adequate Reward for the Akedah?" In *The Crucified Messiah*, 146–160. Minneapolis: Augsburg, 1974.

———. "The Particularity of the Pauline Epistles as a Problem in the Ancient Church." In *Neotestamentica et Patristica. Eine Freundesgabe, Herrn Professor Dr. Oscar Cullmann zu seinem 60. Geburtstag überreicht*, Supplements to Novum Testamentum, vol. 6, edited by A. N. Wilder et al., 261–271. Leiden: E. J. Brill, 1962.

Darr, K. P. *Far More Precious Than Jewels: Perspectives on Biblical Women*. Louisville, Ky.: Westminster John Knox, 1991.

Dodd, C. H. "Atonement." In *The Bible and the Greeks*, 82–95. London: Hodder & Stoughton, 1935.

———. *The Epistle of Paul to the Romans*. New York: Harper, 1932.

———. *The Meaning of Paul for Today*. London: G. Allen & Unwin, 1958.

Duff, N. J. "The Significance of Pauline Apocalyptic for Theological Ethics." In *Apocalyptic and the New Testament: Essays in Honor of J. Louis Martyn*, edited by J. Marcus and M. L. Soards, 279–296. Journal for the Study of the New Testament Supplement Series 24. Sheffield: Sheffield Academic Press, 1989.

Dunn, J. D. G. *Romans*, 2 vols. Word Bible Commentary 38. Dallas: Word, 1988.

Elliott, N. "Romans 13:1–7 in the Context of Imperial Propaganda." In *Paul and Empire: Religion and Power in Roman Imperial Society*, edited by R. A. Horsley, 184–204. Harrisburg: Trinity Press International, 1997.

Fredriksen, P. "Judaism, the Circumcision of Gentiles, and Apocalyptic Hope: Another Look at Galatians 1 and 2." *Journal of Theological Studies* 42 (1991): 532–564.

Funk, R.W. "The Apostolic *Parousia*: Form and Significance." In *Christian History and Interpretation: Studies Presented to John Knox*, edited by W. R. Farmer, C. F. D. Moule, R. R. Niebuhr, 249–268. Cambridge: Cambridge University Press, 1967.

Gaventa, B. R. "Romans," *Women's Bible Commentary*, Exp. ed. with Apocrypha, edited by C. A. Newsom and S. H. Ringe, 403–410. Louisville: Westminster John Knox, 1998.

———. "The Singularity of the Gospel." *Pauline Theology I*, edited by J. Bassler, 147–159. Minneapolis: Fortress, 1991.

Getty, M. A. "Paul and the Salvation of Israel: A Perspective on Romans 9–11." *Catholic Biblical Quarterly* 50:3 (1988): 456–469.

———. "Paul on the Covenants and the Future of Israel." *Biblical Theology Bulletin* 17 (1987): 92–99.

Gollwitzer, H. *The Way to Life: Sermons in a Time of World Crisis*, translated by D. Cairns. Edinburgh: T&T Clark, 1981.

Grieb, A.K. "Affiliation with Jesus Christ in His Sacrifice: Some Uses of Scripture to Define the Identity of Jesus Christ in Romans" (Ph.D. diss., Yale University, 1997).

Harnack, A. *What Is Christianity?* 1901. Reprint, New York: Harper, 1957.

Hays, R. B. *Echoes of Scripture in the Letters of Paul*. New Haven, Conn.: Yale University Press, 1989.

———. "'Have We Found Abraham to Be Our Forefather According to the Flesh?': A Reconsideration of Rom. 4:1." *Novum Testamentum* 27 (1985): 76–98.

———. *The Moral Vision of the New Testament: Community, Cross, and New Creation: A Contemporary Introduction to New Testament Ethics*. San Francisco: HarperCollins, 1996.

———. "Psalm 143 and the Logic of Romans 3." *Journal of Biblical Literature* 99 (1980): 107–115.

———. "'The Righteous One' as Eschatological Deliverer: A Case Study in Paul's Apocalyptic Hermeneutics." In *Apocalyptic and the New Testament: Essays in Honor of J. Louis Martyn*, edited by J. Marcus and M. L. Soards, 191–215. Sheffield: Sheffield Academic Press, 1988.

———. "'Who Has Believed Our Message?' Paul's Reading of Isaiah." *Society of Biblical Literature Seminar Papers* (1998): 205–225.

Hock, R. F. *The Social Context of Paul's Ministry: Tentmaking and Apostleship*. Philadelphia: Fortress, 1980.

Hooker, M. D. *From Adam to Christ: Essays on Paul*. Cambridge: Cambridge University Press, 1990.

Jervis, L. A. *The Purpose of Romans: A Comparative Letter Structure Investigation*. Journal for the Study of the New Testament Supplement Series 55. Sheffield: Sheffield Academic Press, 1991.

Johnson, E. E. *The Function of Apocalyptic and Wisdom Traditions in Romans 9–11*. Society of Biblical Literature Dissertation Series 109. Atlanta: Scholars, 1989.

———. "Romans 9–11: The Faithfulness and Impartiality of God." *Pauline Theology III: Romans*, edited by D. M. Hay and E. E. Johnson, 211–239. Minneapolis: Fortress, 1995.

Johnson, L. T. *Reading Romans: A Literary and Theological Commentary*. New York: Crossroad, 1997.

Käsemann, E. *Commentary on Romans*, translated by G. W. Bromiley. Grand Rapids: Eerdmans, 1980.

———. "Justification and Salvation History in the Epistle to the Romans." In *Perspectives on Paul*, translated by M. Kohl, 60–101. London: SCM Press, 1971.

———. "Principles of Interpretation of Romans 13." In *New Testament Questions of Today*, translated by W. J. Montague, 196–216. Philadelphia: Fortress, 1969.

———. "The Righteousness of God in Paul." In *New Testament Questions of Today*, translated by W. J. Montague, 168–182. Philadelphia: Fortress, 1969.

Keck, L. E. *Paul and His Letters*. Rev. ed. Philadelphia: Fortress, 1988.

———. "The Absent Good: The Significance of Rom 7:18a." In *Text und Geschichte*, 66–75. Marburg: N. G. Elwert, 1999.

———. "The Letter of Paul to the Romans." In *The HarperCollins Study Bible*, New Revised Standard Version, edited by W. A. Meeks, 2114–2138. New York: HarperCollins, 1993.

Keesmaat, S. C. *Paul and His Story: (Re)Interpreting the Exodus Tradition*, Journal for the Study of the New Testament Supplement Series 181. Sheffield: Sheffield Academic Press, 1999.

Koenig, J. *Rediscovering New Testament Prayer: Boldness and Blessing in the Name of Jesus*. San Francisco: Harper, 1992.

Kümmel, W. G. *Römer 7 und die Bekehrung des Paulus*. Leipzig: Hinrichs, 1929. Reissued as *Römer 7 und das Bild des Menschen im Neuen Testament*. Munich: Kaiser, 1974.

Levenson, J. D. *The Death and Resurrection of the Beloved Son: The Transformation of Child Sacrifice in Judaism and Christianity*. New Haven, Conn.: Yale University Press, 1993.

Lorde, A. *Sister Outsider: Essays and Speeches*. New York: Crossing, 1984.

Luther, M. *Lectures on Romans*. LCC XV. Translated and edited by Wilhelm Pauck. Philadelphia: Westminster, 1961.

———. "Preface to the Letter of Saint Paul to the Romans." In *Luther's Works*, vol. 35. Saint Louis: Concordia, 1960.

MacMullen, R. *Roman Social Relations*. New Haven, Conn.: Yale University Press, 1974.

Marcus, J. *Jesus and the Holocaust: Reflections on Suffering and Hope*. New York: Doubleday, 1997.

Martyn, D. W. "A Child and Adam: A Parable of the Two Ages." In *Apocalyptic and the New Testament: Essays in Honor of J. Louis Martyn*, edited by J. Marcus and M. L. Soards. Journal for the Study of the New Testament Supplement Series 24, 317–333. Sheffield: Sheffield Academic Press, 1989.

Martyn, J. L. "Epistemology at the Turn of the Ages." In *Theological Issues in the Letters of Paul*, 89–110. Nashville: Abingdon, 1997.

———. *Galatians: A New Translation with Introduction and Commentary*, Anchor Bible 33A. New York: Doubleday, 1997.

Meeks, W. A. "'And Rose Up to Play': Midrash and Paraenesis in 1 Cor 10:1–22." *Journal for the Study of the New Testament* 16 (1982): 64–78.

———. "Judgment and the Brother: Romans 14:1–15:13." In *Tradition and Interpretation in the New Testament: Essays in Honor of E. Earle Ellis*, edited by G. F. Hawthorne and O. Betz, 290–300. Grand Rapids: Eerdmans, 1987.

———. "On Trusting an Unpredictable God: A Hermeneutical Meditation on Romans 9–11." In *Faith and History: Essays in Honor of Paul W. Meyer*, edited by J. T. Carroll et al., 105–124. Atlanta: Scholars, 1990.

———. *The First Urban Christians: The Social World of the Apostle Paul.* New Haven, Conn.: Yale University Press, 1983.

Melanchthon, P. *Loci Communes Rerum Theologicarum (Melanchthon and Bucer)*, edited by W. Pauck. Philadelphia: Westminster, 1969.

Micks, M. H. *Deep Waters: An Introduction to Baptism.* Cambridge, Mass.: Cowley, 1996.

Mitchell, M. M. *Paul and the Rhetoric of Reconciliation: An Exegetical Investigation of the Language and Composition of 1 Corinthians*, Hermeneutische Untersuchungen zur Theologie 28. Tübingen: Mohr Siebeck, 1991.

Morgan, R. *Romans.* Sheffield: Sheffield Academic Press, 1997.

Morris, L. "The Meaning of ἱλαστήριον in Rom III,25," *New Testament Studies* 2 (1955/56): 33–34.

Mosher, S. *God's Power, Jesus' Faith and World Mission: A Study in Romans.* Scottdale, Pa.: Herald, 1996.

Nygren, A. *Commentary on Romans*, translated by C. C. Rasmussen. Philadelphia: Muhlenberg, 1949.

Origen. *Commentary on the Epistle to the Romans. Commentarii in Epistulam ad Romanos*, edited by T. Heither. New York: Herder, 1990.

Osiek, C. "Paul's Prayer: Relationship with Christ." In *Scripture and Prayer: A Celebration for Carroll Stuhlmueller*, edited by C. Osiek and D. Senior, 145–157. Wilmington, Del.: Michael Glazier, 1988.

Peterson, D. G. "Prayer in Paul's Writings." In *Teach Us To Pray*, edited by D. A. Carson, 84–101. Exeter: World Evangelical Fellowship, 1990.

Rajak, T. "Inscription and Context: Reading the Jewish Catacombs of Rome." In *Studies in Early Jewish Epigraphy*, edited by J. W. Van Henten and P. W. Van der Horst, 226–241. Leiden: E. J. Brill, 1994.

Rowe, C. K. "Romans 10:13: What Is the Name of the Lord?" *Horizons in Biblical Theology* 22:2 (2000): 135–173.

Sanders, E. P. *Paul and Palestinian Judaism: A Comparison of Patterns of Religion.* Philadelphia: Fortress, 1977.

———. *Paul, the Law, and the Jewish People.* Philadelphia: Fortress, 1983.

———. *Paul.* Oxford: Oxford University Press, 1991.

Schottroff, L. "Die Schreckensherrschaft der Sünde und die Befreiung durch Christus nach dem Römerbrief des Paulus." *Evangelische Theologie* 39 (1979): 497–510.

———. "'Give to Caesar What Belongs to Caesar and to God What Belongs to God': A Theological Response of the Early Christian Church to Its Social and Political Environment." In *The Love of Enemy and Nonretaliation in the New Testament*, edited by Willard M. Swartley. 223–257. Louisville, Ky.: Westminster/John Knox, 1992.

Schubert, P. *The Form and Function of the Pauline Thanksgivings.* Berlin: Töpelmann, 1939.

Schütz, J. H. *Paul and the Anatomy of Apostolic Authority*, Society for New Testament Studies 26. Cambridge: Cambridge University Press, 1975.

Setzer, C. J. *Jewish Responses to Early Christians: History and Polemics, 30–150 C.E.* Minneapolis: Fortress, 1994.

Soards, M. L. "The Righteousness of God in the Writings of the Apostle Paul," *Biblical Theology Bulletin* 15 (1985): 104–109.

Spiegel, S. *The Last Trial: On the Legends and Lore of the Command to Abraham to Offer Isaac as a Sacrifice: The Akedah*, translated by J. Goldin. New York: Pantheon, 1967.

Stendahl, K. *Final Account: Paul's Letter to the Romans.* Minneapolis: Fortress, 1995.

Stringfellow, W. *A Simplicity of Faith: My Experience in Mourning*. Nashville: Abingdon, 1982.

———. *Conscience and Obedience: The Politics of Romans 13 and Revelation 13 in Light of the Second Coming*. Waco: Word, 1977.

Stuhlmacher, P. *Paul's Letter to the Romans: A Commentary*, translated by S. J. Hafemann. Louisville: Westminster John Knox, 1994.

Tamez, E. *The Amnesty of Grace: Justification by Faith from a Latin American Perspective*, translated by S. H. Ringe. Nashville: Abingdon, 1993.

Wagner, J. R. "The Heralds of Salvation and the Mission of Paul." In *Jesus and the Suffering Servant: Isaiah 53 and Christian Origins*, edited by W. H. Bellinger and W. R. Farmer, 193–222. Harrisburg: Trinity Press International, 1998.

———. *"Who Has Believed Our Message?": Paul and Isaiah "in Concert" in the Letter to the Romans*. Leiden: E. J. Brill, 2002.

Wesley, J. *The Works of John Wesley, Vol. 18, Journal and Diaries I (1735–1738)*, edited by W. R. Ward and R. P. Heitzenrater. Nashville: Abingdon, 1988.

Whittaker, M. *Jews and Christians: Graeco-Roman Views*. Cambridge: Cambridge University Press, 1984.

Wiefel, W. "The Jewish Community in Ancient Rome and the Origins of Roman Christianity." In *The Romans Debate*, Rev. and exp. ed., edited by K. P. Donfried. Peabody, Mass.: Hendrickson, 1991.

Wilckens, U. *Der Brief an die Römer*, 3 vols. Zürich: Benziger, 1978, 1980, 1982.

Wiles, G. P. *Paul's Intercessory Prayers: The Significance of the Intercessory Prayer Passages in the Letters of St. Paul*. Cambridge: Cambridge University Press, 1974.

Williams, R. "The Dark Night." In *A Ray of Darkness: Sermons and Reflections*, 80–84. Boston: Cowley, 1995.

Wright, N. T. "Romans and the Theology of Paul." In *Pauline Theology, Volume III: Romans*, edited by D. M. Hay and E. E. Johnson, 30–67. Minneapolis: Fortress, 1995.

———. *The Climax of the Covenant: Christ and the Law in Pauline Theology*. Minneapolis: Fortress, 1991.

———. *The New Testament and the People of God*. Minneapolis: Fortress, 1992.

Yoder, J. H. *The Christian Witness to the State*. Newton, Kans.: Faith & Life, 1964.

———. *The Politics of Jesus: Vicit Agnus Noster*, 2d ed. Grand Rapids: Eerdmans, 1993.

———. "The Use of the Bible in Theology." In *The Use of the Bible in Theology: Evangelical Options*, edited by R. K. Johnston, 103–120. Atlanta: John Knox, 1985.

Index of Biblical References

Boldface locators indicate sections or extensive treatment of a topic.

Index of Names

Printed in the United States
120197LV00003BA/107/A